# CHRIST

## IN YOU THE

# HOPE OF

# GLORY

# CHRIST

## IN YOU THE

# HOPE OF

# GLORY

WRITTEN AND EDITED BY
ANDREW FLESSA

Colossians 1:27 KJV

*Christ In You, The Hope of Glory*

Published by Words of His Grace, an imprint of His Grace Redeems

Nashville, TN

Unless otherwise noted, all Scripture quotations are from the King James Version or American Standard Version of the Holy Bible.

Visit the author's website at https://hisgraceredeems.com/

Facebook @hisgraceredeemsyou
Instagram @hisgraceredeemsyou
TikTok @hisgraceredeemsyou
YouTube @hisgraceredeemsyou

International Standard Book Number: 979-8-218-74685-8

Front cover photo credit to Dennis Jarvis
"Garden Tomb" Jerusalem, Israel October 10, 2016

25 26 27 28 29 30 31 32 33 - 9 8 7 6 5 4 3 2 1
Printed in the United States of America

*Thank you for selecting this book. It is likely the book selected you through the power of the Holy Spirit.*

*May it bring you the healing, truth, and freedom you have been searching for, for years, if not decades.*

*The book is written for nonbelievers in Christ, yet believers in the body of Christ will also find value and spiritual nourishment in the text.*

*If you are not currently a believer, I wrote this book as a bridge for you to better understand the Bible. Many people, even if they grew up in church, have only seen a fraction of what an authentic relationship with Jesus is.*

*I encourage you to approach the text with an open mind, as you may discover that you are God's hope of glory and He wants to dwell inside you and redeem you to eternal glory.*

*The Greek word for redeem is "lytroó" (/loo-tro'-o/). This word is used in the New Testament to describe the act of setting a captive free through the payment of a ransom or a high price. It signifies the process of buying back or rescuing someone from captivity in a spiritual sense.*

*Without God we cannot be redeemed, without us God has nothing to love and God is love.*

*1 John 4:8 "He that loveth not knoweth not God; for God is love."*

Let those who have ears to hear, hear,

I used to be involved in witchcraft, the occult, yoga, Eastern meditation and Jewish mysticism. I was trained how to "manifest" in the traditions of secret societies and mystery schools.

I frequently encountered "angel numbers" and pursued them eagerly, as if I were on a journey to catch them all, seeking for deeper meaning and guidance behind each one.

I was working as hard as possible to alchemize my best life.

I paid for rituals, numerology reports, horoscope feeds, tarot readings, and strange spiritual healing sessions like group reenactments and spiritual surgery.

I read oracle cards, tarot cards, and consulted with online psychics to do tarot readings. I talked to psychics when I had a crucial decision to make. I did yoga weekly. I did four ten-day silent meditation retreats in a two year span. I had a room full of expensive crystals.

I believed in and studied horoscopes and consulted with online astrologers. I burned sage. I attended a mystery school. I thought shadow work needed to be done under full moons to increase the magical manifestation powers of releasing what I didn't like and receiving exactly what I did like.

I thought mercury retrograde was something to be feared.

I thought if I followed their prescriptions, their rituals, their rites and their teachings then I would start to have an increase of abundance and a reduction in suffering. I was gathering new age tidbits here and there, all over the globe, traveling thousands of miles, trying to stitch

3

together the pieces to create meaning. I was preparing for the impending enlightenment of humanity and the new age of aquarius.

In actuality, I was grasping for air. I was paddling against the wind. My faith was placed in my own abilities, how much I could give, how much I could research and how much I could do. I believed I could right my own wrongs.

I bought into the lie for years. I was in pain and earnestly looking for relief. I did "energy" work with my chakras. I chanted "chakra tones" in the car. I took online chakra tests and gave those online tests to others. I took online pop psychology tests. I thought "know thyself" was all I needed to know. I studied alchemy and ascension. I thought the Galactic Federation was a benevolent group of aliens, spoiler alert, they aren't. I thought all I needed to do was level up from 3D consciousness to 5D and beyond. I thought the crystals in my pocket each day were special and had special powers because I selected the exact ones I needed for healing, transformation, manifestation, and ascension.

I was involved with reiki, energy healers, new age shamans, new age midwives, and psychics. Really, anyone and everyone offering the promise of relief. I was pleasure seeking and extremely self-focused. I thought twin flames were real. I thought Greek gods and goddesses were real, and not only that, right there on the other side cheering me on. I had a minor obsession with Hercules, the fabled Greek god. I was starting to believe I was Hercules incarnated yet again for the beginning of the new age, the new earth, enlisted by the universe to help heal the planet and solve the problems of humanity.

I believed I was a starseed: a wunderkind sent here from another star system to fix the broken systems of the planet through new age beliefs and values.

—

4

I thought I was in contact and channeling benevolent aliens, as well as my spirit guides, spirit animals, including eagles, lions, and grizzly bears. I would talk to the universe. I thought God and the universe were the same thing. I once embraced pantheism and believed that God's consciousness could be found in all things, even in something as ordinary as a doorknob.

Mixed in with all that, I believed I was speaking to my higher self. I believed that I created my own reality and that I was my own god, and in complete control of my life and its trajectory through affirmations, visualizations, rituals, and meditation sessions. I was convinced I was "getting it."

I see now, looking back with 20/20 hindsight, I was living in selfishness, pride, and delusion.

This was partly a coping mechanism and partly for self-preservation. I was feeding into and building up my ego, because I thought that's what I was supposed to do to create a sense of self and intellectual superiority.

The world told me I needed to do this to be somebody.

I was trapped in a continuous cycle of healing and "leveling up."

I was constantly seeking the next and even more unique healing session; the next new age mentor to inspire me, and the right course or seminar to unlock my full potential. I had spiritual shiny object syndrome, going from one new age practice to the next.

As I was drifting, I thought to myself, maybe this psychedelic is the key. Maybe this energy healer is the key. Maybe eastern insight meditation is the key. Maybe kabbalah is the key. Maybe I'm just not trying hard enough and not following the rituals I paid for closely enough.

I wasn't sure of what the formula was, it was like I was fervently searching for a way to dismantle an atomic bomb of suffering. I was trying to crack the code. I thought I was superhuman, a superhero god being forged through the trials of life.

I felt a little peace after each healing session I paid for, or I convinced myself I did, and chased that high continually, but then it would wear off. I believed that my next crisis was designed by the universe to have me seek magic and meditation even harder, to ascend my frequency even further.

I was cracking the secret code to the harmony of the collective consciousness of myself and the planet and nobody was going to tell me otherwise. My religion was oneness, also known as the law of one. While I believed all of this, I was suffering and in a valley of despair, depression and anxiety, reaching for weed and alcohol to turn the volume down and merely survive.

The truth is, I longed to feel loved, heard, and understood.

My soul felt fragmented, adrift without a sense of belonging. I believed I was like a unicorn, too rare to live, too rare to die, leading me to feel disassociated and disconnected from others and the world around me.

I was a homesick alien starseed longing for my home planet, just like Clark Kent. I couldn't see I was taking in kryptonite in various forms and was believing it was going to make me feel better.

My body was in a constant state of fight or flight. I had a spirit of fear over me about my health, purpose, and finances, constantly.

There were lots of days I had wished I wasn't alive. I was being tormented by the demonic realm, and I didn't know it. I thought I could burn a little sage, say some "I am affirmations" and load up my room with expensive crystals to put the dark forces at bay, when sage and crystals were really giving the demonic realm access to me. Modalities like that give the demonic realm an open door to enter… but more about that later.

Then I realized if I said enough self-affirming affirmations, I could fill up my personal reserves of self-trust, self-worth, and self-love and then everything would suddenly work out.

Eureka! I cracked the code!

However, I was wrong about all of it. I had no idea how much deception I was inside of.

What I was doing was laying down a welcome mat for darkness, false religion, false gods, illusions, delusions, deceptions, and all the chaos that follows those things.

I felt allergic to the J-word. Jesus. I unfriended an online friend in Utah who was half in the new age and half in Christianity who spoke of Jesus. Of all people, she began to tell me on phone calls that "Jesus is looking for you." That didn't sit well with me at the time. I didn't want Him, but guess what, He still wanted me.

Can you imagine God knocking on the door of your life, and you refuse to answer the door? God. The Creator of everything and everyone. The master orchestrator of all biology, all world civilizations, the Maker of the Heavens and the earth, all the cosmos, all the souls, and all the matter in existence. The one and true God knocking on the door and you don't answer.

It's a miracle this female friend was still focused on Jesus, because it's near impossible to ride two horses at the same time. I have come to learn that Jesus followers and new agers are on two very different paths that lead an individual to two very different destinations.

When it comes to the spiritual tradition you select it will have an all-encompassing effect on your whole life and life path. It can be reasonably said, that the spiritual, the supernatural, dictates the rest of your life. All parts of your life including, who you talk to, who you marry, what media you take in, where you live, what you do for work, what your legacy is and what your daily lifestyle looks like. All areas of life start in the spiritual. In the new age this principle is "as above so below." There is truth to that principle, however it's not what you think.

Plato expounded on this concept in various dialogues such as the "Republic" and "Symposium" 400 years before Jesus arrived, illustrating that everything found on earth, whether a table, a chair, or a person, points to a supreme and divine blueprint—a perfect form emanating from the unseen and divine realm, but this is not to say a doorknob and Jesus are the same. That's inaccurate. The divine and perfect form of the threefold God in Heaven has dominion over everything and everyone in the created world. The one and true God of the Bible is alive, and He is the ultimate form of forms. That's why Jesus is described as the King of kings, and Lord of lords... but more on that later.

The new age movement frequently mixes genuine truth with falsehood, a deceptive strategy employed by the enemy to present partial truths, resulting in temporary relief, similar to an oppressive drug habit, and this lures individuals into seeking more, just like an alcoholic or a sugar addict that can't get enough. The enemy can distort truth but can never create or deliver real truth.

This can be likened to mass-manufactured processed foods that resembles food but are actually food-like products filled with chemicals, artificial sweeteners, and additives.

In addition to blending half-truths, the dark side distorts and inverts things to make light appear dark, and dark appear light.

Isaiah 5:20 KJV

*Woe unto them that call evil good, and good evil; that put darkness for light, and light for darkness; that put bitter for sweet, and sweet for bitter!*

The enemy of life, satan, also known as the great deceiver, employs various strategies to deceive people. The evil one's top solder is lucifer, a fallen angel who was once the light bearer and the music leader in Heaven, he succumbed to pride and was cast out of Heaven by God. Together with legions of demons and people under his influence satan works ceaselessly to normalize sin and present holiness as something unconventional. This deceptive agenda promotes half truths and false gods through cultural mediums like social media, television, movies, and music. He is the enemy and he largely lives through the airwaves and the screens.

Satan's deceptive tactics to normalize sin and distort holiness are part of a larger spiritual battle that extends beyond the earthly realm. As believers and nonbelievers in Christ navigate the challenges of this world, it's essential to grasp the ultimate truth that Heaven transcends earthly limitations. The war here on earth is related to the war in the Heavens. The full realization of Heaven on earth occurs at the culmination of the upcoming seven year tribulation when satan loses the war in the Heavens. After satan is defeated, the Kingdom of Heaven will merge with the earth, and the old earth will pass away.

While some new age authors mention an upcoming new earth, where everyone is somehow enlightened, the ultimate truth lives in the understanding that a future new earth is one and the same as the Kingdom of Heaven on earth. It has nothing to do with the new age of aquarius. Heaven is a place today, but the Kingdom of Heaven merging with the natural earth is a supernatural progression of the story God wrote at the beginning of time… but more on that later.

By the grace of God, I was pardoned from my life of destruction.

He met me in my stubbornness. In my sin. In my depression. In my chaos. In my addiction. In my depravity. In my delusions. In my pride. In my lust.

Everything reset and changed after I reluctantly accepted prayer one morning in Boston when I was thirty years old, and I never saw it coming – if someone handed you this book and said to read it. Please pay attention. It could be the personal "great reset" you have been diligently looking for.

So, I was on the back porch of my apartment in Boston, and I began to have a conversation with a Christian I had never met before.

I lived with multiple roommates, and one of the roommates brought over one of her friends for morning coffee, August 22, 2020.

We were talking about spirituality right off the bat. I was advocating spirituality is an experience. She was advocating for absolute truths and the Bible. Something that felt antiquated to me at the time. We were starting to butt heads in our thirty minute conversation. We both sensed this. Then, she paused. I remember the moment vividly. She looked at me in my eyes and said, "Can I pray for you?"

In that deeply significant moment, I surrendered and accepted her invitation, and she prayed for me for what seemed like twenty minutes, yet it felt as brief as two minutes. Her prayers transcended earthly constraints, carrying a divine blessing that surpassed time and space. The presence of God permeated her words as she fervently unleashed powerful prayers on my behalf.

By the end of the powerful prayers, I looked up, and she was crying, and so was I. We were both overcome with the glory of God resting on us. In an instant I was undone. The revelation of who God is met me. I saw myself for who I really was, worthless apart from His grace. In spite of it all, in spite of my pride, in spite of serving false gods, the Lord Himself came to me. My eyes were opened and the veil was lifted.

I accepted Jesus into my life in that moment. I was met with a deep surge of wonder and the realization of the truth of God and who He is.

Jesus is God.

Something shifted. Something changed. The rest of that day all I could keep saying to myself was "wow… whoa… what just happened?" I was met by Jesus with a sign and a wonder, just as the Bible promises. He had all my attention and still does to this day.

The wonder I was experiencing felt like new "air space" and "new territory." In essence, a new spiritual awareness I had never had before. This was the kind of love that I was desperately seeking for in all the wrong ways, and for many years. The eyes of my heart were opened.

Psalm 84:5 ASV

*For thou, Lord, art good, and ready to forgive, And abundant in lovingkindness unto all them that call upon thee.*

Ephesians 1:18 ASV

*...having the eyes of your heart enlightened, that ye may know what is the hope of his calling, what the riches of the glory of his inheritance in the saints*

That's when I knew my old friend who told me Jesus was looking for me was right. Jesus was after my heart. He was chasing after me. He was right under my nose the whole time, all the way back to my birth in 1989.

That's when I knew why the years leading up to 2020 I had many seemingly random older ladies in public places taking a spiritual interest in me, praying for me, and handing me Bibles on the street. Minutes after I accepted salvation in Jesus, I showed the girl that prayed for me how many Bibles I already had awaiting me in my bookshelf.

Salvation is the acceptance of Jesus as God. This is achieved through faith in Jesus Christ's redemptive sacrifice, resurrection, and supernatural blood. Accepting His work and His blood result in forgiveness, repentance, and reconciliation with God. Sin and its consequences are removed, all equaling right standing with God and ultimately equaling the future state of eternal life in Heaven. I immediately changed and no longer had an interest in sin like I did before. Six months later I made the decision to move away from Boston.

In 2021, I made the road trip to Austin, TX and approximately six months into living in Austin while on a dating app, a girl I had never met in person extended an invitation to a church. The service was scheduled for that Saturday evening at 6 PM, presenting me with a sudden decision to make it from North Austin to South Austin in time. I chose to attend. Although I have never met this girl, I believe that God worked through her to direct me to a church where I could experience a direct relationship with Jesus and pursue spiritual growth. God is fantastic at working through people, but so is the enemy... but more on that later.

Upon walking into this church, I immediately knew something very special was happening. It felt much different than the Catholic churches I grew up in. I hadn't been inside a church in about 17 years.

The Holy Spirit focused church I walked into in Texas was also met with a sign and a wonder. This is where I started to develop a relationship with God through praise, worship, prayer, healthy community and studying the Bible for the first time in my life.

I began seeking only Him and praising only Him for all the times He kept me alive. He led me to salvation and brought me into an entirely different life in a few short months. I was most definitely in new territory spiritually and physically.

While Austin and Boston share some cultural similarities, they are different in many ways. Texas has a much stronger church culture than Boston because it's part of the Bible Belt. Before my church attendance, I had not experienced the depth of a direct and personal relationship with Jesus and what it means. While in the new age I looked at Christianity as an outdated religion, not knowing it's a relationship with the God of the universe Himself more than it is a boilerplate religion to control people. It's not just another path; it's the highest path and many are called, but few hear the call.

Now that I have come to the knowledge of the truth, I am determined to never let go of Jesus. My prayer is that He won't let go of me either. Religion provides the framework of tradition, yet its essence lives in the relationship with the Holy Trinity – God, Jesus, and the Holy Spirit. Similarly, marriage offers a structure, but it's true significance is reflected in the health of the relationship.

The satisfaction and rest in my soul from seeking the presence of the Lord is unlike anything else I have ever experienced, and I have had a lot of "spiritual" experiences, as you can tell.

After taking that first step into church and sincerely seeking Jesus and the Word of God I have become released of all the bondage of sin, addiction, depression, anxiety, and negative demonic spirits I didn't even know I had tormenting me. I went through the fire and have come out the other side with the clarity I desperately needed for decades.

Over the years since walking with the Lord He has been telling me, "I am healing every single area of your life" and I'm by no means a perfect Christian, there's no such thing, I didn't earn this gift, Jesus lovingly died to make me new, so I do my best to not take His sacrifice for granted. I make mistakes, I screw up, I'm still human so I so follow what the Bible says so I'm no longer a screw up: I crucify my flesh daily, that's the fallen Adam nature all men and woman have, I pick up my cross daily, I receive God's new mercies each day (Lamentations 3:22-23), and I repent frequently. I feel convicted of sin and convinced of holiness each day by following the Holy Spirit who now dwells inside of me.

Only Christianity has the promise of the God of the universe. The Creator of everything, living inside of you. Healing you. Loving you. Guiding you. Ensuring you make it home to Heaven.

There have been peaks and valleys in my Christian walk since 2020, but I wouldn't change it for a thing. I would not trade the deep meaning I get from being a son of God and on the road to Heaven. Not even for all the riches and kingdoms of the world. I would never trade away what I received and do anything to risk forgoing my salvation and my relationship with Jesus. I understand why thousands of martyrs during early Christianity were willing to die for their faith rather than renounce it, that's how important finding Jesus is.

I did not understand Jesus. I do now and I can tell I will understand much more about His glory once I get to Heaven.

God Himself does not make mistakes. God is perfect. He is always blameless. That's why Him dying on the cross to set me free is so remarkable. I'm unremarkable, but it turns out we have a remarkable God. God loves Himself and that's why He placed His image, yes Himself, onto humans. That mapping can either be embraced or rejected. If it's embraced, you do become refined into the image of God. Who is God? God is agape love. The Greek word "agape" (/ah-gah-pay/) refers to a selfless, sacrificial, and unconditional form of love. Agape is used to describe the highest form of love that exists and that is the very same love God has for humanity, and His believers can embody this love and share it with others. God loves Himself and He wanted to extend Himself onto and into His creation, human beings. This design gives humans the free-will opportunity to learn to receive God's love, love themself, extend that love to others, and in return, closing the loop, love God back.

Agape love is cosmic, relentless, and unconditional. That's the love God always has for us. In the relationship He is always at 100%. Each human has the conscious choice to embrace that love or reject it. If He is rejected by you time and time again, eventually, He won't recognize you, because all the qualities of God inside you have been eroded through sin, depravity, pride, self-absorption, and idolatry.

This is referred to as being turned over to a reprobate mind. A reprobate mind is a state of being that is morally corrupt, unprincipled, and devoid of moral values or real love. Essentially, a monster. It is a state of being where one is completely unrecognizable by God due to persistent unbelief and immorality. It signifies a spiritual condition where an individual has turned away from God entirely and has embraced a life of sin to the point where their hearts and minds are completely hardened against the truth of God. Many individuals today find themselves in this state.

His love is unconditional, but He doesn't stay where He is unwelcomed. God's grace for a lost individual is large but not endless. Having said that, we are currently in the Grace Covenant because of Jesus. In today's world people are sinning left and right without immediately being struck down by God like God used to do in the Old Testament. The God of the Old Testament is saving up His wrath for the seven year tribulation… but more on that later.

He loves us more than we know. His interest in humans and human affairs is good news, that's why He provided Jesus as a merciful way out. With your permission He can do some heavy lifting with you in terms of healing, restoration, redemption, revelation, and truth.

———

I humbly acknowledge that the blessings I am experiencing now are not a result of my own strength or efforts, it's His Grace. When we invite the one and true God into our lives and nurture a personal relationship with Him, we will witness a supernatural transformation in our lives. I know God is real because I hear His voice in prayer and there is a distinct transformation in my life from following His commands. Prior to the cross, my life was a mess. After embracing the cross, I am being shaped by Jesus into a masterpiece that looks closer to the image of Jesus each day.

Isaiah 64:8 KJV

*But now, O Lord, thou art our father; we are the clay, and thou our potter; and we all are the work of thy hand.*

When faced with the temptation to return to old sinful habits, I turn to prayer in the name of Jesus. I fix my focus on Him, surrendering all to His will. I always keep in memory the omnipresence of God and then I experience supernatural relief from any desires that want to creep in and create distance from Him. I have tasted and seen His glory, so I am never letting go.

1 Corinthians 10:13 ASV

*There hath no temptation taken you but such as man can bear: but God is faithful, who will not suffer you to be tempted above that ye are able; but will with the temptation make also the way of escape, that ye may be able to endure it.*

I have been washed on the inside and made free by His Word, His blood, His love, and His promises written in the Bible.

I have encountered the Bible as a living, breathing Word—a text to be studied, embraced, and lived out. As I draw closer, my life takes on a supernatural quality, marked by divine appointments, messages I need to hear, and meaningful synchronicities. I see His divine orchestration in all of it now.

I have deeply experienced the power of His Holy Spirit. I have felt waves of deep love from Jesus, a type and form of love I was always craving for and didn't know I needed. A type of love that is supernatural and goes far beyond the potency of human love, agape love.

I am forever transformed and deeply impacted by His love and His grace that embraced me in my brokenness. His acceptance of me as I was extends beyond mere inclusion; it signifies my place within His Church, His family, and ultimately His eternal Kingdom, which transcends way beyond earthly limitations.

Some new agers are interested in God and what's beyond the created world. Some are not and place all their focus in pagan spirits (demons) and the four elements. The new agers that are interested in God often think there are multiple paths to reach God. They believe the myth that all religions are equal – the myth says all religions and spiritual practices will lead you into a direct and personal relationship with God. This goes with the myth that if you were a good enough person you go to Heaven. Another popular myth is there is neither Heaven nor hell, only void and endless cycles of reincarnation until enlightenment is reached.

If you have been holding onto any of these myths, not judging you. I was inside of that for about a decade. I am simply shedding light on these myths to give you the opportunity for your personal great reset, to come to the knowledge of the Truth while there is still time.

---

James 4:14 ASV

*...whereas ye know not what shall be on the morrow. What is your
life? For ye are a vapor, that appeareth for a little time, and then
vanisheth away.*

We don't have unlimited time to find right standing with God. Many
individuals in the new age movement believe it's about discovering
the healing modality that suits them perfectly. They search for the one
that strikes the balance between comfort and growth, looking for the
one that offers some comfort but not too much, so it feels like
progress. It's akin to the fad diet mentality, where individuals hop
from one trend to another in search of the perfect fit. This behavior is
reflected in how spiritual enthusiasts shift from one modality to the
next, no different than binge dieters that move from one diet to the
next. Once again, it is spiritual shiny object syndrome. That's the core
of new age spirituality. It presents a wide variety of enticing options
to explore, yet it lacks the depth needed for true transformation. That
is all the work of satan to keep you stuck in a loop of fruitlessness.

Many in the new age movement dabble in a wide variety of spiritual
experiences but never go that deep in each modality, because each
modality isn't that deep. New agers miss out entirely on enjoying the
depth and richness that a direct relationship with God can bring into
their lives.

Following Jesus is the highest path, hardest path, and deepest path.

Psalm 42:7 KJV

*Deep calleth unto deep at the noise of thy waterspouts: all thy waves
and thy billows are gone over me.*

New agers often tout things like, you can access "christ consciousness" or "universal energy" through meditation, crystalline pyramids, ascension practices, and become an ascended master yourself. This is akin to being offered the path toward buddhahood, in eastern meditation.

If one wants to taste real, not artificial, "Christ consciousness" you can select humility and surrender to the truth of Jesus. This will provide a mainline to the mainframe, so to speak, a direct avenue to greater tiers of access to the sound mind of God in your life, in other words, greater measures of His mapping into your mind. He can wholly remap your mind to the divine patterns that align with Him and who He is, so when your final day comes, and you meet your Maker, He recognizes you as His own, and accepts you into His Kingdom for eternity. He is perfect so He requires perfect submission to the knowledge of Christ. This is the only way to fully heal.

Jesus is the light, the truth, and the way. Nobody comes to the Father through any avenue other than Jesus. Any myth otherwise is a lie. Jesus is not a spiritual modality. He is a person, the Son of God, a man, still alive today, miraculously born to a virgin, with the blood of the Father flowing through His veins, making Him the perfect sacrifice to release humanity from the chains of sin, sickness, and death, as well as the sin nature inherited from Adam that affects all humanity. Our perfect God died for us, far from perfect people, to give us all of this, to set us free from the bondage of sin and death.

The Father so loved humanity that in order to reverse the curse that originated in the garden of Adam and Eve because of satan, He Had to provide the highest blood sacrifice possible, His Son, Himself. Jesus followed the Father's will perfectly and died the most terrible death possible to set you and I, and anybody with ears to hear, free, free from sin, free from bondage, free from trauma, and free from death

—

20

and hell. A nonbeliever that rejected Jesus their entire life and the sacrifice He did for them will not be reabsorbed into the Father at the end of their life, for everlasting life in Heaven, where our true life begins. They will spend their afterlife in their own personal hell they were sowing for decades. We all know someone like that. It sure seems like from the outside they are living in their own personal hell. They usually aren't kind, just like Ebenezer Scrooge. They are not in touch with truth. They project their pain onto others. They play the victim and focus on hurt and betrayal. If only they could open their ears to the truth that there is victory in Christ, a way out, a way to unlock freedom, a way to unlock a spiritually safe and fulfilling existence in this life and the next. His name is Jesus.

Billions of individuals are unaware that the payment for sin is death, a sooner death than God intended, and then eternity in hell, a place you never want to go. The only remedy to overcome death is through life, and the ultimate form of life in this realm is blood.

Here is why Jesus' blood that was and is alive pays the fine for you:

Countless individuals find themselves in a state of separation from the Father due to the consequence of Adam's fall. Even those unsaved people who outwardly exude contentment, prosperity, and stability are ensnared by the depraved sin nature passed down from Adam, they might be good at hiding it. Adam's transgression caused the curse of man, he became separated from God because he allowed satan to manipulate him. God needed a way to correct that for all humankind. As the Son of God, Jesus had the Father's life-giving blood coursing through His veins 2,000 years ago, this made Him the actual highest expression of life on earth, so Jesus, the worthy blameless Lamb became a spiritual offering through His blood and His sacrifice to completely nullify the effects of sin and the curse through His supernatural blood. Through the spiritual covering of His blood there is complete redemption and reconciliation with the Father to anyone who accepts the work that Jesus did on the cross for them.

Through Jesus' sacrificial act, individuals are declared innocent through faith in His work on the cross. Allowing the blood of Jesus to wash over you each day declares you blameless in both this life and the next. The exchange of death for life was already done for you. Jesus' victory over death, hell, and the grave, all accomplished in three days after thirty-three years of preparation, stands as a testament to God's unparalleled dominion and His grace for humanity.

Hebrews 9:22 KJV

*And almost all things are by the law purged with blood; and without shedding of blood is no remission.*

The sins you committed in this life and the sin you were born with, including all generational curses including but not limited to the fallen Adam nature from the original fall of man, is what needs to be paid for. The blood of Jesus makes you exonerated so there is the remission of sins and you too are innocent and blameless.

Adam and Eve would have never died if they didn't sin. Their sin set the curse of death into motion. The reason the sacrifice was needed by Jesus is because the wages of sin are permanent death, hell forever. The wages of accepting salvation are eternal life in Heaven with the Father. The only way to pay for the toll of death is with a superior payment of life, this is why the triumphant life of the Father's blood, also known as Jesus' blood, was needed.

The fine for sin, death, needs to be paid for with the ultimate form of payment, life. One of the facts of reality is you can't escape the principle of cause and effect, wrongly labeled as karma. You reap what you sow in this life. If you sow death into yourself and others those will be your wages. If you sow life into yourself and others those will be your wages. The only actual way to sow life into yourself is to be in touch with the truth of what "life" is. If you keep reading you will come to know that God is not only love, but He is also life. The book of life here on earth is the Bible, it allows you accept Jesus' work on the cross and find a direct relationship with God, the author of life itself.

You must come to embrace God and God's love because you can't give what you haven't got. How do you sow life into yourself and others without knowing who or what life is? You can't transmit what you haven't got. Without knowing the source of life and love, you can't provide that to yourself and others. When you find the source, you realize His name is Jesus.

The individuals known as so-called ascended masters, none of whom speak of the remission of sins, include figures like Gautama buddha (one of many buddhas in a line of buddhas), Sai Baba, Confucious, Quan Yin, Kali, Shiva, El Moyra, Metatron and Saint Germain among others. The new age tells you to aspire to become like them, but they are all traps. False idols. False gods and dead people without eternal life. Some of them are fictional characters that never even existed.

When people refer to "ascended masters" and include or compare them to Jesus, they are alluding to enlightened individuals who have supposedly reached a higher level of consciousness and mastered earthly limitations. Well, by that definition Jesus leads the field. He is the most advanced and set apart from any of them. The main reason being He is still alive today. He is the only one who is God, provides freedom from bondage and death and leads to right standing with God.

Jesus is the most in touch with reality because when He walked the earth He was fully God and fully man. He is the cornerstone of the greatest miracle humanity has ever seen. He rose from the dead after three days in the grave through the resurrection power of the Holy Spirit. Jesus was brought back to life, in a glorified body, and visited the disciples. He walked around in person after His earthly death to prove the reality of eternal life through Him. It was historically documented, 500 people saw Him walking around, alive again. It was miraculous and jaw-dropping to all that witnessed Him alive once again. God defeated death, hell, and the grave all in three days 2,000 years ago. That's resurrection power. That's Jesus.

Any powers that the ascended masters supposedly exhibited came from the demonic realm. The demonic has a power set of their own, but as you can see if you know how to be coherent and align with truth, God is much more powerful than the principalities of death and darkness. That's good news.

In Christianity, Jesus Christ is the Holy and set apart Son of God, God the Son, the Savior of humanity, and the only way to salvation. The Gospel is the death, burial, and resurrection of Jesus—all the divine, distinct, and supernatural operation of God.

The foundational tenets of the Christian faith encompass the profound belief in the divinity of Jesus Christ, His sacrificial and redemptive death to reverse the curse inherited from the fall of Adam, and His triumphant resurrection proving the existence of eternal life as a possibility for man. These pivotal events serve as the cornerstone of Christian theology, all illustrating the ultimate love and salvation that God has for His worldwide base of believers. Jesus' sacrificial death on the cross is the single most pivotal moment in human history because it reveals the promise – the promise of redemption and eternal life to all who embrace His truthful message of grace.

---

All of these components are what compose His story, the story of God, who He is, and who we are. We are in God's story. These truths of the timeline of humanity and who God is, is distributed through the Bible. It was written by forty authors that didn't know each other, were separated by location and time, wrote in three different languages, and were inspired through the resurrection power of the Holy Spirit to write it. It has over 63,000 cross references, so it miraculously all connects to itself. No other spiritual book has this much credibility. The New Testament was written across 1,500 years from the time of Jesus' death to about the year 1,533 AD. The fact that the Bible confirms itself and does not contradict itself is absolutely miracle of God. The Gospel of the death, burial, and resurrection of Jesus sets Him apart from every other spiritual figure or supposed ascended master, again most of the others are more fiction than fact.

The Bible says we have 2,000 years of the age of grace, the Church Age, that was ushered in by Jesus. We are rapidly coming near to the end of the Church Age, this will result in the rapture of the Church where the true believers are resurrected into Heaven in the twinkling of an eye and spared from the wrath of the seven year tribulation… but more on that later.

Jesus is the most widely documented spiritual figure in the history books. He is arguably the most famous man in the world, still to this day. He is Holy and set apart when it comes to the spiritual realm. There is nobody else like Him. There is nobody else that defeated death like Him. He is inviting you to become more like Him by learning about Him and then hopefully after this book making the choice to be born again by committing to behold Him and carry Him.

There are not multiple ways to God. There's only one. His name is Jesus.

John 14:6 ASV

*Jesus saith unto him, I am the way, and the truth, and the life: no one cometh unto the Father, but by me.*

I know some of you will think the same thing that I thought about my friend that said, "Jesus is looking for you."

"Stop annoying me with the J-word." The reason His name may be irritating is because demons tremble at His name. This is because the new age opens doors to the demonic. But the good news is Jesus has the ultimate authority and final say over angels and demons.

I will explain what deliverance from all evils is later in this book.

Man at his worst is demonized, man at his best is still embattled with the Adam nature, man at his better than best state is surrendered to God, is allowing the healing operation of God, and is on the road to Heaven.

The truth is, if you are destined to read this book and claim true freedom, become born again, and be on fire, you will. It is written, those who have ears to hear the truth will hear, adhere, and abide.

Revelation 2:7 KJV

*He that hath an ear, let him hear what the Spirit saith unto the churches; To him that overcometh will I give to eat of the tree of life, which is in the midst of the paradise of God.*

There's nothing that compares to the faith, hope, and love that comes from knowing Jesus and placing all your faith in Him. He will never let you down.

He will supply to you supernatural peace, joy, and righteousness. This peace is a peace that surpasses all understanding (Philippians 4:7).

My prayer is that this book plants a seed in your heart and that you recognize the absolute Truth in this book, and that may you be open minded enough to the idea that Jesus is chasing after you too.

You are a soul. You matter. In the eyes of God, no matter how much trash you are surrounded by, you are treasure. You are worthy. You are worthy of the love of the Father. The reality is His blood washes anyone clean of their dirt. If you hear the call and step forth, He can claim you as the treasure you are to Him.

Nobody comes to the Father spotless. Come as you are and let Jesus meet you in your mess. He will never forsake you nor condemn you for coming home to Him. He is for you. He is a good Father.

It's by His might, His grace, and not by my power that you may feel the poke in your heart to let Jesus in.

Salvation is a gift of God. The gift works through the power of the Holy Spirit to bring a man or woman to conviction and repentance. I will never take credit for a new salvation. I'm just a servant in the Kingdom of God, on a co-mission with Jesus, to present the Truth and then allow God to do the heavy lifting. Only He can overcome someone with the glory of Himself.

I am humbled, honored, and deeply fulfilled to be a conduit for the Holy Spirit; for intercession, for teaching, for scattering the Word of God, for your healing, for your deliverance, and for your salvation. I'm humbled He could take someone like me, a former mess of sin, pain, lust, pride, new age vegetable soup spirituality, and then stand me upright, dust me off, turn me around, lift my chin, and use me to bless others and expand His eternal Kingdom. The fact that He met me in my mess, worked on my heart, and now sees me worthy to be sent on His behalf to be an ambassador of His truth and His love is mind blowing.

If you have ever wanted nearness and connection with God, meaning and purpose, a glimpse behind the veil, and a new lease on life this is your invitation. Consider yourself formally invited to the wedding feast in Heaven.

Once in a lifetime opportunities only come once in a lifetime.

This book you are to read is a distinct blend of personal testimony, spiritual concepts, keys to your true identity, and an explainer for some of the absolute truths in the Bible.

You will receive a discourse on the dangers of the new age and more importantly on the flipside you will get a further understanding written on your heart of the glory of God, and what knowing Him can mean for you.

Blood, sweat, and tears were shed for over a decade to obtain the discoveries enshrouded in this book. I blindly stumbled for years while seeking for the doorway to healing and redemption. This book is your fast lane to the door handle so the doorway to God fully opens.

A door that no man can shut.

Revelation 3:8 ASV

*...behold, I have set before thee a door opened, which no one can shut*

## Dedication

Dedicated to Jesus Christ my Lord and Savior, for pulling me out of the harmful fire and placing me in His Holy fire. All through and by Him. For loving me better than anyone ever can or ever will.

Malachi 3:2-3 KJV

*But who may abide the day of his coming? and who shall stand when he appeareth? for he is like a refiner's fire, and like fullers' soap: And he shall sit as a refiner and purifier of silver: and he shall purify the sons of Levi, and purge them as gold and silver, that they may offer unto the Lord an offering in righteousness.*

Hebrews 12:2 KJV

*Looking unto Jesus the author and finisher of our faith; who for the joy that was set before him endured the cross, despising the shame, and is set down at the right hand of the throne of God.*

By His grace alone He rescued me and claimed me as His own just in time.

I now see what my life was like before Jesus and now after. The difference is massive. I now see why He kept me alive and safe during several moments of near death.

He has removed depression and anxiety, and I live in a consistent state of peace and joy that can only come from Him. I have obtained salvation and a place in the mansions of Heaven.

John 14:2 KJV

*In my Father's house are many mansions: if it were not so, I would have told you. I go to prepare a place for you.*

*Numbers 6:24-26 KJV*

*The Lord bless thee, and keep thee: The Lord make his face shine upon thee, and be gracious unto thee: The Lord lift up his countenance upon thee, and give thee peace.*

Isaiah 61:1 KJV

*The Spirit of the Lord God is upon me; because the Lord hath anointed me to preach good tidings unto the meek; he hath sent me to bind up the brokenhearted, to proclaim liberty to the captives, and the opening of the prison to them that are bound.*

Psalm 24:1 KJV

*The earth is the Lord's, and the fulness thereof; the world, and they that dwell therein.*

John 14:20 KJV

*At that day ye shall know that I am in my Father, and ye in me, and I in you.*

## Acknowledgement

My personal Bible teacher and esteemed elder in the faith, brother John. He was trained by the late "Holy" Hubert Lindsey.

John has patiently and compassionately brought me into a deep understanding of Bible theology.

He has properly shown me how to rightly divide between the Jewish mosaic law and the grace that Jesus brought when His blood started to flow down that day on Calvary 2,000 years ago.

I now know that through Jesus purchased the Church with His blood, He was resurrected on the third day, fulfilled the Jewish law, and opened salvation to the entire world. Forty-seven days after the resurrection Jesus sent the Holy Spirit and fire baptism to His people as a guide and comforter for everlasting righteousness.

Because John has so deeply discipled me, I now see the truth that I am no longer my own, I am Jesus' purchased possession; therefore, I never deny the omnipresence of the Holy Spirit.

John has shown me the difference between the Kingdom of Heaven and the Kingdom of God. He has shown me where the Old Testament Covenant ended and where the New Testament Covenant began. He has shown me where the religious and indoctrinated operation of man has no eternal value and where the operation of God begins to have eternal value in a man's life.

The best part about John is He always gives the credit to God.

"Never deny the omnipresence of the Holy Spirit." -Brother John

---

# Contents

CH. 1 HAVE YOU BEEN SEEKING SPIRITUALLY SEEKING? .......................................39

CH. 2 GOD'S WILL: IT IS WRITTEN, YOU HAVE A HOPE AND A FUTURE...............45

CH. 3 HUMANITY FELL FROM GRACE ................................................................55

CH. 4 THE RAPTURE RESURRECTION EVENT: HIS CHURCH IS NOT APPOINTED TO WRATH ....................................................................................................................69

CH. 5 HOW TO BE A SAINT IN THE KINGDOM OF GOD .......................................95

CH. 6 THE HOLY SPIRIT ...................................................................................115

CH. 7 THE LAW OF ATTRACTION GURUS HAVE IT ALL WRONG..........................151

CH. 8 DO YOU DESIRE TO BE PURIFIED?..........................................................161

CH. 9 THE POWER VACUUM..............................................................................179

CH. 10 YOUR UNSHAKABLE IDENTITY IN CHRIST..............................................207

CH. 11 MAN'S SEARCH FOR MEANING .............................................................231

CH. 12 ENERGETIC SIGNATURES ......................................................................255

CH. 13 APPRECIATION OVER EXPECTATION......................................................273

CH. 14 THE WONDERFUL COUNSELOR...............................................................297

CH. 15 THE WORD OF GOD................................................................................307

CH. 16 HOW TO IDENTIFY FALSE CHRISTIANITY ...............................................333

CH. 17 STEP IN ALL THE WAY YOUR DESTINY AWAITS .....................................345

CH. 18 SALVATION PRAYER ..............................................................................359

THE NAMES OF GOD: WHO GOD IS ..................................................................365

## Introduction

Have you been focused on healing yourself?

Welcome home! Take rest.

You are truly blessed to have discovered this book, not merely lucky but blessed. Your encounter with this book was not a coincidence; it was by divine appointment. Jesus desires to have a personal relationship with you, and through Him, you can experience abundant blessings. Those who accept Him into their lives are truly blessed beyond measure, blessed in this life and in the eternity that awaits.

I sincerely apologize if you come from a background of being hurt by a local church or a so-called Christian. There is a big difference between the condemnation, rituals, and rules of man-made religion and the very human, very real relationship you can begin to develop with Jesus, the Son of God, through the power of the Holy Spirit.

The term religion is a loaded word because it's two sided. Meaning there is the indoctrination of man, that puts on the outward image of holiness, follows man-made traditions and rituals and has a self-focused worship. And on the other side you have the authentic operation of God, which happens to be Jesus Himself. Man gets directly in the way of God and creates a misrepresentation of the truth of who God is. Only Jesus Himself can come in and clean up the mess that man has made. He does this through giving you a direct relationship with Him that surpasses any man-made attempts at religion.

Again, one side consists of rituals, rites, regulations, false humility, and a brash treatment of the body of Christ, while the other side

---

involves the transformative operation of God that can overcome the flesh, bring healing to any wound, and mend the brokenhearted.

The Scripture that shows the difference between religion and relationship is found in the book of Colossians in the New Testament.

Colossians 2:23 ASV

*Which things have indeed a show of wisdom in will-worship, and humility, and severity to the body; but are not of any value against the indulgence of the flesh.*

The operation of God in a man's or woman's life can make the impossible, possible. Overcoming the flesh and the wickedness baked into the human body is impossible without the direct operation of God in a person's life. This means it's only God that can set a man free.

Jesus is the alive and He is the direct operation of God in a person's life. He made such a splash in human history because He was fully God and fully man. He walked the earth like we do, so He intimately understands the human condition and what it's like. He intimately understands our thoughts, emotions, and all that the human experience entails.

He can provide a different type of love and healing… an astronomical love that we have been seeking after our entire lives. I say that with complete confidence because I was spiritually seeking and very broken inside for decades. I was searching for this type of love in all the wrong places. I didn't find the healing and the love I needed in those sources because it was never possible.

Where I did find the love I was desperately needing was through Jesus and the new life He pours in.

---

His love can be viscerally experienced through direct and personal encounters with Him, where wave after wave of His healing and restorative love is crashes over. During encounters like there are tears of joy, healing, and relief. All you must do is show up and enter into His presence with praise and thanksgiving.

Psalm 100:4 KJV

*Enter into his gates with thanksgiving, and into his courts with praise: be thankful unto him, and bless his name.*

If you keep an open mind that Jesus could be who the Bible says He is, then you also give yourself the joyful opportunity of being undone by the face to face reality of His love, the love you desperately need, and what a beautiful love it is.

He is always so close by, nearer than your own skin, so He speaks gently and kindly to His children.

You will know you experienced an encounter with Him if you felt a deep surge of love, peace, joy, comfort, affection, appreciation, satisfaction and gratitude, and not only that, it wasn't anything you manufactured. You simply allowed His grace to rest on you.

His love feels like a warm blanket wrapping around your whole body. A feeling that you would dwell within for eternity if you could.

Well you can. Your future with Jesus is very bright. Allowing His love in now, a love better than any other human can provide, is just the start.

This is the blessed hope: His presence in your life.

# Ch. 1 HAVE YOU BEEN SEEKING SPIRITUALLY SEEKING?

If you have been going from tradition to tradition and looking for peace, looking for relief, seeking freedom, and looking for self-knowledge look no further because all self-knowledge is found in the Father.

Philippians 4:7 KJV

*And the peace of God, which passeth all understanding, shall keep your hearts and minds through Christ Jesus.*

The image of the eternal God of the universe, the Maker of Heaven and earth, has been mapped onto all humans, and it's up to us to claim our identity in God, and enter into our divine heritage.

Genesis 1:27 KJV

*So God created man in his own image, in the image of God created he him; male and female created he them.*

When you are observing yourself or another person you are also studying the image and likeness of God.

God is intimately connected with us, is for us, and wants to know us. God wants to give us a hope and a future.

We have a good Father in Heaven that wants to see you completely healed - whether spiritually, mentally, physically, emotionally, or financially. Our God will bring you back to life and restore you to the condition that God intended for you, in other words; God's will for you. He actually wants a relationship with you, and not a surface level one either, a deep and real one.

God doesn't want to see you down and out and suffering. He wants you to realize He will give you a purpose, a hope, and a future with the actual blessing being a real relationship with Him and salvation in Heaven. The Lord will indeed provide for you, but it's important not to equate God's blessings solely with provision or physical possessions.

The Bible wants Christians to be doing Kingdom work, and that will take specialized tools and resources. Christians must be able to handle resources without turning those resources of the world into idols. Idols are anyone or anything given greater priority than your direct relationship with God.

People seek new age false gods and idols because they are on a quest for personal power or financial gain or both.

The book of Acts in the Bible demonstrates a story about a sorcerer who uses sorcery for personal gain and then he comes to realize that there is much more power in the Holy Spirit than his sorcery work, and he could harness it to make a profit.

The book of Acts is placed during the early Church, beginning three days after His death on the cross. Jesus was resurrected, went to Heaven, and immediately came back to earth to walk among His disciples. He was walking around with holes in His hands where the nails where in His glorified body. One of inheritances of the saints of God is a glorified body, we will review all of the inheritances of the saints in later chapters.

A saint of God is anybody that has heard the call to be holy and set apart from the world and dedicated to God's purposes on earth.

In Acts 8:9-24, Simon the sorcerer was amazed by the miracles that followed the disciples and wanted to purchase the power of the Holy Spirit from them, yes with physical money. The Apostle Peter rebuked Simon for his wicked plan to purchase the Spirit of God with mere money with the intention of personal gain. Simon's first instinct was to treat the indwelling of the Spirit of God like a business transaction which was clearly out of order. Peter urged Simon to seek repentance and turn away from his learned habit pattern of manipulating others for personal gain.

The early Church worked diligently to create distance between the path of following Jesus and the alternative paths paganism, sorcerery, divination, and witchcraft. All of which were common at the time and are still common to this day.

Even though the dark arts have been consistent across time, God is much more consistent because He is the same yesterday, today, and into forever (Hebrews 13:8). Satan and his demons have a fast approaching expiration date, so they are on death row. God is the eternal Creator to forever behold. He is still in operation today just as He was in the book of Acts.

The early believers in the Church accomplished the goal of setting the path of following Jesus apart from sorcery and other pagan practices by collectively and openly renouncing their former false gods and idols. This act of renunciation was a profound and public demonstration of their commitment to following Christ wholeheartedly and rejecting any form of idolatry or sorcery that was contrary to the teachings of the Bible.

Acts 19:18-20 ASV

*Many also of them that had believed came, confessing, and declaring their deeds. And not a few of them that practised magical arts brought their books together and burned them in the sight of all; and they counted the price of them, and found it fifty thousand pieces of silver. So mightily grew the word of the Lord and prevailed.*

This account displays the decisive actions taken by many believers in the early Church, not just a few of them, to strongly forsake and renounce their previous involvement with magic, witchcraft, and the occult and instead embrace a new way of life in alignment with the teachings of the Lord. These early believers were followers of the way of Christ.

In the Book of Acts, the term "followers of the Way" was used to describe the early Christians. This term was likely used by both believers and outsiders to refer to the followers of Jesus Christ. It emphasizes the idea that Christianity is not just a set of beliefs, but a "way" of living and being – an entire lifestyle of passionately following Jesus as the way, the truth, and the life (John 14:6).

Just as the early Church realized, you will also come have a greater awareness around the gap between "holy living" that places you into right standing with God and the alternative paths that place you into "sinful living" and therefore direct opposition to God. One way brings you home and the other brings you astray.

The alternative paths are weaved all throughout modern society. Modern day witchcraft and idolatry take many different forms. Well intended spiritual seekers quickly end up finding themselves in the alternative paths because of how common they are.

The primary focus of the early Church was centered on proclaiming the Gospel with conviction. The unfiltered Gospel message stirred the hearts of the people. The disciples declared the fulfillment of the prophet Joel's prophecy about the Holy Spirit pouring out on all flesh (Acts 2:16-21), they shared many other prophecies that were confirmed through Jesus, and they boldly proclaimed Jesus as the crucified and risen Messiah, the anointed one that the Jesus people were looking for because He was prophesied to come. They explained to the Jewish crowds their role in Jesus' crucifixion and lead them to a state of holy repentance. The call to repentance coupled with the receiving of the baptism of the Holy Spirit and fire, and the fervent cries to save themselves from a corrupt generation were all key to showing the crowds that the Way was very different than Judaism, paganism, and any other alternative path out there.

It was only talk either, they showed the authority Jesus bestowed upon them to bring salvation, healing, and deliverance. They demonstrated the direct and life-changing operation and impact the Holy Spirit can have, this placed following the Way, way above anything else.

Simon ultimately came to repentance too and acknowledged his request to buy the Spirit of God was unholy and asked Peter to pray for him. Simon did come to authentic repentance and at some level recognized his need for God in his life. He saw the conviction in the disciples; he saw the demonstration of the Holy Spirit. He could not deny the power in the Spirit of God was superior to his practices in the dark arts. He had a Holy conviction come over him and he realized he would rather not be in any opposition to God. The veil was lifted, and he clearly saw sorcery and manipulation were in infinite opposition to God.

The takeaway from Simon's story is surrendering to faith in Jesus instantly facilitates a sincere change of heart. Naturally, it occurs as a result of the operation of God, and when that operation takes hold in a person, the fallen desires of the heart including the desires to practice anything in opposition to God falls away.

God's will is never to manipulate people for personal gain, but instead to create mutually beneficial outcomes that benefit many. One that fully comes to Christ receives the benefits of salvation and spiritual gifts, God benefits by gaining another soul into His Kingdom, and others that are also saved, healed, and delivered through the Spirit of God also benefit. God creates triple win scenarios and not win-loss dynamics.

As you can see, God wants a person to emerge into their highest and best form.

Jeremiah 29:11 KJV

*For I know the thoughts that I think toward you, saith the Lord, thoughts of peace, and not of evil, to give you an expected end.*

# Ch. 2 GOD'S WILL: IT IS WRITTEN, YOU HAVE A HOPE AND A FUTURE

Just like how God had a plan and a will for his Son, Jesus, while He was here, God has a will for you too.

You matter to him a lot! More than you could ever know!

When a nonbeliever accepts Jesus into their heart then He celebrates just like a dad would celebrate if they got a child back from the dead that died suddenly.

Think of a parent that lost a child at a young age due to birth complications or an accident or another health issue. If you completely turn your life to Jesus, then it's like God got a child back from the dead! It's just like that! That's how much your restoration matters to Him. He is a good God!

The new age and all other false belief systems can't offer this type of redemption, this type of freedom, and this type of salvation!

Salvation simply means you are saved from hell and are now on the road to Heaven. It means you just changed teams and became a saint of God, and now personally have Jesus in the throne room of Heaven, alive, day and night, watching over you, guiding you, and praying for you.

Ephesians 2:8-9 KJV

*For by grace are ye saved through faith; and that not of yourselves: it is the gift of God: Not of works, lest any man should boast.*

---

Acts 4:12 KJV

*And in none other is there salvation: for neither is there any other name under heaven, that is given among men, wherein we must be saved.*

The name above all names is Jesus. There is no higher name. Through His name and His blood, His authority is here.

Rest assured that your resurrected (post-salvation) life purpose is bigger and better than anything you could have imagined. On the other side of giving your life to Jesus is a new level of satisfaction and meaning that your life never had before.

We have powerful imaginations, so just stop and wonder… how much more powerful is God's imagination?

Consider God's birds eye perspective for a moment.

He can see across the past, present, and future, transcending time and space to perceive how the events of your life intertwine far more clearly than you ever could. Therefore, seeking His wisdom and guidance is a wise choice. You can only see today, He can always see your tomorrow.

He can see which people in your life are blessings and which people are dead weight. Seek His presence through prayer and praise and your life will start to take on the supernatural power of God. You can't get the power of God in your life until you seek the presence of Him.

He can comprehend your special talents and abilities better than any other person can because He made you. He made you in the womb so He knows your life purpose and life plans better than you do.

Jeremiah 1:5 KJV

*Before I formed thee in the belly I knew thee; and before thou camest forth out of the womb I sanctified thee, and I ordained thee a prophet unto the nations.*

Psalm 139:13-14 KJV

*For thou hast possessed my reins: thou hast covered me in my mother's womb. I will praise thee; for I am fearfully and wonderfully made: marvellous are thy works; and that my soul knoweth right well.*

Your mom was taking care of her body with exercise and good nutrition while you were being formed in the womb, but God birthed your soul and shaped your heart and neurons together in the ways that He best saw fit for the life design that He wanted for you.

At the moment of conception there's a medically documented flash of light and the soul entered the womb – a miracle of God all on its own. That same day you were being formed by God.

God knew everything about you when were two cells rubbing together, don't you think today while you are a full-grown human made of trillions of cells, He has your back? He knew everything there was to know about you then and He knows everything there is to know about you now. From the start you had a God written will to follow to give you a life of victory and satisfaction. He didn't promise it would be easy, but He does promise He's always there with you and His way is worth it, in this life and into the next.

After seven weeks of growing in the womb you were the size of a coffee bean, already with a heart and brain being formed.

He has always had an interest in you and wants to bless you and prosper you with life and life more abundantly (John 10:10). He promises the resurrection and healing of your soul from the damage of this world. He wants to love on you and show you how much you are loved by Him, His Son Jesus, and the Holy Spirit. He can only do this with your full permission to allow in His will. You must let him speak over you with His Word and His voice in order to rewrite you and bring you back to the will He's always had for you.

Regardless of how well your earthly parents were able to love you, the Father wants you to feel the unlimited waves of love that He has for you, and at any hour of the day, and without condition. His love is not something you have to work for. It's something to be surrendered to.

The proof He loves you and wants you was His death on the cross for you. He died in your place, He showed His worthiness to you and reversed every curse in your life, for you to be set free from all oppression.

You happen to be God's highest form of creation, so start to take joy in that knowledge. The Father is for you. He loves you beyond belief. Many people think God is either evil or nonexistent, because evil things occur on earth at the hand of man, but they must understand man has free will mixed with a fallen nature that can only be fully overcome through the blood of Jesus and His work on the cross.

God gives each individual free will out of respect for each person. How each souls stewards this free will is up to them. Life without free will would be meaningless and without any creativity. God did not create robots. He created humans with the ability to think, act, perceive and grow in goodness, truth, and beauty. To Jesus, there is no greater beauty than a believer who reflects the image of God and is journeying towards the wedding feast in Heaven with Him. Heaven celebrates over a soul that has found their way home (Luke 15:7).

God has a plan to save you from the wreckage of the past and put you back on your feet, with nourishing food in your belly, His Word in your mind, and purpose in your step. Only He can do this, nobody and nothing else can. We are talking about the operation of God in your life, not the operation of man. Every other solution falls short of the power and glory of God.

Not college. Not psychologists. Not psychics. Not tarot readers. Not online courses. Not personal development gurus. Not self-help books. Not even your closest friends and family can turn you around and place you on the road to Heaven. This journey is about having faith and stepping into the supernatural operation of God in your life. Your only job is to allow it.

You will discover as you progress through this book the supernatural and profound significance of following Jesus and adhering to the teachings of the Bible, and I'm not referring to rigid religion. I am referring to a personal relationship with Jesus as your Lord and Savior. So much of the world says you must work for transformation, God says, "Let me blow your mind and love the hell of out of you."

Only He can do this because He is somebody who knows you. Somebody who will encourage you. Somebody to lean on when times are great and when times are tough, and not only that, any time of the day. He is real. He is Jesus. He's alive just like you and I are and just like your best friend is. He can also become your new best friend, I know seems farfetched, I understand, but as you get deeper into the supernatural Word of the Bible and deeper into His presence then the

---

49

Holy Spirit will be flowing through you, and you will start to have clear communication with God. It's a real relationship, not an imaginary friend., and you will come to realize He is more real than life itself. He really cares about us that much and wants to know each of us personally. That's why the Gospel is good news.

Engaging with God through a direct and honest relationship is crucial to how God can come in and operate in your life. This is because He wants to know you and be in close communication with you. It's each person's choice to surrender and seek Him and be close to Him.

Those that are close to Him in this life will be close to Him in the eternal life. Those that are far away from Him in this life will not be able to spend eternity with Him, because frankly He does not know them. That's how personal the God of the universe really is. This is good news. He is not a remote, cold, and impersonal simulation as some people believe.

He is beyond capable to be with us each day so that we can come to know Him more and He can come to know us more. If He recognizes you now, He will recognize you upon entry into Heaven. Being with Him in Heaven is obviously of eternal importance. We are only alive on the earth for a tiny blip in time.

As mentioned, religion has really placed a bad taste in people's mouths about what Christianity is, what the Bible is about, and who Jesus is.

Showing highly indoctrinated religious people the real Bible and the real Jesus are some of the hardest people to get through to, because it means the whole man-made approach they have been taking for years or decades is wrong. That can be life shattering for some. There are many Christians in the world but only a certain subset of them are born again, they have left their old life behind and have allowed the new life in.

John 3:3 KJV

*Jesus answered and said unto him, Verily, verily, I say unto thee, Except a man be born again, he cannot see the kingdom of God.*

Born again refers to a spiritual rebirth or transformation that occurs when a person accepts Jesus Christ as their Lord and Savior. It means they have tasted the tree of life, the goodness of God, and the reality of God and there is no turning back. It's someone that's realized being connected to the vine, Jesus, is better than the world and anything else in it.

When you have a direct experience of God coming into your life then you will immediately start to turn away from sin and completely embrace the Gospel message of the death, burial, and resurrection of Jesus. The resurrection was a literal event and its simultaneously symbolic of a man or woman being rebirthed, made new, and filled with the gift of new life through the Holy Spirit. Just as Jesus was resurrected a person becomes spiritually resurrected, cleaned, turned around, and ready for the rapture resurrection event of the Church.

Before a man or woman is born again they are not truly alive. They are still under the bondage of finite death rather than eternal life. This has to do with everyone being born under the curse of the bloodline from the fall of Adam and Eve. Only the blood of Jesus and the Holy Spirit completely reverses that curse and births someone anew.

The concept of rebirth emphasizes a renewal of the individual's relationship with God, a renewal of their mind and the desires of their heart, and an entirely new beginning – a new lease on life.

A born again believer places all of their faith in Jesus, because they know they can trust Him. He is God and not an ordinary man so He will never let you down. He is the master mediator between the earthly realm and the Heavenlies.

Only the Lord Jesus can be the ultimate protector and provider of your life. Only placing your faith in Him can turn your life in an entirely new direction that is pleasing to yourself and to God, the Father in Heaven.

Jesus was very close to His Father while He was on earth, that's why He called Him Father throughout the Bible and spoke with Him daily. We can also have the same direct daily relationship with the Father through Jesus and the Holy Spirit, not just a similar one, but the very same intimate connection with the one and true God.

He will kick down doors to save you from the evil one. He will steadfastly go after His lost sheep. The Lord giveth and the Lord taketh (Job 1:21) meaning He provides all blessings in your life whether big or small. Take care of His teachings and embody His Kingdom, the Kingdom of God, more each day, and He will assuredly take care of you and your needs.

The Lord is the ultimate provider, one of His Hebrew names mentioned in the first book of the Bible, Genesis, is Jehovah Jireh (/juh-HOH-vuh ji-REH/) meaning "the Lord our provider."

Read to the end, and you will find a glossary of all the names of God. The names will give you even further clarity on who God is.

This book will help you gain a deeper insight into the nature of God, how to cultivate access to the Kingdom of God, fortify your identity in Christ, and give you the keys to go deeper into your life purpose. Along the way of following God's will for you, you will need to be better equipped to navigate the spiritual battles that come your way, as well as the general ups and downs of life.

You will fortify your faith and you will become better equipped at being effective for the Gospel. You will learn the knowledge on how to enter the Kingdom, become clean, holy, and much more aware of the fundamentals of the faith.

There aren't a million basics to learn, there are just a few, it's about going in deep on those and mastering them. As God says, *study* to show yourself approved unto God (2 Timothy 2:15). The basics always go back to the death, burial, and resurrection – the blood, the Holy Spirit and what allowing in that operation from the throne room unlocks.

Studying and becoming better equipped in the faith is not about embarking on a laborious path of works, rather it's about learning the value of surrender and rest in Him, how much of faith can bring in the miracles of God, rather than thinking it is human works or human striving that gets the result.

He is the God of grace and favor, He just needs your attention. Strap in, step in all the way and you will be reintroduced to the real Jesus, the real faith, and the real transformation you need for your destiny in Christ.

Haggai 2:9 KJV

*The glory of this latter house shall be greater than of the former, saith the Lord of hosts: and in this place will I give peace, saith the Lord of hosts.*

If you've been wandering and seeking meaning in all the wrong places, welcome home! Pause, breathe deep, and take rest in Jesus.

You are invited to take a moment, kneel down, talk to God, and let go of your heaviest burdens. Turn them over and He will take them. Give Him what's been weighing you down and He will lift you from it and bring you instant relief. He can only do this if you take the first and hardest step – to surrender, to lay down your worries, to lay your down shame, to lay down your pain, to lay down your pride, and lay down your heart. The only requirement is to come as you are.

Your heart won't feel as heavy and you will immediately feel the effects of prayer. That is the power of prayer. His burden is light, and His yoke is easy. He wants you to feel His peace rest on you and not the heaviness of life.

Proverbs 10:22 KJV

*The blessing of the Lord, it maketh rich, and he addeth no sorrow with it.*

Nothing else will ever be able to satisfy and fill the God sized hole that each human has. No pleasure. No reward. No person. No dollar amount. No possession. Only Jesus can satisfy.

He can see things that you can't. He can see the people in your life for who they really are. This is because He knows their thoughts, intentions, and actions, especially the ones you haven't seen.

Billions of humans are lost and really don't want to believe that God can observe their intentions, thoughts, and actions. This is largely because deep down they know they aren't living right so they prefer willful ignorance over the truth. This is no different than Adam and Eve willfully ignoring the command that God provided in Genesis 2, "And the Lord God commanded the man, saying, Of every tree of the garden thou mayest freely eat: but of the tree of the knowledge of good and evil, thou shalt not eat of it: for in the day that thou eatest thereof thou shalt surely die." Adam and Eve were in glorified bodies and would have lived forever. The garden was built for them and they didn't have to labor for any of it. The animals (other than the snake) and the weather weren't trying to kill them. They had it made.

God provided for them a perfect garden, but they willfully chose to ignore God's command and live in willful ignorance (disobedience) leading to the fall of humanity. God called Adam and Eve "Adam" reflecting how they were one because they were married. Adam had a duty to protect his wife, she being his flesh, however when she was alone, she was disobedient to God even though she knew the one rule. The snake deceived Eve into disobeying the one rule through lying to her that tasting the forbidden fruit would not result in death, instead it would bring enlightenment and godlike knowledge. The snake's tactics aimed to undermine God's trustworthiness, His perfect identity, and sow seeds of rebellion and disobedience. The snake successfully built-up Eve's pride, which was her and Adam's downfall. Paradise was lost, innocence was lost and the generational curse of death and destructive tendencies entered the bloodline of humanity. This is why today we have evil people, torrential weather, and vicious animals.

Things would have turned out better for them if they had faith that God knew better than them. This is why a believer lovingly embraces the truth that God can provide protection against people, places and things not meant for them and conversely, He can make Kingdom connections to people, places, and things meant for them, all in accordance with His will.

A nonbeliever living in sin will hate the idea that God can see everything. A believer living in holiness will love the idea that God can see everything.

As you turn away from a sinful lifestyle and embrace the lifestyle of righteousness, that one that God designed for you, then your new life in Christ will arrive and align with God's beautiful and meticulously crafted plan for you. That plan is written and is awaiting you.

Nobody that is born and given life and breath in their lungs is a mistake. He has a will for them all, the overwhelming majority reject it.

Everyone that is conceived has a God-given perfect will and a life plan. He is that good. The eighty million babies that were tragically aborted prior to Roe v. Wade being overturned in America each had a will, a hope, and a future that was destroyed. All those people that died in world wars had a will and a future that the evil one destroyed.

Their futures were cut short. God authors life. The devil authors death. God knows every individual who is responsible for all those deaths and He will never forget.

God cares about life, a lot. I do believe in the all those babies are in Heaven awaiting their parents, and if their parents do not make it to Heaven then God will continue to take care of those babies. Across the Bible God's love for babies and children is evident. They are innocent. They get to choose if they embrace God or reject at the age of accountability.

---

57

The age of accountability is where children reach a point of understanding their actions in relation to sin. This age is believed to be when children become responsible for their choices. Theologians derive this idea from passages like Isaiah 7:16. It signifies a time when children can discern between good and evil. Children before the age of accountability will go up in the rapture of the Church.

If you are past the age of accountability that means God will hold you accountable for your actions, good and bad. He will make a way for you to enjoy eternal life in Heaven if you turn away from the life of sin, because sin only leads to death and destruction, as we see in the story of Adam and Eve.

Isn't a peaceful and satisfying life better than a stressful and uncertain one?

Categorically, yes!

Proverbs 28:13 KJV

*He that covereth his sins shall not prosper: but whoso confesseth and forsaketh them shall have mercy.*

Isaiah 55:7 KJV

*Let the wicked forsake his way, and the unrighteous man his thoughts: and let him return unto the Lord, and he will have mercy upon him; and to our God, for he will abundantly pardon.*

Drink in the above and below Scriptures that help convey the blueprint that Jesus brought to the earth through His life, His work, His sermons, His disciples, and His ultimate sacrifice.

Righteousness is holiness and that is who God is.

John 3:15-17 KJV

*That whosoever believeth in him should not perish, but have eternal life. For God so loved the world, that he gave his only begotten Son, that whosoever believeth in him should not perish, but have everlasting life. For God sent not his Son into the world to condemn the world; but that the world through him might be saved.*

Adam and Eve failed the test. In Christian theology, it is believed that God, being omniscient (all-knowing), had foreknowledge of Adam and Eve's eventual disobedience in the Garden of Eden. While God knew that they would disobey, it does not mean that He caused or forced them to do so. God granted them free will to make choices, even though He knew the outcome. The disobedience of Adam and Eve played a crucial role in God's plan for redemption through Jesus Christ, demonstrating His mercy, grace, and love for humanity despite our shortcomings.

Were they always meant to fail? I don't know, but what is certain is that Jesus is the redeemer that came back for the souls of earth to clear the sin debt of past, present, and future – for anyone willing to surrender to His work on the cross. God wasn't going to leave His children to the command of the evil one. This is why Jesus is called the last Adam. He came and reversed it all.

He loves His children so much that He did not hesitate to lay down His life for them. The Father generously gave His only Son, Jesus, to give everyone eternal life in Heaven and to provide true freedom from the curse of the fall of Adam. He did this because He loved us first. Loving Him first was not a requirement for Him to send His only Son for the redemption of all the souls that would hear the call, in other words, He came back for His children. He doesn't have a clenched fist. He has open arms for those that belong to Him through hearing the call to surrender.

Jesus opened Heavenly access, meaning through Him we can enter the Kingdom of God to heal ourselves and to positively affect humanity.

Jesus shared this prayer openly to teach the lost sheep of Israel, the Jewish people, how to pray and welcome in the Kingdom of Heaven on earth. The lost sheep of Israel rejected the Messiah, Jesus, and the opportunity right then to bring in the Kingdom of Heaven on earth. This was just like Adam and Eve rejecting God's one command. The acceptance of the prophesied Messiah would have led to the restoration of a perfect garden-like state, Heaven on earth. However, due to the presence of evil in the bloodline of humanity from the fall, they rejected the Messiah who spoke these words.

Matthew 6:9-13 KJV

*After this manner therefore pray ye:*
*Our Father which art in heaven, Hallowed be thy name. Thy kingdom come, Thy will be done in earth, as it is in heaven. Give us this day our daily bread. And forgive us our debts, as we forgive our debtors. And lead us not into temptation, but deliver us from evil: For thine is the kingdom, and the power, and the glory, for ever. Amen.*

Jesus returned with the mission to restore the lost paradise for the strayed sheep of Israel, but overall, they rejected Him because He sounded heretical, He didn't come as a thunderous warrior to save the Jews from the Romans, and He threatened the power structure of the religious establishment.

Evil may be in the bloodline of humanity from the fall, but Jesus came back for the Jewish people, and after their rejection and the cross, then the Gentiles (all people groups in the world) we're granted access to the Kingdom of God and deliverance from evil.

Acts 28:28 KJV

*Be it known therefore unto you, that the salvation of God is sent unto the Gentiles, and that they will hear it.*

The evil nature in humans is from the fall but God sent Jesus because He saw the greater potential in us. He saw us in Heaven one day.

God desires for each person to hear the call and embrace righteousness and holiness, rather than surrender to sin. Sin is a direct a departure from God's flawless intentions. The adversary thrives on distorting truth, sowing doubt and leading individuals astray from the path of righteousness. The evil one distributes sin on a silver platter. The enemy is a parasite on the planet to be eviscerated. A parasitical pest that's attempting to organize and consume its host – just like a snake eating itself, which snakes do indeed do. Totally incoherent. It's no wonder that the snake eating itself is a satanic symbol.

You can observe if the enemy is operating in yourself or someone else by how much self-destruction they involve them self in. A Holy Spirit filled Christian is not embarking on self-destruction. Sin is like a court charge the devil can have against you. He wants to bring you to hell with him and his demons.

A born again person no longer has this for that lifestyle that separates them from God. The death drive is no longer there. The fleeting desires to no longer be alive and no longer deal with life is no longer there. The desires for self harm in the guise of pleasure is no longer there.

Like a parasite the evil one toils to see the demise of its host even though when they consume the host all the way, they also die. Where is the logic in that? There is no logic in that. That's incoherence. The devil hates you, hates life, and hates humanity. He is in a state of maximum separation from God and he is incoherent. He wants to see you guilty of sin so he can have you in hell for torment.

This is why the Bible emphasizes that self-harm and harm towards others is sin, and sin leads to death and destruction. It always does. It's straightforward. It's simple cause and effect. Each action in the world causes a ripple effect. Humanity is still dealing with the ripple effect of Adam and Eve sinning.

A trans person for example has distrusted God's Word about there only being two genders. They are walking in sin. Some fallen churches actually celebrate this sin.

They think God screwed up with their gender. God is infinitely smarter than humans, so God didn't screw up.

This type of trans or homosexual person has fallen for fallen agendas, again all of this is because of the fall of Adam, and now they are on hormone drugs of the opposite sex, considering gender reassignment surgery, and their body is extremely confused.

That type of behavior leads to mental health deficiencies, a loss of truth, and a shorter life. Hormones are extremely important to health and should be honored. They are so important in fact that a lot of the fast food in America has hormone disrupters to feminize the male

---

population. Male testosterone has decreased decade after decade for many decades now. Nobody can directly pinpoint the reason why, but it's a mix of poisons in the food, water, air and clothing.

In the same vein of culturally accepted sin, new age feminism, is a lie from the enemy to get women against men, dependent on their day job, and ultimately isolated and dependent on themselves rather than a loving husband. Godly women know it is part of God's design to submit to the right husband, not just any man, the right husband, that honors her as a child of God and waits for marriage for sex.

A wife submits to her own husband, and he also submits to her (Ephesians 5:22-33). Also, a Godly women knows that prioritizing family over corporate career is important and part of God's design. Women need to nurture a home environment, birth children, and love and care for the family. Men need to provide and protect, as well as love and care for the family. That's God's plan for men and women to be joyful together and in their given design.

In Genesis, we clearly see it is written Adam is the first man, and Eve is the first woman, and she came from man. Meaning, they are distinctly different genders, are attached at the rib, and woman was created to serve man. She has a biblical role as a servant helper, and he has a biblical role as a servant leader. They are both embracing the Jesus in them to selflessly serve.

None of that means a woman is weak, but rather it means God gives her strength and security inside of a healthy, God honoring marriage Covenant, one that is aligned with His will.

Male and female hormones are extremely different, yet powerful, with entirely different purposes. Men and women think extremely differently and that is all part of God's design. They are stronger together. The new age feminism movement is working to get women to be more masculine and independent like men. Feminism is ironically the opposite of real femininity.

The man walking in God's will is to model Jesus and embody the character of Jesus. He must be willing to lay down his life for his wife and family, just as Jesus did. The woman is to model the church and be an accommodative and loving nurturer, she adores and respects the man she beholds, and she is Holy Spirit filled.

They are both Holy Spirit filled because holiness demands excellence and keeps any sinful ways at bay.

Sharing testimonies and sharing the Word of God into society will allow more people to find refuge and relief in Jesus, one by one. Especially those, that have been lost in fallen agendas that distort gender identity and gender roles.

It's always been about identity.

When satan wanted to have Jesus fall down and worship him, he questioned the identity of Jesus. He said, "If you are really the Son of God" three times to get Jesus to question His identity. Jesus didn't fall for it because He well knew He was and is the Son of God.

There is nothing new under the sun. The evil one is still doing the same thing today especially with young people. They are under constant attack through the media and social media, pushing them towards the normalization of gender distortion. The enemy works through various agendas to create deviation, distortion, and perversion of God's designs for harmony and order. Both the word deviant and deviation have roots in the Latin word "deviare," (/de-vee-AH-reh/) meaning to turn aside or stray. The shared origin of both these terms reveals the adversary's goal to lead one astray and to cause one to stumble, diverting them from the path aligned with God's design and will from them.

Isaiah 53:6 KJV

*All we like sheep have gone astray; we have turned every one to his own way, and the Lord hath laid on him the iniquity of us all.*

Man is fallen but can be redeemed through the blood of Jesus. It can't be said any more simply than that. Only His blood pays the sin debt and provides a restored identity.

The amount of chaos and disorder that has been caused by satan and his demons on earth has been obvious. Thankfully, in God's grace He foretold us in the Bible it would this way, especially in the last days before the Church is raptured. This is why the Bible instructs us to be able to observe the signs of the times, because the signs of the times reveal that tribulation, judgement from God, and the return of Jesus is soon. The Greek word for judgement is "krisis" and we all know how to pronounce that. As you can easily see the worldwide crises are ramping up in frequency and magnitude. World peace is a worthy ideal on paper, but its not coming until after the rapture and the seven year tribulation, only Jesus Himself literally reigning on the earth after the tribulation will bring true peace.

World peace is an oxymoron because "the world" is fallen because of the fall of Adam. It will keep being that way until Jesus turns it around. The unholiness across society is just like in the days of Noah and it needs to be purged. It will be purged during the seven year tribulation. There are many perilous signs of the end times given in the New Testament and specifically the book of Revelation.

Some Christians think one or more of the seven seals of the scrolls mentioned in Revelation may have already been opened, signifying the tribulation has started, but the Holy Spirit and the Church is still here, the Bible calls this the Restrainer.

After the Church disappears one day and goes home to Heaven in the rapture event, the seven year tribulation starts, and the Restrainer goes up with the Church. When this occurs the end of the Church Age is confirmed and the literal antichrist "man of sin" will be given reign for seven years to cause destruction. The world will be reduced down to rubble through wars and the world population will be narrowed down to through plagues, wars and martyrdom to 144,000 Hebrew people from the 12 tribes of Israel and a handful of others from around the world that have accepted Christ. Then the millennial reign of Christ begins.

The Church Age is the time of grace where the door is still open to receive the Grace Covenant. We are simply observing a foreshadowing of the seals of Revelation now. If you think the world is in turmoil now, then what will occur during the tribulation will be nothing short of jaw dropping. There will death and destruction of billions. The end of the world as we know it truly hasn't started yet, but it's getting extremely very close, the signs of the end times are amplifying by the day. Those with the Holy Spirit can see it. Those without the Holy Spirit can't.

The first seal says there will be false prophets and false religion rampant in society. The scrolls represent judgement, God's wrath, and Jesus coming back for His true remnant, His Church. Not His religious remnant, not His remnant trying to gain favor through the appearance of good works. Not, His lukewarm, believers. No. He is coming back for His embattled officers and soldiers in the true army of God that always operate from a place of submission to the knowledge of Christ. They are consistently repentant and truly surrendered to His leadership, guidance, and grace. These are the few born again believers that persisted, faced adversities, and never lost their faith and hope despite the efforts of satan to rip away it all away.

This is His innocent, spotless bride, He died for, to be with in Heaven.

Matthew 24:35 KJV

*Heaven and earth shall pass away, but my Words shall not pass away.*

Titus 2:13 KJV

*Looking for that blessed hope, and the glorious appearing of the great God and our Saviour Jesus Christ.*

# Ch. 4 THE RAPTURE RESURRECTION EVENT: HIS CHURCH IS NOT APPOINTED TO WRATH

Matthew 24:7 KJV

*For nation shall rise against nation, and kingdom against kingdom: and there shall be famines, and pestilences, and earthquakes, in divers places.*

This verse from the book of Matthew is describing the upcoming seven year tribulation to the Jewish people. This is where the two kingdoms reach an ultimate collision point with each other. What humanity is heading into is of biblical proportions. Prophecy that is thousands of years old is coming true before our eyes. That's why there is so much instability in the world, and that uptrend is going to continue to escalate into the seven year tribulation. The culmination point humanity is rushing toward is the end of the Church Age, the end of the age of grace. Right as the tribulation begins, and the fire of judgement falls down upon the earth, the Church, His bride, will be raptured by Jesus Himself to go home to be with Him in Heaven. This is the rapture resurrection event where His Church is caught up into the clouds together to be with the Lord for eternity. It is a singular event in time. It is also set in stone on a certain date in the future.

1 Thessalonians 4:16-17 KJV

*For the Lord himself shall descend from heaven with a shout, with the voice of the archangel, and with the trump of God: and the dead in Christ shall rise first: Then we which are alive and remain shall be caught up together with them in the clouds, to meet the Lord in the air: and so shall we ever be with the Lord.*

1 Corinthians 15:52 KJV

*In a moment, in the twinkling of an eye, at the last trump: for the trumpet shall sound, and the dead shall be raised incorruptible, and we shall be changed.*

If you miss the rapture of the Church and are left behind you can still be saved and go to Heaven but there is an extremely high chance you will have to die for the name of Jesus. The people left behind are those who outright rejected Jesus as well as those who were religious but never formed a direct relationship with Him and were ultimately lukewarm rather than bought all the way in on the Bible and Jesus.

Jesus died for you and paid for all the charges against you with His blood 2,000 years ago, this opened up the Church Age, and as of the writing of the publishing of this book, we are in the final moments of the Church Age. In the final moments while the door to the Church Age is still open, you can still get on the Ark of Salvation by accepting His grace and pleading the blood over your life and your past sins. It's the only way to be found holy and blameless.

After the Church Age ends, and the Church goes to Heaven in the blink of an eye and the tribulation starts then you will need to die for Jesus by professing the name of Jesus no matter what comes against you. The places trade. Since you decided to be lukewarm during the Church Age, you will need to be an on fire believer and die for Him.

After the rapture of the Church, there will be war and turmoil and strange beings walking the earth. These beings will be demonic and not of God. They may appear as angels walking the earth and they may have the appearance of light but they are evil and made of false light. They will proclaim things that go against the Bible, such as there's more than one path to Heaven or there are many ways to

Heaven. Those are satan's lies. Faith in Jesus Christ and His blood is the only way into Heaven (John 14:6, 1 Corinthians 15:1-4).

If you missed the rapture and are reading this, this is a warning to be on the lookout for antichrists and fallen angels - many will be deceived (Matthew 24:24). If angel or any person preaches anything other truth than salvation through Jesus Christ, the one that was crucified for the sins of the world, then they must be forsaken. Those are angels that are sent by satan to deceive many. People have had dreams of these beings spreading a false Gospel during the tribulation.

Galatians 1:8-9 KJV

*But though we, or an angel from heaven, preach any other gospel unto you than that which we have preached unto you, let him be accursed. As we said before, so say I now again, If any man preach any other gospel unto you than that ye have received, let him be accursed.*

This may occur because satan will have total reign over the earth during the seven year tribulation. God allows this because His wrath has been stored up for the last 2,000 years of the age of grace. The God of the Old Testament consistently pours out His wrath on the ungodly. The world has enjoyed the God of the New Testament the last 2,000 years where God's grace has been abound, but that time is quickly coming to an end when the Church Age ends and the Holy Spirit goes to Heaven with the Church: the sanctified saints of God.

The wrath will be poured out on all the ungodly people that forsook the work and blood of Jesus during the Church Age, including the Hebrew people that have continually forsaken Jesus, the righteous King, the Messiah, God's only Son.

Jesus was and is the Messiah prophesied about in Isaiah 53 in the Old Testament.

The upcoming tribulation will be the most tumultuous seven year period that humanity has ever seen. It will be much larger than WW2 in scope and scale. God, in His grace, was kind enough to provide to the world His Son to spare His people from wrath. The Bible is a guidebook of clear prophecy and warning to the whole world. For those who have ears to hear: He consistently provides a way out for the righteous, to be spared from wrath. The only way to be righteous is to accept, plead, and embrace the blood of Jesus in your life.

It goes without saying many in modern culture have ignored or outright rejected the Bible. Rejecting any of the Bible is the same as rejecting the Son.

If you are reading this after the rapture of the Church, after the Holy Spirit has left the earth, know you must endure. You must go through the greater endeavor and hold onto the name of Jesus no matter what. I repeat, NO MATTER WHAT. They will threaten, manipulate, and torture and kill Christians to make you renounce your faith. They will have drones and the AI beast system to hunt down Christians and round them up and place them into prisons. Hold fast, saint. Do not renounce the name of Jesus and who He is. He is Lord and Savior.

If you are reading this before the rapture of the Church, before the Holy Spirit has left the earth, and while the door to accepting the grace of Jesus and the salvation He offers is open, read this, repent, and plead the blood over your life and past sins, just know the door of grace is coming to a close very soon. If you accept Jesus then unashamedly tell others about Him and how to be set free while there is still time.

As of my final edits of this book there is worldwide biblical flooding. The birth pains of the end times are in full effect. Some are theorizing "the water just broke" and we going Home to be with Jesus anyday.

Only through accepting His blood and Jesus' work on the cross can you be washed clean and made blameless in the sight of God.

The people that are telling you a golden age is coming and the best is yet to come are not being truthful to you. Politicians lie. Man lies. Jesus never lies. The Bible never lies. You deserve the truth authored by God and not the counterfeit deception authored by satan.

Since the year 2000 there has been an uptick in wars, diseases, economic and geopolitical instability, earthquakes, and natural disasters. All of this is a *mere* foreshadow of what is to come in the tribulation.

The escalation of these trends has only grown more pronounced since 2020, and the trends are not letting up any time soon. These are the birth pains of the impending tribulation, when at the start King Jesus "crowns" on the clouds and brings His Church home. We go to Heaven to be with Him and then we come back with Him at the end of the seven years for the battle of Armageddon, Jesus and the saints win, and we reign for 1,000 years on earth and there is actual peace.

The birth pains of 2025 are only going to continue to escalate, and will become 1,000x worse during the tribulation.

My desire is to share the truth with you out of love for your soul and your impending eternity.

You must select the Ark of Salvation, the Kingdom of God, now because the day of salvation is today (2 Corinthians 6:2).

We can turn to the prophetic book of Daniel, to receive an accurate representation from God of the two kingdoms here on earth. This is to gain a greater understanding on which kingdom we want to find ourselves in allegiance to on our last day on earth.

There is one kingdom that is made of clay and will shatter in due time and there is one kingdom that is made of iron and is everlasting.

In Daniel 2, the king of Babylon, Nebuchadnezzar, sought after the "wise men" across the city of Babylon to help him interpret a vivid dream that he desperately wanted an interpretation for. The wise men in the city were not able provide this for him so he ordered all of the wise men in the city to death. As one of the wise men in the city Daniel was facing death so he prayed. Daniel was a Hebrew young man, not originally from Babylon, he came forth and confidently stood in front of the king and assured him he could interpret.

What set Daniel apart from the other wise men in the city, that included sorcerers, magicians, and astrologers, was Daniel was not a magician or pagan, instead he got his wisdom from a different source.

Daniel was raised in the traditions of the wise men because He was raised in Babylon against his will, but he had the God of Israel on his side living inside of him. Through his relationship with God he had extraordinary abilities, and these were not from witchcraft or divination, but instead through his direct relationship with God. His relationship with God was his superpower. He had direct access to the source of truth, the extraordinary, one and true Almighty God.

Daniel 2:44-47 ASV

*And in the days of those kings shall the God of heaven set up a*
*kingdom which shall never be destroyed, nor shall the sovereignty*
*thereof be left to another people; but it shall break in pieces and*
*consume all these kingdoms, and it shall stand for ever. Forasmuch as*
*thou sawest that a stone was cut out of the mountain without hands,*
*and that it brake in pieces the iron, the brass, the clay, the silver, and*
*the gold; the great God hath made known to the king what shall come*
*to pass hereafter: and the dream is certain, and the interpretation*
*thereof sure. Then the king Nebuchadnezzar fell upon his face, and*
*worshipped Daniel, and commanded that they should offer an*
*oblation and sweet odours unto him. The king answered unto Daniel,*
*and said, Of a truth your God is the God of gods, and the Lord of*
*kings, and a revealer of secrets, seeing thou hast been able to reveal*
*this secret.*

Daniel's accurate interpretation of the dream spared him and his
Hebrew friends from a certain death at the hand of the king.

The dream interpretation satisfied the king and provided a clear
prophecy, a future description, of the two kingdoms coming into full
contact with each other. The Kingdom of God is the clear winner and
always defeats and consumes the false kingdom.

Hebrews 12:29 KJV

*For our God is a consuming fire.*

The iron and clay kingdoms prophecy is a powerful illustration of the
contrasting nature of placing all your faith in the kingdom of the
everlasting God instead of the temporary kingdom of the world.

Currently, the world is a world of mixture. Iron dwells with clay and everyone tries their best to get along. But there is a day coming when the two kingdoms go in full speed direct contact with each other. The iron will be separated from the clay and the wheat will be separated from the weeds. In ancient Israel, valuable wheat would grow amongst weeds, and the weeds were separated from the wheat on the threshing floor, an agricultural room where the separation between the good harvest and the waste occurred. The judgement day and the start of the tribulation is the ultimate threshing floor for all human history. Whether you are found in one kingdom or the other comes down to allegiance. God already sees who has accepted, plead, and embraced the blood and who hasn't.

The righteous Kingdom is authored by God and the other by the deceiver, satan.

The kingdom of the world, also referred to the kingdom of darkness, is unstable, fragile, and temporary. It's the kingdom of man.

The Kingdom of God is solid and unwavering and always standing firm in the face of any adversity.

These two kingdoms are spiritual in nature. The kingdom of the world manifests in the form of the pride of life, faith in money, personal conquests for power, lying lips, manipulation, false worship, false gods, vanity, lust, and sexual immorality, among other things.

On the other side, the Kingdom of God is peace, joy, and righteousness in the Holy Spirit. It stands as a firm foundation like solid iron. God's Kingdom is everlasting. "Faith, hope, and love those three last forever." He is eternal, mighty, and unshakeable.

The earthly kingdom is temporary and fated to collapse.

The average age of a man-made empire on earth is only 250 years. A drop in the bucket compared to eternity. The American empire is coming up on 250 years right now. It's hotly debated if God's grace is still over the country. It's been the modern Babylon, the star of military and industrial power, but it has many sins to be paid for.

The temporary nature of human kingdoms is very much evident in the face of natural death, natural disasters, unnatural diseases, wars, and the ultimately the pervasive and perverse moral decay found all across humanity. This is still all because of Adam and Eve's free will choice to disobey God and fall from grace and put death and sin on the bloodline of humanity.

Jesus sent His Son to reverse the curse of the fall and to provide access to God's Kingdom, a refuge and a hope in a world of thorns, pitfalls, danger, and decay. God's kingdom is harmonious and is much akin to the pristine beauty found in the Garden of Eden. His Kingdom is not from here (John 18:36) but we can gain full access to it just like Daniel did while we are here. All through a simple, uncomplicated, relationship with Jesus. It's all about allowing His blood.

After the end of the seven year tribulation there will be the supernatural restoration on earth of the garden like state of perfection, this is called the Kingdom of Heaven. The Kingdom of Heaven will literally meet the earth for the 1,000 literal reign of Jesus Christ from Jerusalem from David's throne (Isaiah 9:7) and then at the end of the 1,000 year reign there will be a brand new heaven and a new earth that emerges (Revelation 21:1-2, 2 Peter 3:10). This is all Bible prophecy. This is all God's story. You can't make this up. I would trust it if I were you because there is no greater form of prophecy than Bible prophecy. It is 100% accurate. Thousands of prophecies in the Bible have already been confirmed and came true and many more especially in the book of Revelation are still to unfold.

As of the writing of this book Bible prophecy from thousands of years ago is actively coming true before our eyes, specifically Daniel 9:27, Ezekiel 38:5-6, Psalms 83, Zechariah 12:2-3, 1 Thessalonians 5:3, Jeremiah 30:7 and Daniel 12:1. All of the prophecies have to do with the end of the Church Age and the start of Jacob's trouble in Israel. That's why Israel is in the news so much, and that is only going to continue up until the end of the Church Age. Israel is the time clock. Israel is surrounded by enemies and around the world the Jewish people are terribly disliked because satan hates God's promises to them. The Bible tells us in the last days before and during the tribulation Israel will be surrounded by enemies. The tribulation starts with a peace deal confirmed by the antichrist where Israel gives away its land to the Islam world. God is infuriated with this because Israel land is God's land. The peace breaks down shortly after and the Jewish people are delivered from the hand of the enemy at the end of the tribulation when Jesus comes back in His second coming, He place His feet on the Mount of Olives and goes through the Eastern Gate in the old city in Jerusalem to rule from the throne of David with an iron rod (Revelation 19:15), an "iron fist." The 1,000 reign begins.

Today, we are seeing evil rise up but we are also seeing the Kingdom of God rise up. The opposing kingdoms will escalate the battle with each other right through into the tribulation when the stakes go up and escalate to a maximum until Jesus returns on the Mount of Olives. This event where the tribulation ends is the battle of Armageddon. This is the Second Coming of Christ, not to be confused with the rapture of the Church when He comes on the clouds and snatches up His Church in the twinkling of an eye. For the battle of Armageddon Jesus brings His armies of pre-tribulation and tribulation saints to trample on satan's head, trample on snakes, and defeat Him entirely. This result of the battle is the kingdom of the world, satan, and man loses. The clay is shattered and the iron everlasting Kingdom wins.

Right before the first seal of Revelation is opened and the seven year tribulation starts is when the rapture occurs and the Church is taken home to Heaven for the seven year wedding feast while simultaneously the seven year judgement of everyone on earth directly opposed to God will commence.

Some naysayers that don't study Scripture say the word rapture isn't in the Bible. But in the New Testament the Greek word linked to the rapture of the Church is the verb "harpazō," (/hahr-pah'-zo/) meaning "to snatch away" or "to seize." This term is used in 1 Thessalonians 4:17 in the New Testament, describing the catching up of believers to meet the Lord in the air. The New Testament was originally written in Greek. In the resurrection event, Jesus will authoritatively catch up His people, the Church, His bride for the wedding feast.

As mentioned, we are seeing a foreshadowing of the first seal of Revelation. The first seal is when false peace is rampant. We see this today in the form of new age belief systems that promote peace, love, unity, and respect when its fake peace, love, unity, and respect.

This figurehead of satan, the antichrist, will confirm a false peace among many nations. He is one that finalizes a two-state solution between many nations and Israel (Daniel 9:27). The Jewish people will think that is their Messiah, when the real Messiah already came 2,000 years ago. This two state deal is done in the name of peace and safety (1 Thessalonians 5:3) to establish stability in the middle east. The first seal is opened and false peace as a result of the deal then spreads across the middle east between Israel and all of the Islamic countries (aligned with Iran) that wish to destroy Israel (Ezekiel 38:5-6). Even though there may be a short bubble of peace for Israel, the rest of the world will be consumed by war and other problems.

All of this sets the stage and begins the opening of the seven scrolls by Jesus and the wrath of the Lamb on earth begins. The false peace for Israel is short lived and the second seal of war across the world is unleashed. Sudden destruction comes upon those who put together the deal to help Israel give away her land to the Islam world. Currently, America and the Abrham Alliance is putting this together with the help of other NATO countries. The third seal is famine and scarcity, this is likely to be where the mark of the beast to buy or sell (Revelation 13) is introduced, because without it you can't buy or sell. The fourth seal is death and plagues. The fifth seal is martyrs dying for the name of Jesus and becoming tribulation saints, as opposed to pre-tribulation saints, which they could have been if they carried their cross before the rapture. The sixth seal is cosmic disturbances, including earthquakes, the sun turning black, the moon turning red, and stars falling from the sky. The seventh seal is seven trumpets of major judgements on the earth including a great star called wormwood hitting the earth causing even more calamity.

Now that you can see the contents of the seven year tribulation you can see the false peace and fake new age religions we have today are foreshadowing the false peace that marks the end of world as we know it. The only authentic peace comes from the prince of peace, Jesus, that's why His reign after the tribulation will be marked by peace across the whole earth while he rules with an iron fist. This is the Kingdom of Heaven on earth. It was postponed through the Jewish people rejecting their Savior. Considering humans have free will in theory they could have accepted the Kingdom of Heaven 2,000 years ago.

As we lead-up to the tribulation, the kingdom you align yourself with is beyond crucial. You are either an earth dweller, bound to the kingdom of the world, or you are filled with the Holy Spirit and the realization that your true home is in Heaven, and you belong in the Kingdom of God. There is no middle ground between these two infinitely opposed kingdoms. The friction between these two kingdoms is, in effect, spiritual warfare – just like oil and water, they can "coexist" but they don't mix, and they will never mix.

To embrace the Kingdom of God surrender to these things: the peace of Jesus, the oil of His anointing, the oil of joy, the oil of gladness, receiving salvation through faith alone in the death, burial, and resurrection of Jesus (what He did for you because you are worthy), washing yourself with the blood of Jesus so He can blot out of all of your sins, and allowing the Holy Spirit and fire baptism to engulf you. When you have the Holy Spirit on board you have a ticket to be redeemed by Jesus on your last day on earth, and not only that while you are here now you suddenly have the urge to make holy changes in your life and lifestyle. All of this results of this results in taking rest in God's love for you and God's will for you.

It certainly makes you wonder why people resist the Kingdom of God so much, it's all pretty great. The great deceiver, satan, has worked tirelessly to keep people bound to sin, to their flesh, to pride, and the fleeting pleasures of life, he has done a big number with the religion of man to push people away from the authentic operation of God, he has tricked unsaved people into thinking they're saved. Not only that he has made it a personal mission to bring persecution against those who do walk in holiness.

James 1:2-4 KJV

*My brethren, count it all joy when ye fall into divers temptations; knowing this, that the trying of your faith worketh patience. But let*

*patience have her perfect work, that ye may be perfect and entire,*
*wanting nothing.*

It's your choice if you want take rest in His Kingdom or be part of the kingdom of the enemy. Nobody wants to go to hell, but the fact is you are picking your destiny each day whether you know it or not. Each day you are playing for the winning team or the losing team. On judgement day, at the start of the tribulation, God will find you on one team or the other. Those in the Kingdom of God go home early in the rapture of the Church.

When God does enact His judgement upon the start of the tribulation those that are made from iron, the faithful and righteous ones that are covered under the blood of Jesus will be seen as ready, and those made out of clay, seen as evil and full of the world and will shatter into a million pieces, literally and metaphorically. The seemingly timeless conflict between good and evil has endured since the ancient times, even preceding the days of Noah and the construction of the ark. Generations before Noah, the tragic story of Adam and Eve unfolded, with their son Cain committing the heinous act of murdering his righteous brother Abel.

From the moment Eve bit the fruit the spiritual battle began between the forces of light and dark throughout human history. The ongoing struggle between good and evil stands as a foundational theme in the biblical narrative, showcasing the persistent nature of this cosmic clash and ultimately highlighting God's victory due to His sovereignty over all creation. It concludes when Jesus reigns with an iron fist.

Adam and Eve had a third son, Seth, that was righteous like Abel was. Seth's bloodline after several generations leads to Noah. As most people know, he faithfully delivered a warning of the impending flood, signaling God's impending judgment upon the earth. Despite the ridicule and disbelief from the unbelievers, Noah and his family remained steadfast, faithful, and obedient in executing God's spoken command to build the giant wooden ark because a flood was coming. Noah's ark stands as a symbol of God's Covenant with His people, offering safety and salvation to those who trust in His Word.

Every person owes their life to God because He is the Creator of all things (Colossians 1:16). Everyone will be held accountable for their actions (2 Corinthians 5:10). Those who have not accepted Christ and continue to live in sin will face God's judgment, while those who belong to Him will be spared from His wrath (Romans 5:9, 1 Thessalonians 5:9).

The rainbow, as mentioned in Genesis after the flood, is indeed a symbol of God's covenant with His people, promising not to destroy them through a global flood again (Genesis 9:13-16). It is a reminder of God's faithfulness and love towards His children. While the rainbow has been misused and distorted in recent times, Christians still claim its true meaning and significance as a symbol of God's covenant and care for His people.

The subsequent arks of God's promises include the tabernacle and the ark of the Covenant, both representing God's presence among His chosen people. The ark of the Covenant, a wooden vessel containing the Ten Commandments, served as a tangible reminder of God's covenant with Israel. Looking ahead, the ultimate promise of God's Covenant is fulfilled in the return of Jesus for His bride on the rapture day, that's the Ark of Salvation for the faithful and redeemed global Church. This future event symbolizes the union between Christ and His followers that have accepted His grace. This is a promise of God just like the rainbow is a promise of God.

Noah put his head down and built God's ark, and then the rain came. God closed the door of the ark and those that did not believe screamed, drowned, and perished. We are in similar times to the days of Noah because many mock and many don't believe Jesus is coming back for His bride, including so-called Christians.

Hebrews 11:7 KJV

*By faith Noah, being warned of God of things not seen as yet, moved with fear, prepared an ark to the saving of his house; by the which he condemned the world, and became heir of the righteousness which is by faith.*

Noah was obedient and faithful, and that was pleasing to God, literally everyone else on earth was unrighteous and sinful. Noah and his family were spared from the flood for their obedience plus each kind of animal. Noah operated on pure faith that the instructions from God were truly from God. He took Him at His Word instead of being hesitant or rebellious. He had the faith that nothing is impossible with God and he had the wisdom to see it's much wiser to obey God than hesitate and doubt. If He said it, it must be believed.

God, seeing the corruption and violence prevalent among people, was deeply grieved and chose to bring a flood as a divine judgment to cleanse the earth. Among a population that may have numbered in the millions or billions, a significant concern arose from the intermarriage between the "sons of God" and the "daughters of humans," leading to the birth of the Nephilim—described as fallen giants in Genesis 6. Some interpretations suggest that these "sons of God" were fallen angels, contributing to the moral decay that prompted God's decision to send the flood. In this backdrop of moral decline, only Noah, found favor in God's sight, leading to his preservation and that of his family through the ark. The Nephilim/fallen angels are most likely going to be the strange beasts that walk the earth again during the book of Revelation because satan will have full reign on earth again (Revelation 6:7-8).

God wanted to sweep away as much of the demonic realm as possible through the flood. A sifting was needed to restore the purity of humanity. Are you see the connection to iron and clay, wheat and tares, and oil and water? God repeats Himself in patterns.

The flood worked, Noah's ark worked, and the demonic was largely placed at bay so that Noah's righteous bloodline could continue, the very bloodline that led to Jesus.

The four wooden arks can be seen as representing different aspects of God's redemptive plan through history to place evil at bay. They are different because God deals with humanity differently across time.

The Ark of Noah: Symbolizes God's protection and deliverance from judgment. A wooden boat for Noah and his family.

The Ark of Moses: Represents God's preservation and deliverance of His chosen people from danger and oppression. A small wooden basket for baby Moses. Includes same aspects of previous Ark.

The Ark of the Covenant: Signifies God's presence, covenant, and guidance among His people to walk away from sin and immorality. A wooden chest to house the 10 commandments written on stone tablets. An eye for an eye. Includes same aspects of previous two Arks.

The Ark of Salvation: Symbolizes God's ultimate act of redemption, salvation, and love for humanity through the sacrificial death of Jesus

Christ, offering forgiveness and reconciliation with God for Jew and Gentile alike. A wooden Roman crucifixion cross. Grace Covenant and God's commandments written on the fleshy tablets of man's hearts. An eye for an eye makes the whole world blind. Includes same aspects of previous three Arks.

Even though this has been a long back and forth war of the Kingdom of God vs the kingdom of the evil one, that does not mean it's an endless war.

Revelation 20:10 KJV

*And the devil that deceived them was cast into the lake of fire and brimstone, where the beast and the false prophet are, and shall be tormented day and night for ever and ever.*

In Revelation 21, the ultimate victory of Christ and the establishment of a new heaven and a new earth are described. After the events of the tribulation, the 1,000 year millennial reign of Christ on the earth from Jerusalem, and the sinners and satan are permanently judged, then the Father creates a new Heaven and a new earth. This chapter is the absolute culmination of God's plan for redemption and the restoration of all things in Christ. At this point the Kingdom of Heaven and New Jerusalem merge completely with the new earth.

Revelation 21:1-4 KJV describes the vision of a new heaven and a new earth:

*And I saw a new heaven and a new earth: for the first heaven and the first earth were passed away; and there was no more sea. And I John saw the holy city, new Jerusalem, coming down from God out of heaven, prepared as a bride adorned for her husband. And I heard a great voice out of heaven saying, Behold, the tabernacle of God is with men, and he will dwell with them, and they shall be his people, and God himself shall be with them, and be their God. And God shall wipe away all tears from their eyes; and there shall be no more death, neither sorrow, nor crying, neither shall there be any more pain: for the former things are passed away.*

As you can see God is in complete control and always has been. The prophecy in Revelation confirms God will reconcile everything. His heart is for the redemption of all things into Christ to create a new state of holiness, goodness, and blessing. This is the eternal character of God. He is a good Father, He is fair with His children, and He wants the best for His children. He is not the author of confusion (1 Corinthians 14:33) or chaos. He is the answer to all of the darkness that has ever existed on the earth and He has always been the answer. The new heaven and the new earth won't have day and night. Only light. He already has the plan in place for no more darkness, spiritual or otherwise. It's our duty to take Him at His Word.

Revelation 21:5 KJV

*And he that sat upon the throne said, Behold, I make all things new. And he said unto me, Write: for these words are true and faithful.*

Considering the new Heaven and new earth have total illumination, no darkness, no sun, no moon, the station we are in now, the earth, with its interplay of light and dark is a training ground for the procurement and refinement of souls that purify into saints. The challenges presented by light and dark provide opportunities for growth, shaping them into saints who reflect the light of God's truth. Gold can't be refined and purified without fiery trials. The complexities of light and dark create dark gray, but that's until Jesus refines, purifies, and sanctifies the saints who embody the virtues of faith, perseverance, and holiness. Remember, the wages for the saints is eternal life with God, from glory to glory.

2 Corinthians 3:18 KJV

*But we all, with open face beholding as in a glass the glory of the Lord, are changed into the same image from glory to glory, even as by the Spirit of the Lord.*

Mark 11:23 ASV

*Verily I say unto you, Whosoever shall say unto this mountain, Be thou taken up and cast into the sea; and shall not doubt in his heart, but shall believe that what he saith cometh to pass; he shall have it.*

This previous passage is always taken out of context. It is referring to the benefits of making it into the Kingdom of Heaven. The saints in their glorified bodies in the Kingdom of Heaven will be able to do things like this. Matthew, Mark, and Luke are the ministry of Jesus offering the Kingdom of Heaven to the Jews. Again, the Kingdom of Heaven arrives after the tribulation. Jesus came first to the Hebrew people to offer them the Kingdom of Heaven but they rejected Him and it. The Kingdom of Heaven meets the earth during the next dispensation, the 1,000 year reign of Christ after the tribulation.

During the age of grace for the Gentiles, known as the Church Age, access to sainthood has never been easier. This 2,000 year grace period in human history offers a presently abundant opportunity for individuals to pursue holiness and spiritual growth. The Church Age is rapidly coming to a close, as mentioned.

Once the saints go to Heaven in the rapture the world will be in a fragile and confused state, this will give the antichrist the opportunity to instantly rise through the ranks all the way up to world governance, he will be charismatic, manipulative, and slick with his words, he will provide satanic solutions to the world's problems and he will demand to be followed and worshipped (2 Thessalonians 2:3).

The enemy is on death row, on borrowed time, and during his time here his goal is to cause strife, he is trying to do anything to cause dissent and distraction in order to prevent new people from turning away from the wicked ways of the world and accepting salvation in Jesus. His primary goal is to distract and prevent new souls from learning the Gospel of the death, burial, and resurrection.

The reality is, you are either being made into the image and likeness of the Holy God in Heaven each day, Jesus, or you are becoming more like the fallen, dark, demonic world each day (Revelation 3:15-16).

After a new believer enters the Kingdom of God then they can become disciples and embark on the meaningful work of sharing the truth of Jesus with others so they too can become disciples of Christ.

The only things satan can do through willing agents (human or AI) is cause division, virality, chaos, strife, war, plagues, turmoil, and distraction, all of this is ultimately to spread fear and inhibit people from sharing about what Jesus did. Unfortunately, the evil one wants as many people as possible to miss the Ark of Salvation, so they have to endure the wrath of the tribulation. If you accept the blood, the work He did on the cross, and rest in His grace you will not be one of the left behind.

Matthew 28:19-20 ASV

*Go ye therefore, and make disciples of all the nations, baptizing them into the name of the Father and of the Son and of the Holy Spirit: teaching them to observe all things whatsoever I commanded you: and lo, I am with you always, even unto the end of the world.*

This was the final marching order from Jesus. He spoke these words while He was in His glorified body after His resurrection and before His ascension into heaven. All nations means all the Gentiles. Again, the Gentiles are all people groups that have never heard the truth of the Gospel of Jesus Christ. Jesus died for anyone willing to hear the call to follow the truth. He died for all people groups before they ever even heard about Him, knowing that some would accept Him and many would deny Him. Yet, He saw His chosen children that were destined to hear the call. It's pure love on behalf of the Father, knowing Jesus would lay His life down for the just that would accept Him and the droves of unjust that would deny Him. The saints have been made justified by Jesus' blood and the unjust will be found guilty for denying the blood, because all have fallen short of the glory of God and have sinned (Romans 3:23).

Catholic-style missions have fallen short in fully bringing the Gospel of Jesus to all people groups. This is due to a blend of a watered down message of the Gospel, not preaching the death, burial, resurrection and what Jesus did, and because making disciples is not a singular event. It is a deliberate and transformative process. Jesus provided the model of how to multiply disciples, but the Church so far has largely missed the model and has preferred drive by missions and evangelism. Disciple making involves intentional and personal, one on one teaching to show a disciple what the Bible says. It's the Paul and Timothy relationship. Paul was the main apostle to the Church, an elder, seasoned in the faith and Timothy was a growing disciple. In Jesus' model of multiplication, when a Timothy is trained up then he can train new disciples.

A disciple studies the Bible, walks forward in faith despite any adversity, makes sacrifices, and has a deep commitment to loving Jesus. A disciple crucifies the flesh, the world, and the fallen desires of the human heart all in order to fully embody the nine aspects of God (Galatians 5:22-23). A disciple is undoubtedly born again.

This barely practiced model is the heart of the Great Commission. Tragically, many modern churches have strayed from this foundational model and completely ignore it in favor of the Catholic style mass and missions. This results in shallow teachings, a flock of believers that barely know their Bible, and a lack of lasting spiritual fruit. The Catholic style missions and mass services of the last 1,500 years have failed to make disciples. This was all the work of satan to delay, detract, and defer.

A disciple is looked at from the outside world as a highly committed Christian, but really a disciple is much closer to a recruit that has agreed to embrace a new life in Christ, reach the end of himself or herself, take up their cross, and be willing to learn how to reform into the new creation in Christ God always wanted for them.

No other spiritual tradition offers the promise from the living God to perform a miraculous transformation: to restore you, dwell within you, and lead you into a completely new version of yourself and your life; to guide you towards a more abundant, holy, and purposeful life in alignment with God's will.

God sets His real believers apart for holy living while they are still alive and sets aside a place for them in Heaven. God is fair and He simply can't allow unholiness to be allowed into His perfect and eternal family. Earth is the training ground for eternity, and everyone will either hear the call to truth, or they will not. The blood of Jesus must be accepted embraced and pled to be justified.

Entering His holy family, again, is open to anyone that hears the call, it's a process of leaving your old life behind, leaving sin behind, and walking the walk. Walking the walk means believing and behaving the Bible.

The door to the Ark of Salvation will close soon just like how God shut the door on Noah's Ark after he was inside and safe and the floor waters began. God opens doors no man can open and shuts doors no man can shut (Isaiah 22:22, Revelation 3:7).

You can see why Christians that realize the truth of Jesus feel a pressing need to step all the way in and become disciples, tell others about Jesus, spread the Gospel, baptize others in the Holy Spirit and fire, heal others, and deliver others from spiritual oppression.

Being saved, being truly born again, is called being saved for a reason. Saving just one other person from eternal death (eternal pain, turmoil, torment in hell) is a big deal. It means through you and the operation of God a soul has been pardoned from a sinful and painful life they were sowing into for years, knowingly or unknowingly.

Everyone is guilty of the Adam nature because the first two humans bit the forbidden fruit in the garden and were obedient to the devil's instruction, but aside from the original fall on humanity's bloodline, if you have ever lied, stolen, cussed, gossiped, gotten drunk, masturbated, had sex outside of marriage, became involved in occult practices, placed faith in astrology, placed faith in celebrities or politicians, placed faith in money and participated in yoga at the local yoga studio, among many other things then you have sinned and have turned away from God. These are common sins, you will know what you need to repent about.

The wages of sin is death. Most people fail to realize how many things in the culture, that are culturally accepted, are way outside of the Bible and the holiness of God. Most people don't realize that everything outside of the approval of God is a distraction that leads to further bondage, even when at times it can feel like growth. That's how subtle the enemy is. Picture social media content, much of the content causes comparison, makes people idolize other people's lives, and further places bondage on someone.

Romans 6:23 KJV

*For the wages of sin is death; but the gift of God is eternal life through Jesus Christ our Lord.*

God is also a God of grace and fairness. That's why He sent His Son. To pay for the charge against you, so you didn't have to, because the wages, the payback, for sin is death and hell.

I take no pleasure in saying this, but most people are in the fast lane on their way to hell, whether they know it or not. The fallen worldly culture places people on a fast track towards hell by default. I do not want to see anyone left behind in the tribulation, that's how bad it will be.

In summary: Jesus Christ is coming back for His Church. Many Christians don't even believe this because they don't study their Bible.

Plead the blood over your life, your sins, and forgive anyone you need to so you aren't weighed down by any of that.

He is looking for a spotless bride, so make sure you are consistently repenting and pleading the blood when you stumble, and make sure you are crucifying the flesh daily and not living from the flesh.

His grace is what redeems, so stay focused on loving Him and allowing Him to love you. Religious works are not what make you justified, only the Grace Covenant, His blood, and resting in the truth of what He did for you can keep you ready.

Walking as a saint of Jesus Christ is a daily commitment. Jesus cares a lot about how you are living today so you are found spotless and blameless to go home in the rapture before the seven year tribulation.

# Ch. 5 HOW TO BE A SAINT IN THE KINGDOM OF GOD

We are in the final moments before Jesus returns for His Church. That's why the spiritual warfare is so intense in the world right now. Humanity is going through the deep throws of birth pains until the 1ˢᵗ seal of Revelation is opened and the terrible tribulation begins.

A wide scale revival in faith is already breaking out, especially among young adults. But the enemy is also on the move, setting traps, authoring deception and confusion, and creating distractions.

The enemy doesn't need to destroy you if he can sufficiently distract you.

The fallen culture's descent into darkness seems to deepen with each passing day, an increasing array of demonic content saturates TV shows, news programs, movies, songs, and social media content on various platforms. Paradoxically, there is also a surge in media that honors Jesus, with a growing presence of TV shows, movies, songs, and social media content that celebrates Him and Christianity. The simultaneous rise of the Kingdom of God and the kingdom of darkness is emboldening each side, pointing to an eventual culmination of opposing forces as discussed in the previous chapter.

It's always been a battle over each soul. The war is a war for the dominion of each individual soul, and it has come to everyone's doorstep. Classrooms, school board meetings, families, social circles, but mostly the internet and social media have been invaded as the main battlefield to cause corruption, corrosion, and distortion of each precious human soul. The easiest way to corrupt a soul is get them ensnared in sin so their holy identity enters into a state of jeopardy.

When an identity begins to drift further and further away from its original God-given design a soul is corrupted and lost.

A soul is incredibly precious, undeniably priceless, because it comes directly from God. Each soul can't be bought. Each soul that is corrupted by choice or through manipulation (witchcraft) will have a journey of finding their way back to purity and innocence. They can be redeemed in an instant through Jesus but they must be ready and willing to accept the truth. That's why the youngest generation is always the most valuable to God, and to the enemy. God wants you for the long run, but so does the evil one.

Churches and pastors are thought of first when bringing people to Jesus however the ministry landscape is more than that. In the book of Acts, the model of the New Testament Church, we see apostles, deacons, evangelists, teachers, prophets, and missionaries serving in various roles in the early church.

The overall goal of the saints in the Church is to have new souls turn to Jesus as their Lord and Savior, get baptized in the Holy Spirit and fire, and start to study the Bible and walk the walk of becoming a disciple in the Kingdom of God. Once someone is a trained disciple they are equipped to do the work of the ministry.

Here are additional aspects of being part of the Kingdom of God:

Upon receiving the baptism of the Holy Spirit and fire, a transformative empowerment occurs as the divine power of God descends upon a new soul. This infusion of spiritual strength equips a person with a heightened level of spiritual authority and capability, surpassing the limitations of their previous self.

Acts 2:38 KJV

*Then Peter said unto them, Repent, and be baptized every one of you in the name of Jesus Christ for the remission of sins, and ye shall receive the gift of the Holy Ghost.*

When the Holy Spirit of God descends upon you through the power and authority in the name of Jesus you become a truly born again new creation.

Matthew 3:11, 3:16-17 KJV

*I indeed baptize you with water unto repentance. but he that cometh after me is mightier than I, whose shoes I am not worthy to bear: he shall baptize you with the Holy Ghost, and with fire:*

*And Jesus, when he was baptized, went up straightway out of the water: and, lo, the Heavens were opened unto him, and he saw the Spirit of God descending like a dove, and lighting upon him:*

*And lo a voice from Heaven, saying, This is my beloved Son, in whom I am well pleased.*

John 1:29 KJV

*The next day John seeth Jesus coming unto him, and saith, Behold the Lamb of God, which taketh away the sin of the world.*

John the baptizer who said these words was a high priest, a prophet and a forerunner of Christ, meaning he was not only Jesus' cousin, he was considered a forerunner because he was chosen by God to prepare the way for the coming of Jesus Christ. John the baptizers role as a forerunner was to proclaim a message of repentance, prepare the hearts of the people for the arrival of the Messiah, and fulfill the prophecy of Isaiah 40:3, which states, "The voice of him that crieth in the wilderness, Prepare ye the way of the Lord, make straight in the desert a highway for our God."

John baptized Jesus with water because that was part of the Jewish law – to be baptized with water by a high priest. Jesus came to fulfill the Jewish law so that the rest of the world could enjoy a better covenant. The Old Covenant required perfection, you had to follow all 613 laws perfectly through sheer willpower. It showed man his problem with sin and the need for a Savior because following the 613 laws was impossible to follow to satisfy God's requirements for holiness, only Jesus could walk out the Jewish law perfectly.

Jesus' death on the cross and the New Covenant in His blood provides better holiness and better access to God than the Jewish law, that's why Christians are not appointed to look back at the laws and assume 613 Jewish laws need to be followed. Not only that the saints shouldn't nibble on the Jewish law because it says you must do all 613 laws or there is condemnation upon you. It's not worth overcomplicating the Gospel of the death, burial, and resurrection of the Savior by nibbling on the law that wasn't meant for the Church under grace. Jesus did the work on the cross once and for all through His blood. He truly did. Do not take it for granted. To be on the Ark of Salvation you let God write his laws of morality directly onto your heart and allow the Holy Spirit to take over.

John was preaching about repentance and the coming of the Kingdom of Heaven because if Jesus was accepted by the Jewish people He would have brought the Kingdom of Heaven to the earth right then and there. Since He was rejected and crucified, the Kingdom of

Heaven's arrival became postponed until the end of the seven year tribulation. The saints have been given the massive gift of the Grace Covenant through Jesus' death, burial, and resurrection.

Jesus and John's relationship to each other started when they were both in the womb, yes while preborn, John recognized Jesus as the Messiah. Mary, who was pregnant with Jesus, visited Elizabeth her relative, who was pregnant with John the baptizer. Baby John leaped in Elizabeth's womb upon hearing Mary's greeting. This event is known as the visitation and is described in Luke 1:41-44. It was through the Holy Spirit that John in the womb recognized the presence of the preborn Jesus, and this led to Elizabeth's proclamation of Mary as the mother of the prophesied Messiah. Jesus and John were related by blood and recognized each other before birth. When Jesus was thirty He was water baptized by John. As mentioned, water baptism is part of the Jewish law. Jesus was Jewish and not Christian. He was born under the law, lived the law, taught the law, preached the law, and got His earthly authority from the law, thus making Him the perfect sacrifice because He walked in holiness and followed the law perfectly, something no man before Him could do. This made Him the perfect spotless Lamb to end the Old Covenant and bring in the New Covenant, grace through His blood, where following the Jewish law was no longer required for holiness and innocence. Instead, the laws of morality become written on a believer's heart through the Holy Spirit.

Hebrews 8:10 KJV

*For this is the covenant that I will make with the house of Israel after those days, saith the Lord; I will put my laws into their mind, and write them in their hearts: and I will be to them a God, and they shall be to me a people.*

Galatians 5:4 KJV

*Christ is become of no effect unto you, whosoever of you are justified by the law; ye are fallen from grace.*

The original Christians and Christians of today have embraced the Holy Spirit and fire baptism; a supernatural transformation done by God.

Acts 1:8 KJV

*But ye shall receive power, after that the Holy Ghost is come upon you: and ye shall be witnesses unto me both in Jerusalem, and in all Judaea, and in Samaria, and unto the uttermost part of the earth.*

Acts 2:1-4 KJV

*And when the day of Pentecost was fully come, they were all with one accord in one place. And suddenly there came a sound from heaven as of a rushing mighty wind, and it filled all the house where they were sitting. And there appeared unto them cloven tongues like as of fire, and it sat upon each of them. And they were all filled with the Holy Ghost, and began to speak with other tongues, as the Spirit gave them utterance.*

This passage from Acts 2:1-4 describes the momentous event of Pentecost, when the Holy Spirit descended upon the disciples while gathered in one Spirit. The sound of a mighty wind and the tongues of fire symbolize the powerful presence of the Holy Spirit permanently filling the believers, similar to how the dove and the column of light descended upon Jesus at the time of his water baptism. Again, in the Old Covenant Jesus was baptized in water and promised to send the

Holy Spirit in the New Covenant. At Pentecost the disciples were baptized with the Holy Spirit and fire thus fulfilling Matthew 3:11.

This enabled new gifts and abilities to come upon them so much so, they began speaking through the fire of God in a new tongue. The manifestation of speaking in other tongues signifies the gift of speaking in a Heavenly language that was not previously known, all enabled by the Holy Spirit dwelling inside. It's a holy language only God can understand, as well as those who have received the gift of interpreting the Heavenly language. I have heard many testimonies of the Holy Spirit allowing people to speak in languages foreign to them without consciously knowing the language.

The event of Pentecost empowered the disciples to boldly proclaim the Gospel to people of various nations. The arrival of the Holy Spirit at Pentecost fulfilled Jesus' promise to send the Holy Spirit into each born again believer, to empower and equip for the work of being a disciple and spreading the message of the Gospel to the ends of the earth.

When a believer has faith in the Gospel of Paul, has accepted their Holy Spirit baptism and fire, and walks in righteousness then they also walk in Jesus' authority. This gives them the gifts of sainthood such as the ability to command angels and demons and heal the sick.

Through saints using their God-given authority I have heard demons shriek and manifest (make their presence known) and leave an afflicted individual. This is when unclean spirits are calmly commanded to leave a person "in Jesus name." The weight isn't in how forcefully Jesus' name is said, the authority is found inside the name. There are many ways demons manifest when they are commanded out in the name of Jesus, one of them is shrieking.

I have seen the devil lose the battle at the individual level many times. No matter how evil you think you have been, no matter how much you have sinned, you can be redeemed by the blood and the love of Jesus. Perfect love casts out all fear (1 John 4:18). Jesus is perfect love.

During a salvation hell's army loses another soul and God's army gains another soul. A person really does decide to change teams because they can see the path they have been heading down is bleak.

Deliverances are a continuation of fortifying who you are, who you are loved by, and who you belong to. When you belong to Jesus, He will assure that a work started in you will be finished to completion (Philippians 1:6).

Jesus intends for you to be spotless and freed from the bondage of sin, demonic torment and perhaps most importantly and most often overlooked, the bondage of the flesh, the Adam nature of man, which is only overcome by the Holy Spirit and fire and being discipled and therefore self-controlled and disciplined.

John 8:36 KJV

*If the Son therefore shall make you free, ye shall be free indeed.*

Deliverance and the cleaning of believers is for the body of Christ. Deliverance works at the identity level, so Jesus can only clean those that belong to Him, and have accepted them as their King. He wants His saints to have no demonic bondage. Jesus delivered many people in the Bible, it was a daily occurrence and not an occasional miracle. He completed the miracle of fishes and loaves twice and He walked on water once. However, He cast demons out of common townspeople daily.

The first sign that the Kingdom of God has arrived on earth is deliverance, a major component of the three year ministry of the prophesied Messiah, Jesus.

Matthew 12:28 KJV

*But if I cast out devils by the Spirit of God, then the kingdom of God is come unto you.*

Jesus wants you to be saved and He wants you to be free and clean of addictions and bondage, so you are an effective soldier in the Kingdom of God. He wants spotless saints that have been set free.

He wants your Sprit man to be strong and your flesh and fleshly desires to be weak, if not completely dead. That is holiness. It's through surrendering to His supernatural operation in your life and not through your own willpower. If you think a man (or woman) can be set free without Jesus through philosophy, psychology, and behavior modification techniques you are sorely mistaken. Humanism is a weak foundation to stand upon. Jesus is a strong foundation to build upon. One way is endless toiling, the other way is through rest.

He wants you living in deep peace without an appetite for chaos or sin. When you take rest in Him you go deeper into Him. Living life through the flesh creates sin and separation and Jesus doesn't want that. He wants us to come to Him through embracing His righteousness, His peace, His joy. He generously supplies all of this. As you become a disciple you will start to have a healthy fear of stepping into the wrong actions that create separation.

Romans 14:17 ASV

*For the kingdom of God is not eating and drinking, but righteousness and peace and joy in the Holy Spirit.*

If you entirely reject the Kingdom He has built for you, and sow into sin, the wages in this life and into the next one are hell forever. God desperately doesn't want that future for you. He wants you to fully come home so there is no separation, He died to give you the way out.

Jesus passionately wants every one of His saints to come home before their last breath and especially before the end of the Church Age. This way you are spared from the wrath of needing to claim sainthood through martyrdom during the tribulation. The antichrist will do everything to intimidate and torture you into renouncing Jesus.

Out of Jesus' kindness for humanity He died for His chosen ones to come home into God's Kingdom. The rapture is on a set date in the future, so Jesus desperately wants as many on board the Ark of Salvation before time is up. The signs are evident the hour is late.

For the lost or wandering sheep that belong to Him, He will go to great lengths to rescue them from the schemes of the devil because of His is that good. If your name is written in the Lamb's book of life in Heaven, He will protect you and make every effort to bring you back into His flock, away from the dominion of the enemy, before it's too late.

Jesus is often referred to as the Good Shepherd because He exemplifies the care and compassion of a shepherd who leaves the ninety-nine to seek out the one lost sheep that has strayed. His deep love for His flock is evident in His desire for their well-being and safety, reflecting the extent of His care for each soul. This profound level of concern underscores the immense value that God places on every single one of His children.

While this next verse was originally directed towards the lost sheep of Israel, the analogy remains relevant for the saints of today, who may have once been lost but now are found. Not all of the parables Jesus spoke to the Jewish people can be applied to modern day Gentiles, but this is one can be.

Jesus sat down with the sinners and tax collectors and the religious Pharisees under the Jewish law found it reprehensible for Jesus to even sit near them.

Jesus responded to the Pharisees with this parable.

Luke 15:3-7 KJV

*And he spake this parable unto them, saying, What man of you, having an hundred sheep, if he lose one of them, doth not leave the ninety and nine in the wilderness, and go after that which is lost, until he find it? And when he hath found it, he layeth it on his shoulders, rejoicing. And when he cometh home, he calleth together his friends and neighbours, saying unto them, Rejoice with me; for I have found my sheep which was lost. I say unto you, that likewise joy shall be in heaven over one sinner that repenteth, more than over ninety and nine just persons, which need no repentance.*

The Father is that good. He seeks out those that need reconciliation with Him. He will passionately go after His lost sheep until He brings them home. The Father is utterly unconcerned with the consequences of His actions with regard to His own safety, comfort, and well-being.

His love isn't crafty or slick, it's not cunning or shrewd, in fact all things considered its quite child-like, with no ulterior motives.

His love bankrupted Heaven by sending Jesus for you, to die in your place. His love doesn't consider Himself first, it isn't selfish or self-serving. He simply puts Himself out there like a shepherd, searching the wilderness until He finds His lost sheep. He goes chasing after on the off chance He finds the lost one, to have that moment where the lost is found. The lost sheep pauses and looks back only to realize how much the Good Shepherd loves him or her.

His love leaves the ninety-nine to find the lost one every time. To many practical adults that's a foolish concept.

What if He loses the ninety-nine in finding the one? What if? …What if finding that one lost sheep is and always will be supremely important.

His love isn't cautious, it's a love that sent His only Son to die gruesome death on a cross, there is no plan B with the love of God. He gives His heart away so completely that if refused one would think it would be irreparably broken, yet He gives Himself away again and again, time and time again.

Make no mistake our sins do pain His heart, but His capacity to forgive a lost sheep and allow Him back in always outweighs the capacity of an individual to sin. With repentance He always allows us back in. He continued to love you in those times when you hated Him, but He paid the cost anyway, of Jesus dying in your place to set you free. He did all of this out of the love the lost sheep.

He did all of this because He wants us to come home, back into a state of total reconciliation with Him. The Greek word for reconciliation is "katallagé" (/ka-ta-la-gi/). This word is used in the New Testament to describe the process of restoring a relationship or bringing about peace and harmony between parties who were previously estranged or at odds with each other.

He so desperately wants us back from the dominion of the lost world and the evil one because we are created in the image and likeness of God, we have a deep and intimate connection with Him, a connection that surpasses even our closest human relationships.

The divine imprint He placed within us establishes a profound bond with our Creator, one that surpasses the ties we have with our parents, our spouses, or even our own sense of self. This intrinsic connection to God shapes our identity of who we are and underscores the depth of His presence within us, guiding us in our journey of life. Once He has our attention He simply wants us to go deeper into His presence within us, to further embrace the image and likeness until we are refined like fine gold. It's all through surrender not strive.

We are wonderfully and painstakingly made in His image, and He is closer to us than our very own DNA. He is even more near than a nano particle. When the Spirit of the Lord is inside of you, He speaks calmly. He whispers because He is close by. His sheep recognize His voice (John 10:27).

As you pray more often your recognition of His voice versus your own becomes more dialed in. His voice starts to feel like a key going into a lock. That's how to discern your thoughts from His voice.

As more souls turn toward righteousness and away from sin and sinful living than we have more advocates and allies in the Kingdom of God – we have one more willing soldier in the army of God ready to share their testimony with others through conversations, books, videos, and public speaking.

The soldier, the disciple, the saint, all one and the same, can be trained. After one is equipped, they will have an overflow of the love of God and that will translate into new salvations, healings, and deliverances all through the blessing and authority of Jesus. It's all emanating from a place of knowing how loved you are by him.

1 Corinthians 13:13 ESV

*But now abideth faith, hope, love, these three; and the greatest of these is love.*

1 John 4:18 KJV

*There is no fear in love; but perfect love casteth out fear: because fear hath torment. He that feareth is not made perfect in love.*

Eventually the evil inside won't be allowed to fester anywhere inside of you because of the perfect love of Jesus that is perfecting you.

That's Jesus' biggest joy, when you fully, not partially, belong to Him. God can promote you, send you on His behalf, and give you deep meaning in your life when you fully belong to Him. He isn't looking for someone to bless, He is looking for someone He can trust to carry the blessing. If He sees you can't be trusted with the blessing He will take it away, that doesn't necessarily mean you aren't saved but it does mean He rescinded the offer to be a minister of the Gospel. He is really looking for faithful committed hearts much more than anything else. He doesn't care what you look like, how rich or poor you are, what country you are from. He sees the heart.

An individual with a humble heart, attentive to God's voice, devoted to studying His Word, and obedient to His guidance, holds great potential for being used by God in significant ways. This readiness to listen, learn, and follow God's instructions can make an unknown disciple extremely effective for enacting God's will on earth, often more effective than a well-known priest or pastor who may have strayed into the worship of wealth and fame.

God values a humble and obedient heart, irrespective of worldly status, and He delights in using those who are willing to serve Him faithfully.

This is why it says God is no respecter of persons, He doesn't look at the external validators most humans look at like social status, career, wealth, or fame. He looks directly into the human heart for holy righteousness or ungodly covetousness. One heart posture is pleasing to God, the other has fallen away.

Acts 10:34 ASV

*And Peter opened his mouth and said, Of a truth I perceive that God is no respecter of persons.*

God often begins by presenting an up and coming disciple with small tests of obedience, allowing them to demonstrate faithfulness in the little things. As he or she proves themselves faithful in these initial tests, He gradually entrusts with greater responsibilities and challenges (Luke 16:10). This progression in testing and responsibility serves as a means of refining character, deepening trust in God, and preparing the disciple for the larger tasks and assignments that He has planned in accordance with His will.

In a military context, consider this analogy: just as a general in the army requires the complete submission and unwavering dedication of his soldiers to achieve success, God seeks our humble submission, faith, commitment, and obedience in order to use us in His army. When God observes these qualities in us, we are recognized as valuable members of His army, effective in the spiritual battle against evil forces, pushing back the gates of hell and actively advancing the Kingdom of God. This imagery underscores the importance of our steadfast loyalty and obedience in serving God's purposes and advancing His Kingdom on earth.

In matters of promotion and advancement in God's kingdom, it is essential to entrust the process to God rather than relying on our own fleshly efforts to seek promotion. By placing our trust in God's timing and plan for our lives, we demonstrate our faith in His sovereignty and wisdom. Allowing God to orchestrate our growth and elevation within His Kingdom ensures that His purposes are fulfilled in our lives, leading to character growth and effectiveness in serving Him.

You must trust that He will elevate you to your proper place and position. You don't have to play the political games of man, and you don't have to strive. In fact, God will promote, where man rejects.

God can see exactly who each person is. He can see their exact character, heart posture, and intentions when it comes to every area of life. God promotes and demotes much more accurately than man and his political based approach. That's why having a healthy reverence of God is wise. The Lord giveth and the Lord taketh (Job 1:21).

In matters of faith, there exists a distinction between having little faith and harnessing great faith. Great faith is exemplified when faced with circumstances that defy human understanding, yet one maintains a supernatural trust in God throughout.

Peter's miraculous walk on water, while a demonstration of faith, was categorized as "little faith" by Jesus. This is because Peter momentarily shifted his focus from Jesus to the storm, leading to fear and he began to sink. Despite this, his initial step out onto the water was an act of faith. Considering little faith allowed Peter to walk on water just like Jesus, one can only imagine the extraordinary impact that great faith can have in transforming and empowering one's life.

Matthew 14:29 KJV

*And he said, Come. And when Peter was come down out of the ship, he walked on the water, to go to Jesus.*

Matthew 14:31 KJV

*And immediately Jesus stretched forth his hand, and caught him, and said unto him, O thou of little faith, wherefore didst thou doubt?*

God loves all His children so much so that He does not want to see any of them harmed. Remember, He is a Good Shepherd. He doesn't want to see anyone of us faithless, tormented, scared, saddened or sinking.

Jesus is a big believer in humanity and always has been. Each one of our souls was made by Him. He came to rescue us, and not to condemn us, and He is still alive, ever praying for His saints.

Romans 8:34 KJV

*Who is he that condemneth? It is Christ that died, yea rather, that is risen again, who is even at the right hand of God, who also maketh intercession for us.*

He came to pull us out of the harmful fire and fill us with His Spirit, His Holy fire. He came to uplift us and rebuild us into mighty warriors, not worriers. He deeply loves us 100% of the time, but in order to befriend Him fully we must turn away from sin and toward a holy life that is pleasing to Him. That means total surrender, reaching the end of yourself, and repenting for all the evil you have already sowed. Plead the blood over sins past and any new ones that pop up.

In the realm beyond this earthly life, the only living Spirit is God the Father, Jesus the Christ, and the Holy Spirit—the triune God.

He is three distinct personalities yet all three are perfectly unified as one Spirit. All other beings or entities in the spiritual realm are not living in the realm of eternal life. Obtaining an in depth understanding of the dynamics of the spiritual world is important because the spiritual its intricately connected to our earthly existence, with various forces at work, and we do not want to be deceived.

Therefore, if one's allegiance and commitment are not fully dedicated to the Holy God of the universe and a life of holiness, one may unknowingly or knowingly be susceptible to the influences of dark forces and unfortunately remain vulnerable to the schemes of the enemy.

God requires total allegiance and submission just like any army general would. In chapter 9 you will learn more about how eager the dark forces are to corrupt an individual.

The spirits that are here on earth outside of the Holy God are demons, which are basically evil, vile, filthy people without bodies looking for a host, meaning somebody to occupy.

The host is a person that has opened doors to satan's demons through a life of sin.

A saint of God has closed off any doors to sin through the Holy Spirit sealing them off and through a disciplined and holy lifestyle.

The enemy is looking for any legal and open door into a person, the enemy is looking for any foothold in a person's life, big or small. Remember, satan is the accuser and he wants to be able accuse you of unrepented sin at the end of your life so he can bring you to hell.

Think of when a door is barely cracked open. A foot can be placed in the crack and the door can be pried opened the rest of the way. That's how the demonic realm works. Even for the saints, the enemy is surveying for cracks. The adversary is constantly prowling to attempt to sow discord and mutiny in the ranks of the saints and the lost.

All lost, secular, pre-saved lifestyles, are sinful, and open doors to the schemes of the enemy. Satan is always plotting and prowling whether saved or unsaved.

Living Holy means that you are walking with the Spirit of God and you are walking a Holy and set apart life, a path that not many people in the world are walking. Being in God's army is an exclusive honor.

Living Holy also means that the Holy Spirit of the living God is dwelling inside of you. A Christian maintains holiness, righteousness, and excellence through always keeping Jesus's sacrifice in remembrance and this sustains the healthy fear of any separation from God. Keeping His authority in memory, keeping on the armor of God, and never denying the omnipresence of the Holy Spirit creates a fusion of protection and assurance of the inheritance of the saints.

The amor of God from Paul's Gospel and how to wear it is in the next chapter.

Paul's Gospel is where the saints of the Church are to study from the most. Paul was appointed by Jesus to equip and teach the Church. He wrote Hebrews, Romans, 1 Corinthians, 2 Corinthians, Galatians, Ephesians, Philippians, Colossians, 1 Thessalonians, 2 Thessalonians, 1 Timothy, 2 Timothy, Titus, and Philemon. In addition to Paul's books the saints should focus on are John, 1 John, 2 John, 3 John, James, 1 Peter, 2 Peter, Jude, and Revelation. These are the books written to the saints about the New Covenant in Jesus' shed blood.

1 Thessalonians 1:3 KJV

*Remembering without ceasing your work of faith, and labour of love, and patience of hope in our Lord Jesus Christ, in the sight of God and our Father.*

2 Timothy 2:8 KJV

*Remember that Jesus Christ of the seed of David was raised from the dead according to my gospel.*

1 Corinthians 15:2 KJV

*By this gospel you are saved, if you hold firmly to the word I preached to you. Otherwise, you have believed in vain."*

Romans 2:16 KJV

*In the day when God shall judge the secrets of men by Jesus Christ according to my gospel."*

# Ch. 6 THE HOLY SPIRIT

The Holy Spirit is a gift to the saints of the Church to live through us, inside of us, and to uplift us. God promises that He will live inside of us and be with us through His Spirit.

When Jesus and the Holy Spirit are on-board then His peace, His guidance, His love, His joy, His righteousness, is always with you, wherever you go and no matter what happens along the way.

Only Christianity has this promise from the one and true Almighty God.

A visual representation of someone becoming a new creation in Christ can be illustrated by combining the color red, symbolizing Jesus' shed blood, with a person's blood, which is blue while in the body. When these two colors are mixed, a new color is formed. The resulting color flowing through the individual's veins is becomes purple, symbolizing the transformation into an entirely new creation. Purple has long been associated with royalty, emphasizing the spiritual rebirth into Christ's royal lineage as a born again Christian.

To experience more of the presence of the Holy Spirit, you can engage by listening to fifteen minutes of worship music. Listen to the lyrics being sung and let the music's rhythm resonate with you. As you immerse yourself in worship, you may start to sense the Holy Spirit's presence lifting your spirit and filling you with a sense of renewal and hope. It only takes a short time to encounter the sacred presence of God to shift your spiritual atmosphere, and receive a fresh touch of optimism, and the truth, when you are in Christ there is hope.

To obtain the full measure of the hope and joy of the indwelling of the

Holy Spirit then accepting salvation through faith and the baptism of the Holy Spirit and fire is the next step (Acts 1:5, Acts 1:8). There is a prayer for the Holy Spirit and fire baptism in chapter 15.

Placing your faith in the work done on the cross for you can shift you from any difficulty you may be dealing with. Allowing the Spirit of God to influence you will come without strive. It's just about allowing the Holy Spirit to come in.

All you need to do is clear your mind and receive Him. You can even start with a prayer during worship that's as simple as, "Holy Spirit come." Repeating this to yourself or out loud will invite the Holy Spirit to further dwell. Surrender control and let Him get to work, then you can lean back and surrender to the love and healing only He can provide. The Holy Spirit isn't anything we have to "work" for, it's someone that we must allow in through preparation, praise, stillness, and prayer.

When we fully surrender ourselves to the Lordship of Jesus Christ, we become spiritually grafted into His bloodline. This connection allows us to partake in the freedom and wisdom that Jesus provided through His sacrifice and teachings. It is through surrender that we can experience the transformative power of His love and guidance.

Ephesians 2:11-13 KJV

*Wherefore remember, that ye being in time past Gentiles in the flesh...That at that time ye were without Christ, being aliens from the commonwealth of Israel, and strangers from the Covenants of promise, having no hope, and without God in the world: But now in Christ Jesus ye who sometimes were far off are made nigh by the blood of Christ.*

Galatians 3:28-29 KJV

*There is neither Jew nor Greek, there is neither bond nor free, there is neither male nor female: for ye are all one in Christ Jesus. And if ye be Christ's, then are ye Abraham's seed, and heirs according to the promise.*

Romans 11:17 KJV

*And if some of the branches be broken off, and thou, being a wild olive tree, wert graffed in among them, and with them partakest of the root and fatness of the olive tree.*

When we invite the Holy Spirit to dwell within us, we also welcome the lineage of prophets and royal kings who have gone before us. This connection enables us to grow and reflect the character of King Jesus more each day. Living in this way, guided by the Holy Spirit and the royal lineage of those who came before us, is truly a remarkable and transformative way to live.

1 John 3:1-2 KJV

*Behold, what manner of love the Father hath bestowed upon us, that we should be called the sons of God: therefore the world knoweth us not, because it knew him not. Beloved, now are we the sons of God, and it doth not yet appear what we shall be: but we know that, when he shall appear, we shall be like him; for we shall see him as he is.*

A Holy Spirit baptized believer becomes a son of God, the same mantle that Jesus walked in as the Son of God. A son allows himself (or herself) to be fully transformed into the image of Jesus.

Being transformed into the image of Jesus through His Spirit equates to being liberated from all forms of mental, physical, and spiritual ailments and this is just the beginning of the profound work that Jesus accomplished for you. His sacrifice paved the way for a life of wholeness, holiness, purpose, and eternal significance.

The Bible is a story of God's love for humanity. He loves us and He does not want us to see us spinning our tires. He wants us to turn over every difficult situation to Him and to trust Him for guidance.

Jesus desires to see His children live free from pain and confusion. When we feel overwhelmed, it may be a sign that we are relying on our own strength and willpower, rather than surrendering it to Him and seeking His guidance. By partnering with Jesus and admitting we need a Savior, we can find strength, clarity, and direction that surpasses the limits of human perspectives and wisdom. He has a thirty-thousand foot perspective on our lives, always seeing the bigger picture we can't see without Him, easily seeing through space and time on our behalf, and guiding us with a full measure of divine wisdom and foresight in all situations. This is all accomplished through the Holy Spirit.

In a very real sense, when you are a disciple of Christ, the Spirit of the Lord goes before you.

Isiah 52:12 KJV

*For you shall not go out in haste, and you shall not go in flight, for the Lord will go before you, and the God of Israel will be your rear guard.*

Today, when I think I may have sinned I have much greater awareness about it and I repent right away rather than drift into shame. Drifting into self-pity and shame never helped anybody. The devil may try and convince a believer they are not able to repent – the extent the enemy plays with people's minds is astounding – that's why we need the Holy Spirit to influence us and complete us.

When the Holy Spirit is inside, you are quickly convicted by unrighteous actions. In other words, the proof the Holy Spirit is dwelling inside of you is you instantly repent and change course back towards holiness. He is the holy tour guide to keep you on the right path and safe from pitfalls.

2 Chronicles 7:14 KJV

*If my people, which are called by my name, shall humble themselves, and pray, and seek my face, and turn from their wicked ways; then will I hear from Heaven, and will forgive their sin, and will heal their land.*

Additionally, the Holy Spirit can also convince you of your holiness. You will be able to clearly see how much you have changed for the better. He will assure you of the improvements in your behavior and character.

John 16:6-8 KJV

*But because I have said these things unto you, sorrow hath filled your heart. Nevertheless I tell you the truth; It is expedient for you that I go away: for if I go not away, the Comforter will not come unto you; but if I depart, I will send him unto you. And when he is come, he will reprove the world of sin, and of righteousness, and of judgment.*

The Comforter is the Holy Spirit. He is who reproves you and the Greek word for reprove is "elencho" (/e-LEN-kho/) meaning to "convict" or "convince." So, it plainly says in John the Comforter will convict you of when you considering sin or have stepped into sin, convince you of when you are righteous and walking in the holiness of Jesus, and convince you of when you are facing judgement. This is to prevent you from facing eternal judgement when you do reach the Courtroom of Heaven, everyone's destiny. In court you are either found justified and set free, or guilty and worthy of punishment.

The Holy Spirit does all of this for you to buffer you against sin and to keep you on the right track and living in peace. The alternative to living in peace and gratitude is living in sin and fear. Both are in lockstep with each other, respectively. Sin and fear are the enemy's currency, and the evil one would delight in nothing more than to see a believer or nonbeliever ensnared in sin and fear.

The Comforter will help you so you do not give fear and worry a home inside your heart and mind. The Holy Spirit completes your mind and provides you with the sound mind of God (2 Timothy 1:7).

If your friends or family are full of small minded, fear-based thinking then you do have permission to create healthy distance.

Proverbs 4:23 ASV

*Keep thy heart with all diligence; For out of it are the issues of life.*

The exceptions that must be navigated with discernment are the Covenant relationships like those between husband and wife, there no exiting that relationship unless there has been evidence of cheating. So that's where a husband and wife must embrace forgiveness, grace, and truth they all need to come together, so that growth and healing occurs and both people are formed further into the likeness and image of Jesus.

The other type of Covenantal relationship is when children are dependent on parents, quite literally for everything, but once the children become adults they are allowed to create distance if there is nothing but toxicity coming from parents. There are unfortunately disciples of Christ out there that have parents and relatives trying to pull them down and away from their faith. Handling this type of challenge all comes down to the leadership and the guidance from the Holy Spirit on what is right.

Part of being a Christian while still living in the world is protecting your ear gates and eye gates, meaning protect what you view and protect what you listen to. The enemy can only get in where he is allowed in. The disciple is called to live holy and set apart from the world. This means a disciple must decide what to let in and what to limit or block.

Having this distance from the world and the negative voices in the world is crucial to the saint as he or she remakes their identity under the dominion and authority of Jesus. The Bible promises you to be a new creation. Jesus is the identity, the master blueprint to emulate and embody.

When you have fully become a new creation in Christ then you are expanding into hope, faith, and love directly from the throne room.

Jesus is the same always and forever so the benefits of seeking Jesus are available for any age, any race, and any nationality.

Hebrews 13:8 KJV

*Jesus Christ the same yesterday, and to day, and for ever.*

Embracing the Holy Spirit and allowing the hope, faith, and love of God to permeate your life brings about a profound transformation.

This includes a heightened sense of inspiration, a revitalized enthusiasm for life, and an assurance of being in right standing with God. When you see the whole picture of yourself and who God is living inside you, then you have a deeper sense of purpose in everyday experiences. As you walk step by step with the Holy Spirit, your daily life takes on a supernatural quality, and you begin to recognize God's hand at work in every area of your daily interactions and circumstances.

As you advance in the ways of the Holy Spirit, do expect changes to occur. The changes will either be all at once or they will be gentle and gradual. Each person's journey toward God is unique to them. Your specific path towards growing in Holy Spirit is all by His design, and not from your own idea of how things should unfold. Trust that His ways are greater. He knows what's meant for you and what's not meant for you. If you intentionally give your whole life over to Jesus then shortly thereafter you may find yourself exiting unhealthy relationships, toxic living situations, and unrighteous habits. Not only that, often instantly and without a struggle. He wants to set you free from any form of slavery or death. He is that good.

You may think I am overselling Jesus, but I'm actually underselling, almost nobody is giving God the full credit due for His total dominion over all things past, present, and future. We will only have the entire revelation of who God is and how much He was watching over us our whole lives until we get to the other side.

As you grow closer to the Lord by spending time in His presence and seeking His guidance, you will naturally become more set apart from the ways of the world. This transformation is God's beautiful design to lead you towards holiness.

Know that your body is the vessel for His blood and His Holy Spirit. your body becomes His body, and you are no longer your own (2 Timothy 1:7), which is paradoxically freeing. He promises you become the temple of the Holy Spirit to steward the eternal and Holy flame.

The Holy Spirit is described in the Bible as a treasure. The Greek word the Bible uses is "thesaurus" (/thuh-sawr-uhs/) in 2 Corinthians 4:7, meaning a "treasure," a storehouse, so rich you can never search it out. That's how magnificent and massive the gift is of the Holy Spirit dwelling inside us. It doesn't matter how long you count and attempt to tabulate; you can never measure the infinite value of the Holy Spirit. That's how much God cares about us. He has extended the most priceless gift, Himself, into His children.

When we allow God to transform us, we become brand new vessels (arks, hope chests) through which His purposes can be fulfilled on earth. Discovering a new sense of purpose in life is a profound journey that believers embark on. While some Christians that are still thinking small may underestimate the significance of our role on earth, God has entrusted us with the treasure of the Holy Spirit to embark on the Great Commission for a divine reason. The Bible itself was brought to us through obedient men who received the Word of God by way of the Holy Spirit, illustrating the vital role each of us plays in the modern-day body of Christ.

In addition to the imagery of the iron and clay kingdoms in the previous chapter, there are various vessels or chambers within you.

Some are constructed from wood and earth, akin to clay, while others are crafted from metals like gold and silver. Unlike materials made from earth, gold and silver do not decay over time.

Gold and silver are long-standing just like the Kingdom of God is long-standing. Gold and silver can maintain molecular structural integrity for many thousands of years.

2 Timothy 2:20 KJV

*But in a great house there are not only vessels of gold and of silver, but also of wood and of earth; and some to honour, and some to dishonour.*

A new believer is in the process of allowing Jesus to burn away and abolish the wooden and earth made vessels inside, so that the gold and silver vessels inside can come forward and shine. Think about if God gives you a special task or assignment. He wants this assignment to go into a long-lasting gold or silver vessel inside of you rather than a temporary and fragile earthen vessel. He wants the treasures inside to be protected and the dross inside to be burned up.

Your body is the chosen temple where the treasures of the Holy Spirit and special assignments are housed. So, protect your temple and protect your assignment He has given you. You only get one body, one lifetime, and one will. You were designed by God to be an overall instrument for the Holy Spirit, His voice, His purposes, and His love.

It is wise to protect your temple from junk food, sugary drinks, fast food, pesticides, GMO food, processed food, seed oils, pharmaceuticals, street drugs, cigarettes, marijuana and alcohol, but not only that refrain from mental junk food from the screens because that ends up inside of you too. Jesus is quite saddened by how much influence the screens have over people.

All these products lower your overall health and your ability to feel the whispers of God which is His nearness. You will come to realize His voice and His presence are the greatest gifts to be found on earth.

While seeking and stewarding the Spirit of God, the eternal flame, your life will take on new power, but it's not your power, it's His power coming upon you, not the other way around. Seek His face, His presence, and His will for you, not the power or the provision you may think you are entitled to. Seek His face before His hand and trust in Him to be a good Father once you allow Him in.

When you begin to steward the presence in your life, you must do your best to continue to steward and maintain the grace on your life. It must be repeated, the Holy Spirit only dwells where there is holiness. Where there is unrighteous activity, He is seemingly absent or at best grieving in the background for taking Him for granted. Just like John the baptizer said, "Prepare the way of the Lord!" The Lord always honors the prepared and without preparing for Him you are not ready for Him – think in the context of the rapture. He is coming back for the prepared saints that have been committed and stewarding holiness.

To have access to the Holy Spirit you must first be a willing steward. The Greek word "oikonomos" (/ee-kon-OM-os/) translates to "steward" or "manager." In the biblical context, a steward is someone entrusted with managing and overseeing the affairs or resources of another, in this case, entrusted with the Spirit of God Himself.

When the Holy Spirit chooses to dwell in you are also entrusted with the gift of grace. The Greek word "charisma" (/khar'-is-mah/) is often translated as "the gifts of grace" in the Bible. It denotes an empowerment bestowed through grace to saints for the edification of the Church and the advancement of God's kingdom. These gifts all come with the Holy Spirit and they are intended to strengthen the body of Christ and to minister to others in love and kindness.

To summarize, a Christ carrier, is a carrier of blessings. The term "anointing" is closely linked to the Greek word "chrisma" (/khrísma/). This noun signifies being consecrated, made holy and set apart, from the fallen world and fallen desires of the heart for a specific purpose. The purpose is in alignment with God's will, and again, this all through the empowering work of the Holy Spirit residing within.

The blessing on your life to live out your God-given will is empowered by the Holy Spirit and that's a gift of grace, given to you for a life of meaning and eternal significance, is not to be taken lightly. If you take it lightly, it means you are stubbornly walking in disobedience, and that opens you up to additional spiritual storms. This is why following Christ is the highest and hardest path – for to whom much is entrusted, much more will be demanded (Luke 12:48).

We can take the story of how a water buffalo manages a storm compared to farm cows, because storms will come, but the key is in the approach. The metaphor encourages individuals to be prepared and to pursue their God-given will directly rather than running away or procrastinating. Cows that choose to run away from the storm end up enduring it for longer periods, but the buffalo wisely charges through, minimizing its time inside the storm. This metaphor emphasizes the importance of taking proactive steps to be prepared with the wisest course of action, leading to quicker outcomes, reduced suffering, and a full transition to God's will, resulting in tangible progress. Remember, spiritual storms will come, but the focus should be on progress rather than perfection. Facing the obstacle head on rather than avoiding it is the way.

1 Peter 5:8 KJV

*Be sober, be vigilant; because your adversary the devil, as a roaring lion, walketh about, seeking whom he may devour.*

Delays can arise in various forms, whether through personal hesitation or chosen distractions. One the most common ways believers impede their progress or disqualify themselves entirely from fulfilling the purposes the Holy Spirit intends for them is through the consumption of alcohol. It's a poison so it grieves the Holy Spirit inside.

Ephesians 5:18 KJV

*And be not drunk with wine, wherein is excess; but be filled with the Spirit*

Proverbs 20:1 KJV

*Wine is a mocker, strong drink is raging: and whosoever is deceived thereby is not wise.*

Isaiah 5:11-13 KJV

*Woe unto them that rise up early in the morning, that they may follow strong drink; that continue until night, till wine inflame them! And the harp, and the viol, the tabret, and pipe, and wine, are in their feasts: but they regard not the work of the Lord, neither consider the operation of his hands. Therefore my people are gone into captivity, because they have no knowledge: and their honourable men are famished, and their multitude dried up with thirst.*

These verses warn against the dangers of drinking and neglecting the ways of the Lord, highlighting the negative consequences that result from prioritizing pleasure and indulgence over spiritual matters. Many Christians in name only today don't deny themselves and still live for the fallen desires of the world and never step into their destiny.

Isaiah 5:22-23 KJV

*Woe unto them that are mighty to drink wine, and men of strength to mingle strong drink: Which justify the wicked for reward, and take away the righteousness of the righteous from him!*

The Bible predominantly portrays wine, wine lovers who partake frequently, and drunkards in a negative light, with only a few instances of positive references to wine used during celebration. Allowing any alcohol in is playing with fire because drunkards will not inherit the Kingdom of God (1 Corinthians 6:10). If you come from a background of alcohol abuse, the phrase one is too many and a thousand drinks is never enough will make sense. You don't want to dim or grieve the Holy Spirit and alcohol is one of the most common slippery slopes to dimming the holy flame inside, remember the Spirit of God inside you is a relationship that has been granted and entrusted from God to us to be stewarded. If you feel no conviction about getting drunk and you believe you are saved, you might be saved through faith, but there is a good chance you are not filled with the Holy Spirit and that's really what God is looking for on rapture day.

On the mental and emotional front, it is essential to focus on things that are uplifting and light rather than dwelling on what is burdensome and dark. Presenting yourself to others with the warmth and love of Jesus is more impactful than embodying the bitterness and darkness of those who are closed off and angry.

Philippians 4:8 KJV

*Finally, brethren, whatsoever things are true, whatsoever things are honest, whatsoever things are just, whatsoever things are pure, whatsoever things are lovely, whatsoever things are of good report; if there be any virtue, and if there be any praise, think on these things.*

Lots of media and social media grieves the Lord, so to see you wasting so much of your time on it, pains Him. So please have strong discernment about who and what you are consistently adding to your mental diet. As mentioned before, protect your eye gates and ear gates. Many today are addicted to scrolling and screentime. Taking in news is a balance between knowing the agendas of the enemy and the signs of the times so you are aware, but also not getting sucked into fear and idolizing the spectacles of disasters. Many Christians are getting sucked into shock and awe politics instead of being compelled by their God-given purpose they need to be executing. As the end approaches its getting harder to focus because of how many end times headlines are rolling out each day.

If you are feeling fearful and distracted it's hard to feel the presence of God – the answer is to focus on and surrender to the presence of God, His face, His peace, His joy, and His righteousness and He will drive out any fear (1 John 4:18). No matter how crazy the news gets, keep your eyes fixed on Jesus. He is always the answer in the face of instability and uncertainty.

Jesus paid the ultimate sacrifice for you to carry the Holy Spirit. He saw you worthy of obtaining access to His holy and royal priesthood, worthy of being humble enough to surrender, take His yoke, and become a Christ carrier. A Christ carrier must be available and not full of the world.

Do not take His sacrifice for granted by partaking in "normal" activities, even if many other Christians are getting sucked in. Remember, satan wants to normalize sin, fear, and chaos and make holiness and focusing on Jesus look abnormal.

Leave normal behind and do not be of the world! Be holy and set apart! When you deeply believe you are His child then you are not living for the ways of the fallen kingdom, the kingdom of the world.

Once again, it must be emphasized the importance of not stumbling into sedatives like alcohol, marijuana, and prescription pills. There is something in the constitution of uppers and downers that eats away at your clarity, your purpose, and your ability to feel and hear the Holy Spirit. The substances place you in your Adam nature and out of your divine nature.

If you numb your vessel out, you will not be able to hear God whisper to you. It is promised, His believers know and hear His voice. There is a reason alcohol has consistently been called spirits. It opens you up to demonic spirits and is toxic to your entire body. When you step into being a blood bought believer your body no longer belongs to you, it becomes the temple of God (1 Corinthians 6:19-20).

John 10:27-28 KJV

*My sheep hear my voice, and I know them, and they follow me: And I give unto them eternal life; and they shall never perish, neither shall any man pluck them out of my hand.*

If you can't hear God or feel God or receive a sense of what He is communicating to you, it means there are distractions getting in the way and causing blockages towards clear communication with Him.

This can be frustrating but please remember, per the Scripture above, it is written, His sheep hear his voice. Each action has an equal and opposite reaction, meaning if you tune into His Kingdom much more than the fallen kingdom of the world, you create more Holy space for Him to dwell and you will hear Him better. He wants your whole heart, body, and mind, not part of it.

God communicates through the miraculous power of the Holy Spirit. Your Holy Helper. Sometimes it's in the form of gentle whispers in your native language, sometimes it's at a feeling level, and sometimes it's at a physical level. God can tap you on the shoulder with His nearby presence, literally. Each person will become aware of how God "talks" to them. For me it's primarily audible in 2-way prayer.

The sensitivity to pick up on how and what He is trying to communicate with you can be reduced through distractions as previously mentioned. Distractions and idols come in a multitude of forms today, whether man-made (fornication, arguments, sex outside of marriage, drugs, alcohol, busyness) or machine-made (social media, streaming platforms, AI chatbots). Any distractions and idols will leave you feeling drained and unmotivated, if not worse.

One of the most common and most damaging forms of distraction, unholiness, and idolatry is pornography and fornication for men or women. Any form of sexual immorality such as sex before marriage is not too different in God's eyes. The dark spirits in the world rejoice in pornography, hookup culture, and sex outside of marriage because these practices directly oppose God's order and design for sex. He wants it kept sacred, inside of a covenantal marriage.

Keeping your vessel clean, consecrated, holy and set apart, and tuned into His voice is like being near a wi-fi signal or a cell tower.

If you are too far away from the router because of noise and unholy distractions, then the signal fades and you don't receive the connection and communication that was intended by the wi-fi designer. God is the ultimate form of "wireless fidelity."

God requires your fidelity. The Greek word for fidelity in the New Testament is "pistis," (/PIS-tis/) which is translated to "faith" or "faithfulness." This word captures what the Lord seeks: trust, loyalty, unwavering belief, and faithfulness in relationship and commitment, with Him primarily and with others in your life. He deserves this level of faithfulness and commitment because His gift of grace saved you and purchased you out of eternal separation (Ephesians 2:8).

Keeping that connection tight is your vital lifeline. Jesus will always protect you and provide you with plans to bless your life. You just must lean in and keep your praise and focus on Him. His voice is always uplifting and never discouraging. His council can always provide a way where you don't see a way. You are at a huge disadvantage when you forfeit this connection through sin, distraction, and idolatry. Conversely, having tight communication with Him places you in a big advantage.

Knowing that the Father will always keep His love on for you is important, you just need to hold up your end up the bargain so He can remain close. His love for you is the same always and forever (Hebrews 13:8). He loved you first, you simply need to show up and abide in Him.

The Greek word for "abide" is "meno" (/me-nō/) which can be translated as "abide," "remain," "stay," or "dwell." It signifies the act of staying in a specific place, continuing in a relationship, or persisting in a state or condition.

Another real-world example of keeping this connection with God tight is white water rafting. The experience of growing up as a human can feel similar to a turbulent white water rafting excursion at times. The ebbs and flows of life can come at us in brutal and unpredictable ways so being in the center of the white-water raft, rather than hanging off the edges, is going to best protect you against the tumultuous waters around you. Being in the center is your buffer.

If you are not prepared and seated correctly you can find yourself falling out at an inopportune moment and the currents can swiftly pull you under. Therefore, it is crucial to adopt a wiser and more balanced approach. This analogy underscores why living a "Christ-centered" life is frequently emphasized when following Jesus.

Spiritually speaking, in Christianity, the seating position you take is known as your heart posture. God can always see your intentions. There is no fooling Him. He can see if you are being a good steward of the Holy Spirit or being foolish.

To make it more applicable, a heart posture is simple to define. Is Jesus on the throne of your heart or are the distractions? Who or what is getting more of your attention? To simplify, distractions in the Christian walk are also known as idols. Is the heart baptized, permanently submerged, into holy desires or is the heart still seeking for pleasures and distractions in a covetous and greedy manner?

Idols have a way of diverting your focus, which is indeed your most precious currency. This is why directing your focus towards someone, or something is often described as "paying attention." Attention could be considered the most valuable currency we possess, as we invest it throughout every waking moment of the day and it's in limited supply. We only get on average 20,000 days on the low end and up to 36,000 days if we are blessed enough to reach one hundred years old.

The point is, only Jesus deserves the seat on the throne of your heart because He created you and breathed life into you. Only He deserves your unwavering faith. He intimately knows you better than any other person ever can or ever will. He deserves obedience above everyone and everything else, yes even close friends and family. If they are pulling you away from God they are not on God's team.

Jesus, who is God, always deserves the top priority in your life. He deserves to be your first thought and your last thought each day.

If the distractions and idols are a consistent deterrent to your relationship with God, then you must pray for renewed vision and renewed focus. Lay down each idol, turn them over to God for reconciliation. Ask for deliverance from all evils in your life. Strong pray for God to expose and remove whatever or whoever is taking you away from Him. Turn each burden over to Jesus. He wants to lighten your load. One by one He will release you from the bondage and confusion of your past. If unrepented sin is holding you back He will show you what you need to plead the blood over.

After you have accepted Jesus and you have been baptized in the Holy Spirit, then you gain the supernatural ability to ask the Holy Spirit what else you need to lay down. He will show you what else has been distracting you from growing in your close relationship with God. He will help you. He will literally tell you. He will convince you of what's in the way toward your spiritual growth.

Developing the personal relationship with Jesus is not rocket science. It is written that if we ask in faith, He will answer (James 4:2). He doesn't want us wandering in the desert for forty years. He wants to help us and lead us all the days of our lives in salvation and eternal freedom while protecting us from all the pitfalls from satan.

Trust that when you turn over the heaviness, Jesus can step in and uplift you, restore you, and restore your identity in Him, as a child of God. You need to give him your time and attention and simply lean in.

Realize the heaviness is not yours to carry. Sometimes you don't have to figure it all out yourself. Instead, you can pray and invite Jesus into the situation and trust that God sees you, the situation, and sees tomorrow before you do and not only that, He has the situation already resolved for you.

The journey of drawing nearer to God is not without its imperfections; setbacks and storms are inevitable, leading to moments of honest repentance. However, the path is always marked by grace. Whether the roadblocks are orchestrated by God or the enemy, God can utilize them as opportunities for growth and wisdom. Every obstacle the enemy intended for harm, God has the power to turn it around transform it for His glory. This book is proof of that.

Genesis 50:20 KJV

*But as for you, ye thought evil against me; but God meant it unto good, to bring to pass, as it is this day, to save much people alive.*

Growing in faith may have moments of weakness, but stumbles do not mean you cease to walk. Stumbling means you have been tempted to go back into the ways of the world, to go back into wandering around Egypt like the Israelites did, to go back into your shell, and to go back into your flesh.

Moments like these mean you temporarily forgot your identity as a child of God, as a son or daughter of the King. It means you went out into the world without the full armor of God on. You forgot you are now a new creation holy and set apart from the fallen world. You must place on the full armor of God and go directly into the daily battle.

Ephesians 6:10-18 KJV

*Finally, my brethren, be strong in the Lord, and in the power of his might. Put on the whole armour of God, that ye may be able to stand against the wiles of the devil. For we wrestle not against flesh and blood, but against principalities, against powers, against the rulers of the darkness of this world, against spiritual wickedness in high places. Wherefore take unto you the whole armour of God, that ye may be able to withstand in the evil day, and having done all, to stand. Stand therefore, having your loins girt about with truth, and having on the breastplate of righteousness; And your feet shod with the preparation of the gospel of peace; Above all, taking the shield of faith, wherewith ye shall be able to quench all the fiery darts of the wicked. And take the helmet of salvation, and the sword of the Spirit, which is the word of God: Praying always with all prayer and supplication in the Spirit, and watching thereunto with all perseverance and supplication for all saints.*

1 Corinthians 10:13 KJV

*There hath no temptation taken you but such as is common to man: but God is faithful, who will not suffer you to be tempted above that ye are able; but will with the temptation also make a way to escape, that ye may be able to bear it.*

When you are inside of a challenge, acknowledge it is a challenge. Know that a moment of weakness and temptation can be flipped into a moment of strength in an instant. It all comes down to discernment and the choices you make. When you feel tempted, know that being tempted is not a sin, caving in is. So, pause and sincerely surrender it to God.

"I surrender all."

If you have had a habit over the years of having poor discipline that will take time. But through prayer and choosing the Holy Spirit over the flesh, He can take you through weakness to the other side, where you are strong in Christ, whatever the challenge may be. He can bring you from being a boy into a great man. From being a girl into a great woman. He can bring you from being lost and outside of Christ to being in Christ and secure, a security money and things can't provide.

All of His strength comes in from a daily faith in following the Lord, not by your power, but by His. Persist and be patient. When you are feeling weak, know that He can come in and be strong. He is the God of the Heaven and the earth, and you are yoked with Him, after all.

Zechariah 4:6 KJV

*Then he answered and spake unto me, saying, This is the Word of the Lord unto Zerubbabel, saying, Not by might, nor by power, but by my spirit, saith the Lord of hosts.*

When you feel like the Holy Spirit is convicting you of sinful activities you can pause and flip the situation into strength. Realize it's a test to do one of two things. You can surrender it to God and take the righteous road or be pulled down by the schemes of the enemy and your flesh. It is written that if you surrender all, resist the devil, then he will flee, and the temptation or evil thoughts will quickly pass by. This is what the Apostle Paul means by crucify your flesh as well as bring thoughts captive to Christ (2 Corinthians 10:5).

Galatians 5:24 ASV

*And they that are of Christ Jesus have crucified the flesh with the passions and the lusts thereof.*

James 4:7 KJV

*Submit yourselves therefore to God. Resist the devil, and he will flee from you.*

Hebrews 1:9 KJV

*Thou hast loved righteousness, and hated iniquity; therefore God, even thy God, hath anointed thee with the oil of gladness above thy fellows.*

When you enter God's glorious family you are suddenly holy and set apart. This means you can turn your burdens over to Jesus and know that the rejuvenation and relief you seek comes from Holy Spirit supernaturally working on your behalf, and nothing else. He places you into a sanctified state, through surrender, and its immediate.

1 Thessalonians 5:23 ASV

*And the God of peace himself sanctify you wholly; and may your spirit and soul and body be preserved entire, without blame at the coming of our Lord Jesus Christ.*

The fulfillment and redemption found in Jesus far exceeds any worldly solutions or desires. His blood carries a supernatural power that surpasses all earthly remedies. Neither psychotherapy, idols, false gods, faux spirituality, mindfulness meditation, rituals, substances, nor self-care practices can match the ultimate power and satisfaction that Jesus provides. Surrendering to only Jesus as Lord of your life and following His teachings leads to a profound transformation that unlocks supernatural wisdom and strength that extends into eternity.

To review so far: we can choose through free will to access the Grace Covenant, receive the Holy Spirit and fire, push the flesh back and have Him guide us in all things, become sanctified wholly, and then upon entry into Heaven we receive our everlasting inheritance.

The journey of carrying Christ is all about accepting Jesus' finished work, embracing God's image that has been mapped onto us, and allowing God to see His likeness and holiness in us.

God's grace has always surrounded you, even when you were unaware of belonging to Him, but His grace extends far beyond that. The fullness of God's grace is experienced through accepting and embracing the Gospel: freedom and redemption are gifts from the Holy Spirit, this is God's operation of breaking any chains that the enemy sought to ensnare you with.

It is important to acknowledge that practices leading into bondage do not align with God's grace. While God may have protected your life while engaging in new age or occult practices that did not fall under His Grace Covenant. Such actions may have been temporarily covered by common grace, but this will stop at the end of the Church Age. The complete measure of His grace did not operate during involvement in these practices, as they are part of the enemy's deceptive tactics to ensnare and entrap individuals. God takes very seriously no other spiritual practices or gods go before Him.

Here is a list of some of the Scriptures that emphasize this about God as the one and true Almighty God. The only one worthy of worship.

Exodus 20:3 KJV

*Thou shalt have no other gods before me.*

Deuteronomy 5:7 KJV

*Thou shalt have none other gods before me.*

Deuteronomy 6:14 KJV

*Ye shall not go after other gods, of the gods of the people which are round about you.*

Deuteronomy 8:19 KJV

*And it shall be, if thou do at all forget the Lord thy God, and walk after other gods, and serve them, and worship them, I testify against you this day that ye shall surely perish.*

Deuteronomy 11:16 KJV

Take heed to yourselves, that your heart be not deceived, and ye turn aside, and serve other gods, and worship them.

Deuteronomy 13:6 KJV

*If thy brother, the son of thy mother, or thy son, or thy daughter, or the wife of thy bosom, or thy friend, which is as thine own soul, entice thee secretly, saying, Let us go and serve other gods, which thou hast not known, thou, nor thy fathers.*

Joshua 24:14 KJV

*Now therefore fear the Lord, and serve him in sincerity and in truth: and put away the gods which your fathers served on the other side of the flood, and in Egypt; and serve ye the Lord.*

It is only through the Holy Spirit's transformative work that genuine liberation and restoration are experienced, guiding us from darkness into the radiant and complete reality of His grace that redeems.

As you journey along the Christian path, Jesus personally intercedes on behalf of His saints, supporting and refining them like a skilled craftsman shaping gold into a beautiful form. He fans the flames within, molding and transforming His followers into His likeness, much like a potter molds clay with precision and care (Isaiah 64:8).

As we have established, God's mercy may have been at work, quietly safeguarding you in ways that may not have been immediately evident. As we journey forward in learning about the Lord, we gradually grasp the various ways in which God watches over both believers and nonbelievers. His grace is lavishly extended to humanity during the Church Age, nurturing a profound connection with Him, all of which emerges through Jesus' blood, the indwelling of the Holy Spirit, and the timeless truths of the Word of God found in the Bible.

This divine connection to the one and true God is never established through occult practices like psychedelic experiences, meditating on emptiness, performing various yoga poses, collecting crystals, hanging dream catchers, consulting with psychics for crystal ball readings or tarot readings, and any other spiritual modalities that may have looked alluring but only lead one astray from the path of the

Holy Trinity. If the enemy can entangle you with darkness he wins.

The prowling enemy sees a legal foothold if you engage in these activities because through your free will choice you opened the door to the dark arts. The spiritual world is this subtle. It is crucial to have high discernment on the source behind spiritual practices and ensure they align with the truth revealed in God's Word. If they don't, they are from the enemy's camp. To say it plainly, if it isn't a person or community that is meeting in the name of the Lord, it's not of God.

The Holy Spirit is known by various names in the Bible, and He plays a vital role in a believer's life. The presence of the Holy Spirit within a believer helps guard against deception and false teachings, including what is often referred to as "false light" or "strange fire" in the Scriptures. The Holy Spirit is a remarkable person that will lead you:

1. Spirit of Truth – He leads us into all truth (John 14:17)

2. Spirit of Wisdom – He reveals God's insight (Ephesians 1:17)

3. Spirit of Promise – He seals our salvation (Ephesians 1:13-14)

4. Spirit of Life – He sets us free in Christ (Romans 8:2)

5. Spirit of Adoption – Makes us children of God (Romans 8:15)

6. Spirit of Holiness – He sanctifies us and sets us apart for God's purposes (Romans 1:4)

7. The Convicter or Convincer – He convicts us of sin and even temptation to sin, He convinces us of righteous behavior, and provides a fair warning of judgement (John 16:7-11)

Do you see the richness and glory by God dwelling inside of you?

Much of the world misses Christ and walks naively into the new age and occult because on the surface it looks light, fun, and healing even though it is a complex deception program designed by satan to further ensnare.

Modern Christians will partake in new age practices like yoga, reiki, burning sage, collecting crystals, collecting ganesh statues, collecting buddha statues, collecting hamsas (evil eyes) and reading horoscopes because they categorize it as harmless. Unfortunately, they are not connecting the dots that the wide deception program is designed by satan. A great example of this is the mystical hamsa symbol, it's supposed to block evil, right? Wrong. It attracts evil. Just about everything the enemy labels as good is evil (Isaiah 5:20).

Yoga for example is worship to very specific Hindu spirits. What you worship is who or what has dominion over you. In the tribulation, the antichrist will demand to be worshipped. If you worship anything other than God, by default you don't belong to God.

You will come to find out on the Christian path there is a gap between "saved" and "truly saved." Another way of saying this is there is a gap between saved and born again. If you are born again, and Holy Spirit filled, all worldly desires start to slip away, and the scales of deception are lifted.

In God's eyes there is a giant gap between casual "consumer" Christianity and committed, consecrated Christianity.

Being truly saved means being born again, living a righteous life, and seriously avoiding sin. Obedience to God stems from the gratitude of being saved, rather than trying to earn salvation through obedience. This aligns you with God's design of grace, where intentional living in the Father's will is key. Additionally, it involves embodying the fruit of the Spirit, which includes showing kindness and love, even to those who may oppose you. The reason you can do things like this is because you are filled with love and kindness directly from God, and that bleeds over into every other interaction. Where emptiness in the heart once attracted fallen pleasures and false gods, now there is an overflow of truth, life, and love. The old life must be left behind.

John 11:25 KJV

*Jesus said unto her, I am the resurrection, and the life: he that believeth in me, though he were dead, yet shall he live.*

The world often promotes new age philosophies through avenues that appear "light" like local yoga studios, reiki sessions, "spiritual" books on topics like the law of attraction, astrology, numerology, tarot archetypes, pop psychology personality archetypes, and the idea of an impending enlightenment of the earth. These ideologies always are self-centered and are always leading individuals astray and away from Jesus. In contrast, Christianity emphasizes dying to self and surrendering to God's will to receive His identity. It ends up being freeing because it's the journey our souls were designed for. Even if a new age practice promises an ego death and dying to self it can't be done through focusing only on yourself. The new age landscape is riddled with these illogical offers that are spiritually unsound.

2 Timothy 3:1-2 ASV

*But know this, that in the last days grievous times shall come. For men shall be lovers of self, lovers of money, boastful, haughty, railers, disobedient to parents, unthankful, unholy.*

God is inherently holy and distinct, as is His Kingdom. When you fully commit your life to Jesus, you are set apart and transformed into a new creation, living in accordance with His holiness. This transformation is a promise from God.

God, Jesus, and the Holy Spirit originate from beyond this fallen world, representing a divine and transcendent reality that surpasses the limitations of this earthly realm. Remember, Plato understood this realm is the realm of illusions and deceptions and the realm beyond is composed of the perfect forms of goodness, truth, and beauty.

John 18:36 ASV

*Jesus answered, My kingdom is not of this world: if my kingdom were of this world, then would my servants fight, that I should not be delivered to the Jews: but now is my kingdom not from hence.*

Jesus was saying in the book of John that He would have had an army of people fighting on His behalf to prevent His crucifixion if this planet was His home. The average person would have been fighting for their King.

However, only a small handful of people knew He was the Messiah, the Son of God, the anointed one, the Savior of mankind. The legacy that Jesus created and is still creating 2,000 years later is testament alone that He was and is the Savior of the world. Jesus is still the most famous person in the world. He is still causing a stir, ruffling feathers, annoying the indoctrinated, the overly religious, and the demonized. He is alive and still on the move spreading revival across all the nations until the quickly approaching end of the Church Age. For the Church the security lives in what He did for the Church.

So, whether the goodness of the Lord compounds slowly in your life or comes roaring at you like a tsunami, the net result will be more peace, more joy, more gratitude, less chaos, more order, more love, and better relations with others (friends and foes alike).

The Kingdom of God is peace, joy, and righteousness, all through His power, and not our own.

As Jesus reigns supreme over all creation, His sovereignty extends above every earthly authority, making Him the King of kings. Even the adversaries in your life will sense the divine power emanating from your presence and will retreat, acknowledging His authority that rests upon you.

Living a life that is holy and set apart encompasses every aspect of your being, reflecting the transformative work of God in your life. This consecrated state draws others to witness the power and presence of God within you, leading to a healthy distance from forces that oppose His divine will. The anointing on you speaks for itself.

The adversaries fear the light, the truth, and the name of Jesus.

Those that previously despised you for changing course with your life and beginning to follow the Lord, will eventually come to study you and ask you why you are doing so well, partly out of jealousy, and partly out of curiosity. They will be able to tell you have found something. You are doing better and you are different. They will want to understand why.

You can say to them, "The difference is Jesus and He is out of this world. He has healed my soul."

You can say to them, "Let me tell you about my friend Jesus."

You can say to them, "I found a new lease on life through Jesus."

You can say to them, "I've been born again."

You can say all the above or what the Holy Spirit direct you to say.

Help them see you have changed course; you are now on the path of redemption. Point to Jesus and not to yourself because it wasn't through your own striving. Jesus paid the fine to set you free from the heaviness of the world and the burdens of your past.

1 Corinthians 6:19 ASV

*Or know ye not that your body is a temple of the Holy Spirit which is in you, which ye have from God? and ye are not your own*

Romans 8:9 ASV

*But ye are not in the flesh but in the Spirit, if so be that the Spirit of God dwelleth in you. But if any man hath not the Spirit of Christ, he is none of his.*

John 14:26 ASV

*But the Comforter, even the Holy Spirit, whom the Father will send in my name, he shall teach you all things, and bring to your remembrance all that I said unto you.*

Acts 1:8 ASV

*But ye shall receive power, when the Holy Spirit is come upon you: and ye shall be my witnesses both in Jerusalem, and in all Judaea and Samaria, and unto the uttermost part of the earth.*

Acts 2:17 ASV

*And it shall be in the last days, saith God, I will pour forth of my Spirit upon all flesh: And your sons and your daughters shall prophesy, And your young men shall see visions, And your old men shall dream dreams.*

Acts 2:38 ASV

*And Peter said unto them, Repent ye, and be baptized every one of you in the name of Jesus Christ unto the remission of your sins; and ye shall receive the gift of the Holy Spirit.*

Not every church believes the Holy Spirit is still moving today as it was in the New Testament. If your church believes in the New Testament and the book of Acts they should be able to see that Jesus was resurrected and He sent the Holy Spirit for His believers.

The fact is not every church reads and follows the Bible. That's why when you are Holy Spirit filled you will only want a Holy Spirit filled church. If you are Holy Spirit filled it means you have the nine aspects of God (Galatians 5:22-23) living inside of you much more than your fallen flesh. If you can't find a Holy Spirit filled local church that's okay, you are the temple of the living God, be the Church and carry Christ everywhere you go.

The fact is, not every local church belongs to God. They will have a name that sounds right, a denominational focused name usually, but the Lord isn't put first and the Bible is twisted and misinterpreted. Most churches are not actually Holy Spirit led, or Spirit filled, this is where a lot of the confusion about Christianity comes from. If the leadership isn't Holy Spirit filled they won't be able to interpret the Scriptures. Even the ones that claim to be Spirit filled might not be.

Many churches today are characterized by the indoctrinated operation of man, self-centeredness, pride, celebrity, and empty promises instead of emphasizing biblical promises. Aside from that only about 5% of churches know how to rightly divide between Covenants. The great majority of them mix the Grace Covenant with the Old Covenant and apply the lukewarm mixture to the congregants. This places the congregants under the condemnation of the Jewish law. Bad teaching, rites, and rituals that were never meant for the Church are what cause blemish. In other words, the leadership preaches from the flesh and places the congregation under the flesh, works, striving, and earning their salvation. The whole operation of satan works to make the congregants feel less than or unworthy when the work was already done on the cross. The Grace message can't be mixed with the lie that Christians are still under the Jewish law. This confuses the congregants, grieves the Holy Spirit, and completely twists end times theology. Only those under the Grace Covenant will be caught up in the rapture. If there's a covenant mix it means that the believer did not fully embrace the work of Jesus: the death, burial, and resurrection for the erasure of sins. It's shocking how many churches have went beyond the Grace Covenant and mix covenants and cause confusion.

Instead of serving the Kingdom of God, they prioritize self-serving agendas that ultimately serve satan. The Holy Spirit feels welcomed in very few churches. This is why the truly saved Christians are the Church, the anointed ones set apart from the world, and carrying the Holy Spirit. Who they are doesn't change with their location, vocation, or local church they are or aren't inside of.

A believer can be in constant contact with the Holy Spirit regardless of whether inside a building or not. If a believer thinks their connection to God is limited to inside a church's four walls, they missed it. Our bodies are the temple of God, not a church building. One way is religion. The other is a devoted relationship to God.

149

Many churches today where the Holy Spirit does not feel welcome are more focused on seat warming, fund collecting, pop psychology, and giving a feel good message that is designed to keep people inside of the four walls. This feeds them false hope and lies rather than accurate Bible teaching.

2 Timothy 4:3-4 KJV

*For the time will come when they will not endure sound doctrine; but after their own lusts shall they heap to themselves teachers, having itching ears; And they shall turn away their ears from the truth, and shall be turned unto fables.*

Many attendees pride themselves on being great local church goers and tithers, but they never truly live as part of Jesus' Church, in the army of God. This is largely because they end up preferring man-made religion instead of the authentic operation of God and this is largely because they end up blindly following a pastor or priest that is a slick talker, but ultimate has a religious or haughty spirit underneath it all. Satan knows if you get the pastor, you get the flock.

These churches often fail to acknowledge the presence and guidance of the Holy Spirit, leading to a lack of His manifestation among them. The Holy Spirit is discerning and chooses to dwell where He is welcomed and honored. His presence is not to be trivialized and is reserved for those who humble themselves and submit to His leadership.

Holiness is attracted to environments where holiness is already present. Stewarding holiness is an intentional process of preparation for greater levels of the power of God to rest upon you through the Holy Spirit.

# Ch. 7 THE LAW OF ATTRACTION GURUS HAVE IT ALL WRONG

Colossians 3:1-2 KJV

*If ye then be risen with Christ, seek those things which are above, where Christ sitteth on the right hand of God. Set your affection on things above, not on things on the earth.*

When I was researching new age law of attraction through Louise Hay and Abraham Hicks and other new age teachers, a lot of it did point to gratitude, but the new age teachers weren't pointing to the source of peace and gratitude.

Peace is a person; His name is Jesus. Following His will He wrote for you is the only way to stay anchored in gratitude and peace.

Philippians 4:6-7 KJV

*Be careful for nothing; but in every thing by prayer and supplication with thanksgiving let your requests be made known unto God. And the peace of God, which passeth all understanding, shall keep your hearts and minds through Christ Jesus.*

The gurus were looking at peace, joy, and gratitude, in essence the wavelength of "feeling good" as something you would generate by your own flesh rather than receiving it through God's grace. They left God entirely out of the equation or would impersonalize Him. Modern churches do the same thing through twisting Scripture through a feel good message that in essence says "give to get" your financial blessings. They promote a "seed faith" principle by twisting the mustard seed parable from the Old Covenant when giving should be done cheerfully not through a desire for personal gain or material wealth. It should be done without ulterior motive and out of the love for God and others.

The gurus and even modern churches look at the effect as something you need to generate yourself while ignoring the cause. If we need to be the daily cause of our own peace, joy, blessing, and gratitude we are in a tiresome and losing battle. You have lost before you started if you think you are going to be your own god, your own siloed vortex of cause and effect. The Lord is the provider in Christianity and you can't manipulate Him, you can't earn it, just like Jesus' work on the cross wasn't anything that was earned.

The "secret" that the new age community and new age leaning churches propagate revolves around the idea that one can manifest their desires through the power of positive thinking and lustful imaginations to generate self-fulfilling prophecies, essentially witchcraft. The churches are doing same thing with having their congregants visualize the "seed faith" offering into a multiplication of the things they want.

The new age and many churches still point to the individuated "self" as the end all be all, which is all a trap of satan. It's a trap because it's based on works, your own willpower, your ability to pay, and your ability to be a little more devoted than the person next to you, rather than from finding and claiming God's will over your life. This is the will that was written ages ago by Jesus, who created everything.

John 1:3 KJV

*All things were made by him; and without him was not any thing made that was made.*

The buck doesn't stop with you as a human, sometimes we wish it did, however, each person is always one breath away from death. God Himself doesn't have that problem. Jesus will always have the final say. He spans the past, the present, and the future, into eternity. He goes before you and can see well into your future. The law of attraction content says repeatedly that you create your own blessing, and you can do this all from your own customized beliefs, efforts, imaginations, statements and affirmations.

God is left out of the picture, intentionally by satan. Following that method is like trying to grow while you are stuck in a cage. It causes you to toil and to spin your tires rather than achieve the greatness you are designed by God for. Following their plan is like trying to grow a tree without sunlight and water. You need the source of sustenance to grow.

The evil one wants to see you discouraged and spinning your tires and living outside the will God has written for you. It's a recipe for feeling worn out, burnt out, and defeated. When you are burnt out you are more vulnerable to sin and the various spiritual attacks of the enemy.

In a nutshell the law of attraction content says, if you say your "I am" (God is the only true I am identity in the universe not us) affirmations often enough, loud enough, and proud enough then you will have all the abundance in the world rushing to you at warp speed. It says stay on a grateful and receptive frequency and then more events that make you feel grateful will come your way. A game of frequency matching to generate a vacuum of abundance, ah-ha sounds easy enough!

All witchcraft. God forbid.

The content was looking at gratitude as the cause rather than the effect. Based on what I know now, gratitude is an effect of Jesus working through you as a vessel for the Holy Spirit.

Living in the joy and gratitude that can only from the Lord will help you feel whole, loved, and complete. Striving to feel peaceful is counter-intuitive, don't you think?

In other words, God's presence and God's will is the cause, and gratitude is the effect. God provides your blessing. He is the source of all provision.

The blessings that rush into a believer or a nonbeliever's life is in accordance with the blessings that God has written for them. It is possible for somebody to mostly be walking in God's will for them without knowing God or being saved.

The key point is God is always responsible for the blessing in someone's life whether they know it or not.

Some nonbelievers do have "abundance" in their life, under the common grace during the Church Age, but that doesn't mean they won't face judgement for denying Jesus at the end of their life.

Mark 8:36 KJV

*For what shall it profit a man, if he shall gain the whole world, and lose his own soul?*

God's will for as many people as possible is to know Jesus, tell others about Him, be Spirit filled, and walk in purity and righteousness; holy as He is holy (1 Peter 1:16).

He only asks for your surrender to His greater way. His only wants your heart.

Those that have blessing but don't realize they are blessed by God tend to lose their blessings, whether that be a spouse, children, health, money, and so on. Pride always comes before the fall (Proverbs 16:18).

People fall into the trap of taking the blessings for granted because they don't connect the dots that the blessings came by the grace of God; they were gifts directly from God. A great example of this is children. They are gifts from God and many evil individuals take them for granted or are willfully evil toward them. It can be assured God has seen all of the evil on earth at the hand of man. The wrath of the Lamb is guaranteed to be poured out on them. Jesus knows exactly who they are.

God often removes things or people that are taken for granted. Taking blessings for granted reflects a lack of gratitude and an excess of pride. The Bible warns that pride precedes a downfall in several places (Proverbs 18:12, Proverbs 11:2, Proverbs 29:23, James 4:6). If one becomes prideful and self-reliant, God will humble them. Pride is commonly seen in both believers and nonbelievers, often manifesting in the pursuit of wealth and attributing success solely to personal abilities. Many individuals pursue money, things, and stuff without considering its meaningfulness. The Bible calls this chasing after vainglory. God sees not only our outward actions but always our innermost intentions and motivations.

If your wealth is earned unethically then it will not last. The foundation will crumble.

God is always the protector, provider and source of all blessing.

Men encounter the most challenge when it comes to relinquishing their pride and acknowledging God is the ultimate protector and provider, as societal norms often emphasize the role of men as the primary protectors and providers for their families. While men are called to fulfill these roles, it is essential for them to simultaneously recognize that all the glory and the honor belong only to God.

Through humbly acknowledging the Almighty God in Heaven as the ultimate source of protection and provision, men can align themselves with God's design and experience the fullness of His blessings and guidance in their lives. Placing God as the ultimate source of protection and provision takes strength in a man, not weakness. The Bible emphasizes in several places that God's strength is made perfect in human weakness, it also highlights the importance of faith and trust in God as a form of spiritual strength, and there is no greater strength because the weapons of our warfare are not carnal (2 Corinthians 10:4).

The right attitude for a man to harness is, "He is the provider, not me. He is the designer of my body, mind, and will, not me. I'm grateful to be here and along for the ride, because I know He has amazing plans and He is steering the ship. I am grateful for all the blessings He has already provided. He is the firm foundation that I stand upon. I approach everything from the place of victory that was accomplished on the cross through Jesus. The more I turn over the reins to Him the more peaceful I am and the more orderly life gets. Thank you Jesus."

Doing mighty feats without partnering with God is tiring, stressful and often doesn't produce much fruit. We can contrast that with stories in the Bible where there was partnership with God and then there was an abundance of fruit despite the improbable odds.

In the Bible there is the story of Gideon. If reluctant Gideon did not step up to defeat many thousands of Midianites with his small army of 300 men, the Israeli people would have been overrun, perhaps permanently. But instead, Gideon had faith in God's ways and God's plans to defeat the opposing army. Gideon and his army were outnumbered 450:1. Gideon defeated 135,000 Midianites with 300 men. None of Gideon's men died. The only way men can do mighty feats especially in the face of adversity is with God.

David's story in the Bible conveys a similar profound message. Starting as a humble shepherd boy, he later became a courageous champion of Israel that secured his destiny as King of Israel. When he faced the seemingly undefeatable goliath, who towered over David at nearly ten feet tall, the narrative showcases David's courage and reveals God's character in supporting Israel and standing by the faithful underdogs.

Through faith, God's glory can rest upon an individual no matter the seemingly impossible circumstances. God's hand over David during his battle with Goliath ensured a triumphant victory for the underdog, altering the course of history for Israel and the world. David's lineage later leads to Jesus. That is why Jesus is also called the Lion of Judah, David was from the house of Judah, one of the twelve tribes of Israel.

The story underscores the importance of seeing beyond outward appearances and relying on faith and courage when faced with formidable giants. This account serves as a metaphor for the victory belonging to those who trust completely in God and walk by faith not sight, especially when the odds appear stacked against them, this is why you must anchor your faith deep down into your soul during everyday battles all the way up to seeming insurmountable challenges. You never know when a goliath will cross your path so you must always be prayed up and prepared in the Spirit.

The more a person can trust that God will grow the tree, then all one must do is be obedient and stay engaged with God's will to see fruit. All one must do is recognize that it is God growing the fruit, and it has always been Him. He has consistently been in the background, safeguarding and providing sustenance, opening doors meant for you, and closing doors not meant for you, orchestrating the pace of your life. He is the one nurturing the tree, guiding the boat, and piloting the plane.

Those are His promises. Take care of His house and he will take care of yours. Take care of His children, your brethren or your actual children, and He will take care of you. Every child, whether born or preborn, every person, that hears the call to step into faith can step into their identity as a child of God.

Again, the process of becoming a disciple is about stewarding the presence of God and understanding God's Word. Worshiping and studying God's Word, in Spirit and in Truth, will create a firm foundation, a rock, to build your life upon.

Your relationships. Your spouse. Your family. Your ministry. Your business. Your health. Your spiritual wellness. Your legacy. Everything.

He will take the mess you've created without Him, blot out the mess, and make you brand new. Your life will change tracks, and it will begin to honor God. All it takes is your surrender.

Your life will improve without brute force effort and toil.

He wants your permission to do this. He wants to lift you up from depression, sluggish living, remove fear and anxiety, and destroy poverty.

Only He can remove demons, remove addictions, remove generational curses and end an unsatisfying and meaningless life. Your only duty is to lay down the old life in order to receive the new life. You must choose to make the exchange and change course.

Matthew 9:17 ASV

*Neither do men put new wine into old wine-skins: else the skins burst, and the wine is spilled, and the skins perish: but they put new wine into fresh wine-skins, and both are preserved.*

The old wine-skins are symbolic of your old life and your old approach that was without God. The old skins must be disposed of in order to receive the new skins that can hold and contain more of the glory of God. If new wine is put into old wineskins, they burst. The new wine skins and new wine include grace, Jesus, the Holy Spirit, faith, His operation, His righteousness, His rest, true freedom through Christ, and eternal life in Heaven.

Just as your life is enriched by inviting God to be a part of it without Him needed coerce you, He respects your free will and will not force or manipulate you into following Him. The choice is yours.

Overall, God isn't looking for someone to bless. As mentioned, He is looking for someone He can trust, and therefore the blessings will come with obedience and adherence to His Word and His will for you.

# Ch. 8 DO YOU DESIRE TO BE PURIFIED?

Many people go toward yoga, tarot, crystals, burning sage and eastern meditation because they want to become liberated. They want freedom. They want relief. But is it authentic relief being offered or further bondage through satan's demons?

People hear through the culture of the world that Buddhism, for example, is about non-attachment and a reduction of suffering. That sounds appealing to many. Most people have had hardships and some have had trauma, so a path that sells the reduction of suffering sounds appealing. Looks can be deceiving this is why the Bible says walk by faith not sight (2 Corinthians 5:7).

The difference here is a pagan versus non-pagan approach. That's the core difference between Christianity and everything else. The pagan works are based in the flesh, in the material, finite world, and the relationship with the Lord is a non-physical purely spiritual relationship.

Paganism is a nice word for witchcraft and satanism. A pagan approach is a works-based approach, a fallen approach stuck in the earth and stuck in humanism. In the pagan paradigm you must work your way toward liberation, only to find out its always out of reach.

The unmistakable sign of paganism is the veneration of physical objects or the created world, rather than the worship of the Holy God in Heaven, the Creator. Additionally, paganism often places personal pleasure above truth or morality. For instance, practices like tantra prioritize personal gratification over spiritual truth. Paganism, just like the demonic has win-loss dynamics and master-slave paradigms.

The polar opposite to an evil, works-based approach is a God-centered and God-ordained perspective that focuses on life quadruple win scenarios. The only submission is to God because He is Almighty, righteous, and eternal. A saved person was won their salvation, a saved person was probably won over because of another saved person, God has saved a soul from hell and brought him or her back home, and now that newly saved person can also help save others.

Romans 6:16 KJV

*Know ye not, that to whom ye yield yourselves servants to obey, his servants ye are to whom ye obey; whether of sin unto death, or of obedience unto righteousness?*

What this verse is saying is the fact is you are either a slave to sin and death or you are obedient to Jesus. There is no middle ground.

The fallen approach to union with God involves ceaseless works in pursuit of freedom, while the true path involves placing faith in the liberating power of Jesus' blood. Christianity stands apart in its exclusive access to God through Jesus and His work on the cross for the remission of sins and the restoration to righteousness, no other world religion or practice offers this or Him.

The pagan approach is always focused on the pride of life, the lust of the eyes, and the lust of the flesh. The holy approach is always focused on faith in Jesus' blood. Blood has always equaled life, and that's why the eternal blood inside of Jesus that was shed on the cross to paid for all sin, the wages of sin is death, and God did not want to see you incur wrath. His blood is the only non-physical spiritual solution that still works and still saves today. This is the only way to be set free and reconciled to the Father for eternity. Anything short of that is unrighteous and does not pay the sin debt. These are God's absolute truths. God is holy and He can only allow holiness back into Himself through the blood of Jesus, which was the Father's blood.

God sent His only Son for the sins of the world. He did the work for us. He gave His only Son to be brutally sacrificed as a worthy blameless spotless Lamb to unlock salvation for His children, to unlock heaven, to unlock baptism of the Holy Spirit, to unlock freedom, and to unlock deliverance from mental, physical, or spiritual afflictions. Since the work of Jesus unlocked all of this, upon your final breath you must be found washed clean by the blood of Jesus inside and out so you too are the spotless and innocent in the Courtroom of Heaven. He is the judge and the juror; the master fruit inspector that can see how blameless and holy someone is. He inspects who has properly plead the blood over their life and sins during their life and lived in a way that honored Him and who didn't.

It makes sense why the core of it all is the removal of sin. People that sin sow seeds of death, destruction, and pain into the world.

Upon accepting the blood, salvation marks the beginning, not the end. Just as death for a believer initiates eternal life, leaving behind your old life signifies the start of the journey to Heaven. Upon entering Heaven your true life commences—your eternal life.

Genuine salvation signifies a true transformation of the heart. This immediate change leads to purposeful living, eliminating doorways to sin, cancelling associations with sinful influences, and watching through the Holy Spirit for behaviors that lead to sin and suffering.

This exchange of desires leads to more peace and joy than you have ever had in your life. It means you have drawn a line in the sand and have set your course on the way to Heaven for eternal life and have thwarted your own personal destruction with a work on the cross you didn't have to personally do, Jesus personally did it for you. That's grace.

In my attempt to right my own wrongs and purity myself in my mid-twenties I attended four ten-day silent meditation retreats. At the start of each retreat the entire cohort of meditators would take a vow of silence and would begin the process of following the instructions for the eastern meditation technique known as vipassana.

This meditation practice, also known as insight meditation or mindfulness meditation, aimed to purify the mind by developing emotional neutrality. The theory was that while observing one's breath and body sensations for six or more hours each day you could alter the habit pattern of the mind, to make it more numbed out to ephemeral change. The goal was to maintain a state of focus on nothingness instead of focusing on changing body sensations because the natural pattern of the mind is to crave body sensations that feel good or avoid body sensations that feel bad.

Did any the mental gymnastics create reconciliation with God in Heaven? No. Instead, it placed me further away from Him because I was buying into a false belief system and buddha-based idolatry. It was doing nothing to provide righteousness or holiness. It produced a strange type of peace because your body produces natural anesthetics to deal with the discomfort of sitting for many hours a day on your legs. It was strange peace compared to the pure peace that comes with Jesus, His peace comes from the throne room and not some flesh based laborious work to get to what felt sort of like peace, but looking back it wasn't real, it was a biological response to pain through anesthetics produced through the flesh to deal with pain.

When a human body has to deal with physical pain for several hours a day it produces endogenous opioids, which are natural painkillers. The pagan fallen technique was to sit on your legs to create pain, then the body produces an internal painkiller response, this is what the meditators get hooked on. In the spirit realm demons are most likely enjoying seeing humans embrace self harm in pursuit of "spirituality."

This is why meditators that would stay at meditation centers for several months at a time and meditate nonstop were called "dhamma bums." Painkiller junkies masqueraded as spiritual gurus. All pagan. All works based. All fallen. All humanism. All feeding the demonic.

The brain wanted to avoid your legs feeling like they were on fire from sitting on them for hours a day, nothing more. This practice was outside of the grace of God. It was making the mind less adapted to the world, not more. What do painkillers do? They make you sleepy and dulled out to your senses and emotions. Is that real peace? No.

After leaving the meditation center the artificial peace fell away quickly, usually within hours. The flesh based demons wanted you to continue self harm and mixed in with that there were chemical withdrawals from your brain no longer releasing painkillers. This pagan fallen approach would make reintegration into the world each time a challenge. The brain was extra sensitive, yet irritated from being in a state of stress masked as peace for 10 days. Looking back, a very weird combination to work so hard for. I didn't know any of this at the time. It's taken years of post-processing to figure out what the meditation technique really is and what it really does.

Makes you wonder, why so many in the world, especially in Los Angeles and New York City, associate the buddha with peace. This is how deceptive satan is. He has all sorts of modalities like this to imitate peace, joy, and righteousness yet provide none.

Creating voids through meditation, trances, or drugs can be extremely dangerous because the demonic realm can slip through the gap and take occupancy. I will explain more about how that works in the next chapter.

Sitting on my legs for many hours a day was dangerous to my knees and the nerves in my legs. Thank God that Jesus, through the power of prayer and the healing authority of Jesus, has restored my knees, returned the richness of my senses, and has recalibrated how sensitive I am to the world around me.

When I am telling you He can restore any hurt I am not joking. Knee problems? Terminal illness? Depression? Anxiety? No problem for Almighty Jesus. He is that good. He is assuredly alive and well.

Paganism never promises anyone instant freedom or healing or right standing with God because it can't provide that. It can't provide resurrection life in this life and the next. Only Jesus can do this.

What you always come across in all pagan approaches is the idea of placing yourself into further bondage: mental, emotional, physical, or financial, to attain pleasure or freedom. Seems counter-intuitive, doesn't it?

Pause and think about that for a moment… enter bondage to become free? That's like placing yourself in handcuffs and believing it is providing you more freedom. Logically it doesn't make sense. Think about when you harm yourself or another person, does that make you feel freer or does that bother your conscience and make you feel remorse? If it gives you that icky feeling inside, then the holiness and the righteousness of Jesus is meant for you. There is no better solution to all morality depravity and sin in the world than Jesus.

As mentioned in chapter 3, thinking that harming yourself or others is your path is spiritual enlightenment and liberation is akin to a snake eating its tail in order to make itself healthier. It makes no logical sense, and snakes do indeed eat themself. It's no coincidence the snake is symbolic of satan in the Bible and in some spiritual circles.

Every step I have taken on the Christian path has been about healing and the reduction of bondage. It's always been about an increase in freedom and never a reduction in freedom to find new freedom.

People that have the wrong view of what Christianity is think it's a rules based, outdated religion, that works through rigid behavior modification and if you don't do it right you go to hell. This is what the work man-made religion has done, at the hand of satan, to remove people away from authentic relationship with Jesus.

The authentic view of what Christianity is, is allowing the direct gifts of God and the supernatural operation of God, through the blood of Jesus, to redeem someone into a new person that is finally alive, has an eternal destiny in Heaven instead of hell, and has discovered God's will for them. Allowing God to come in and do this is how to receive daily measures of His grace, His peace, His joy, and His righteousness. None of it should technically work, but its supernatural, the absolute truths behind Jesus and the simplicity make it work. It's God's design that was meant for humans to embrace to bring them into a state of right standing with the Father.

Jesus breaks the chains. He heals and cleans His sheep. He breaks the yoke that you have had with the enemy when His personal blessing comes upon your life and claims you as His own sheep. The anointing breaks the bad yoke and installs His holy yoke.

The bad yoke can be best seen with yoga. The word yoga is derived from the Sanskrit root "yuj," which uncoincidentally means to yoke, unite, or join. Each yoga pose is a form of devotional worship to a specific Hindu spirit, that is unfortunately part of a polytheistic belief system rooted in untruth. These earthly spirits are not of God, these are demons. The Bible refers to demons as devils or unclean spirits.

Whether yoga or eastern meditation, the instructions given to contort and bind up your body with the hopes of pleasure and freedom. The Bible has never once told me to become less free, mentally, physically or financially, to become spiritually more free. The Bible says we are either a slave to sin and the world, or we are a voluntary slave to Jesus (Romans 6:22). It's either or. It's the bad yoke or the holy yoke.

The is no middle ground, just like in the afterlife there is no purgatory. There is either eternal life with Jesus or hell forever.

I take being yoked up with Jesus any day versus being yoked up with the false gods, demons, and idols of the world. I've been yoked up with Jesus for five years now, my soul is finally at rest, at peace.

They key point is: never once has the Bible been about entering into bondage in order to attain freedom. Do you clearly see the conundrum that the buddhists, yogis, and pagans are offering? It's not by the grace and mercy of God. It's through humanism, works, self harm and chasing the carrot on the end of the stick blended with the false promise of pleasure, enlightenment, and freedom. Spiritual deception and false traditions have been around for thousands of years, spiritual deception is still around today and is worse than ever.

That has not changed.

Ecclesiastes 1:9-10 KJV

*The thing that hath been, it is that which shall be; and that which is done is that which shall be done: and there is no new thing under the sun. Is there any thing whereof it may be said, See, this is new? it hath been already of old time, which was before us.*

Do you know what was inscribed on the entry gate of Auschwitz concentration camp? It was a false promise, it said "work sets you free." This was the cruel falsehood presented to the Jewish people who were forced to pass through the gate against their will.

What could be more insidious than dangling the illusion of freedom before those who suffer under the chains of unjust bondage? This same deceitful ploy mirrors the works-based practices intertwined with the ideologies of the new age movement.

These practices demand your energy, your time, often your financial resources, and your compliance, yet they fail to deliver genuine freedom in exchange.

What is offered in return are satan's demons. That's where your time, effort, and life force energy is going. Being involved in these practices opens doors to the spiritually parasitic demons that are looking for humans to occupy. Literally prowling in the spiritual realm like a lion looking to devour a sheep. You might be getting the sense by now that you are one of the Lord's sheep.

None of the fallen practices and traditions provide the promises of God written in the Bible. They do not provide freedom and redemption like the blood of Jesus actively does. They don't promise salvation and they don't promise the rapture resurrection to avoid the seven year tribulation that's coming.

Esther 4:14b KJV

*And who knoweth whether thou art come to the kingdom for such a time as this?*

Now is an excellent time to be in the Kingdom of God so you are pure and blameless in God's sight so you are ready to be spared from the wrath of tribulation. The false practices out there cannot bring you into the supernatural reality of who God is and what He can do. They do not bring you into the presence of Jesus and the Father that created everything, the very deity that made your soul. They will never talk about Jesus or Him as the only way to Heaven. They will never explain the death, burial, resurrection and the supernatural blood of Jesus that sets the captives free. They will sell humanism and works which are always taxing, burdensome, energy-depleting, and usually financially costly.

The new age practices of yoga, Eastern meditation, kabbalah, witchcraft, tarot, Shamanism, astrology, divination, Hinduism, and Islam and countless others are rooted in works rather than faith in Jesus. These traditions do not align with placing faith in the one and only Jesus, the only one that can clear the sin debt you were born with and you added to during your lifetime.

These practices promote false power and false hope, always leading individuals to rely more on themselves and their deceptive spiritual leaders. These false teachers include yogis, gurus, swamis, shamans, psychics, yoga teachers, imams, witches, wizards, among others.

Their aim is always to distance you from Jesus, leaving you

vulnerable to spiritual and demonic attack. Ultimately, these practices seek to elevate personal pride while diminishing reliance on Jesus, the only one that died in your place for you.

Some of you will not like I included Islam, but its works based and allah is a demon, and Muhammed was a false prophet that was never resurrected. Same with buddha, never resurrected. The list goes on. Only Jesus defeated death, hell, and the grave for you. The prophet Isa that Islamists associate with Jesus is very different than the Jesus of the Bible. Overall the belief system of Islam is rooted in violence and hatred, in other words, demonically influenced.

There are many testimonies now on social media of muslims that converted to Christianity in an instant. The have a common theme, they reveal that when allah was called upon the name only brought darkness, fear, and chaos into the situation. It was never a name of life, joy, freedom, or peace and never can be. It's stuck in humanism, flesh, and works. The Temple Mount, where there is a Mosque today, is where Jesus will sit and reign from. He will sit where David's throne was after the seven year tribulation. In the Second Coming Jesus will open and go through the Eastern Gate and the Mosque will be replaced with where Jesus will sit and reign.

In the accounts of former muslims, they experienced a sense of darkness after invoking allah, but when they called upon the name of Jesus, darkness would dissipate instantly. His name would usher in a powerful presence, a mighty rushing wind (Acts 2:2), bringing truth, joy, comfort, healing, redemption, restoration, and deliverance from surrounding evils, providing instant relief. To hear one of these testimonies from a former muslim look up Afshin Javid.

At the Eastern meditation center they played the same instructional recordings each time. The instructional recordings, recited by the late meditation teacher, S.N. Goenka, would say, "If you admit Jesus is the Son of God. Who cares?" Vipassana meditation centers around the world play these same recordings repeatedly, all year long. Any Bible believing Christian knows that these teachings are blasphemy and in direct opposition to God. A former muslim saved from the pits of hell through the name of Jesus would agree.

When the meditation teacher would say that snide comment with the intention of disrespecting the deity of Jesus, the room of meditators would often laugh. Even though I was not a Jesus follower at the time something didn't feel right inside of me when the meditators would laugh. They were laughing at a Bible truth. To admit Jesus is the Son of God is also to admit He is the Messiah, the Lord, and the Savior of mankind. Each time I heard this recoding, and the new cohort of meditators laughed I would always think to myself, "What if Goenka is wrong? And knowing and admitting Jesus is the Son of God is actually important?"

Well, it turns out knowing that truth is eternally important. Admitting and believing Jesus is the Son of God, and therefore Lord and Savior of your life, is one of the most major tenants of being a believer on the way to Heaven. A saint believes in who Jesus is and what He did for the Church. Revelation says the lake of fire is for the unbelievers.

Revelation 21:8 ASV

*But for the fearful, and unbelieving, and abominable, and murderers, and fornicators, and sorcerers, and idolaters, and all liars, their part shall be in the lake that burneth with fire and brimstone; which is the second death.*

Proclaiming Jesus is the Son of God is a powerful and important statement to strongly believe, that's why the enemy does not want you admitting that truth. Jesus is the only name that makes demons tremble, because they know they can't hold a candle to His authority.

Romans 10:9 KJV

*That if thou shalt confess with thy mouth the Lord Jesus, and shalt believe in thine heart that God hath raised him from the dead, thou shalt be saved."*

Walk down a city sidewalk proclaiming that Jesus is the Son of God. You will be high-fived by a few and chastised by many. That's because His name has power. His name has the ultimate authority on earth. His sheep love His name and can't get enough of it.

The goats balk at His name and spit it out immediately. Search for street preachers on social media, they are consistently heckled, sometimes violently attacked for sharing the simple Gospel with the public, and sometimes even in America their Constitutional free speech rights are infringed, and they are threatened or arrested by the police simply for speaking the good news of what Jesus did. No more, no less. This is in America, the country with the most Christians.

The reason people are irritated by the name of Jesus is because the demons living in their flesh are irritated by the authority the name of Jesus carries. When you accept salvation and belong to Jesus, you carry Him everywhere with you, into every decision, ever situation, every room, so some people are irritated by a believer just being themselves and being a Christ carrier. They can see the light of the world, Jesus, inside and it causes irritation because of their demons.

The traditions without Jesus drain your energy and feed those demons operating in the flesh. You can command the demons in an afflicted Christian to go in the name of Jesus, and the demons will flee, but deliverance is a messy process, so it's better to not open doors to darkness. The deliverance process works and cleans up the messes, but it can be a challenge, some demons are more stubborn than others, with bigger strongholds on a person, so some go undetected until your third or fourth deliverance session or service until they are found, so it's like chopping down hell by the acre to clean a person of demons when it would have been easier if they simply never opened the doors to demons in the first place. The pagan, fallen spiritual practices of the world are one of the primary welcome mats to demons.

Mark 16:17 KJV

*And these signs shall follow them that believe; In my name shall they cast out devils; they shall speak with new tongues*

Demons, the negative spirits of the world, feed on a person's vitality. This is all they know how to do. They are like people without bodies, so they look to inhabit people and cause pain and chaos. Demons do this because they have zero respect for humans because we were created in the image of God. They want to tarnish God's holy creation. They want to cause the total demise of each human.

For the record, in the world of angels and demons, an angel can appear as a human, but an angel will never inhabit a human, and angels are not to be worshipped (Revelation 22:8-9) but they can be commanded just as demons can be commanded. Humans were created one notch lower than angels (Hebrews 2:7), but through the authority of Jesus living inside of us, we can command both angels and demons and they must obey because of the authority in the name of Jesus.

It is crucial to make note that not all instances of deliverance involve the presence of a demon because the fallen nature, the flesh that dies, was inherited on the bloodline of all humanity from the fall of Adam. This "Adam nature" requires the Holy Spirit and fire, disciple training and the full armor of God to be worn, as outlined in chapter 6.

The power and authority of Jesus remains constant, as we are currently living in the era of the Church Age, also referred to as the New Covenant. A clear indication of the arrival of the Kingdom of God on earth is the expulsion of demons through the work of the Spirit of God (Matthew 12:28).

God's desire is for His people to experience freedom, purity, and spiritual cleansing so they are made pure, holy, and innocent again.

The New Testament in the Bible, which commences after Jesus' blood started flowing down on the rocks on Calvary includes the Gospels of Matthew, Mark, and Luke once Jesus blood started to flow down (Matthew 27, Mark 15, Luke 23) Acts, Epistles (the love letters and Word of correction to the Church), and Revelation. His death on the cross was the fulfillment of the Old Testament and the beginning of the New Testament. This pivotal event marked the beginning of a new era for humanity, a New Covenant, and in more ways than one the beginning of time for humanity because eternal life through the Holy Spirit, a resurrection, born again life, was not available prior to Jesus dying on the cross.

Hebrews 9:16-18 KJV

*For where a testament is, there must also of necessity be the death of the testator. For a testament is of force after men are dead: otherwise it is of no strength at all while the testator liveth. Whereupon neither the first testament was dedicated without blood.*

175

In the Last Supper, Jesus specifically refers to the cup of wine as the "New Covenant in my blood" (Luke 22:20), signifying the establishment of the New Covenant through the blood that was shed on Calvary.

After this evet of the blood of God Himself being shed on a rugged cross in Jerusalem all flesh, demons, and death must bow to the new sheriff in town, Jesus. He and the Father were ten steps ahead of the old devil and defeated satan and his demons on the cross. That's why the cross is the central symbol of Christianity. It solidified victory in the name of Jesus from that day going forward. The curse on humanity's bloodline was reversed from that day going forward.

Deliverance in Jesus name is done from this place of victory, and it cleans the generational curses too. If you attend an authentic deliverance service, the demons inside of people in the room tremble, scream, and exit from a person with nothing short of fussiness.

They are foul spirits so they go out with a stink but when they go, they go, and the captives are cleaned and set free by Jesus. Hearing a demon manifest in an oppressed person sounds often like shrieking, that means the demon is extremely irritated and is about to exit the individual. The demon that shrieks most commonly is Jezebel. The Bible talks about her and her husband to warn others about her. The demons today are the same as Old Testament demons because they are ancient spirits that wander looking for a host. They will be judged and locked up at the end of the seven year tribulation. After 1,000 years of peace on earth they are sent into the lake of fire with satan for a permanent death.

Jezebel is a common dark spirit that can manifest in individuals regardless of gender but usually found in woman. Traits are manipulation, fascinating with witchcraft, self-centeredness, control through sex and showing skin, aloofness, and excessive sexuality. When embodied by women, Jezebel seeks dominion over men, their status, influence, wealth, and even their very soul through allure and sexual seduction. In the biblical narrative, Jezebel's influence over her husband, King Ahab, who exhibited a spirit of apathy, allowed her to exert unbridled power without restraint, and not only over him but to multiple men at the same time.

When she is commanded to leave she makes an intense shriek because she goes but she consistently goes with a fight. The blood-curdling shriek is a child of God getting their freedom from the oppressive spirit.

If you were in the new age, it is very likely that authentic New Testament deliverance will unlock new freedom and purity for you.

In the realm of spiritual warfare, it is crucial to understand that demonic forces gain access through sin, and this provides a legal right for the demon to operate. It must also be noted that having an energetic chord to those in your life that are sinning or demonized can also give the enemy some level of access to you.

In a one on one deliverance the powerful name and authority of Jesus serves as the ultimate defense against such malevolent spiritual entities. His authority always surpasses any legal grounds they may claim. While the process of deliverance may vary in duration, the victory always belongs to our sovereign King, Jesus. His authority always reigns supreme.

It works for believers because as believers, it is essential to stand firm in the identity as blood bought child of God, made in His divine image. When we surrender to God and let Him take full ownership of us, as He purchased the Church with His own blood, demons have no choice but to flee. The victory has already been secured by our triumphant Lord and Savior, Jesus, leaving no room for the enemy to prevail.

John 19:30 ASV

*When Jesus therefore had received the vinegar, he said, It is finished: and he bowed his head, and gave up his spirit.*

1 Samuel 17:47 KJV

*And all this assembly shall know that the Lord saveth not with sword and spear: for the battle is the Lord's, and he will give you into our hands.*

*Ephesians 6:12 KJV*

*For we wrestle not against flesh and blood, but against principalities, against powers, against the rulers of the darkness of this world, against spiritual wickedness in high places.*

As you lean further into God, Jesus, and the Holy Spirit then you are creating a larger and larger buffer that defends against the power vacuum, the mechanism that draws the darkness in.

The next chapter helps you realize why when there is no buffer in place the demons rush in.

## Ch. 9 THE POWER VACUUM

Have you encountered the concept of a "power vacuum" before?

It describes a situation where a nation is missing strong and centralized leadership, has no firmly established king or president, and has no clear chain of command.

In such circumstances, foreign invaders perceive an opportunity to enter, establish their presence, exploit resources, and assert authority. This is all due to the absence of effective governance. The absence of authority where there is supposed to be authority creates the vacuum. The same concept applies to your own heart and mind.

It's as if the White House was suddenly empty and any citizen or foreign invader could walk in, sit down in the oval office, and say, "Hey guess what, I declare and decree I am president now. I'm the commander in chief. I command armies to advance. I sign executive orders. I decide who is pardoned. I decide the laws of the land."

Plenty of invaders, foreign and domestic, would rush in to take the seat in the oval office if it was unclaimed. It's a powerful seat on the world stage.

Similar to the White House or Buckingham Palace, you also have a powerful seat inside. It's on the throne of your heart. If it's not completely occupied by King Jesus, the only man that is supposed to be on the throne of your heart, then there is a power vacuum, and idols and demons come in and occupy. Having your heart share space with King Jesus and the idols of the world is committing spiritual adultery. He needs your whole heart and not part of it, and again, this is for an individual's spiritual health. Jesus died for you fully and never took any shortcuts or half measures. The least you can do is give Him your whole heart in return.

Are you seeing how the throne of your heart is the most important spiritual seat inside of you?

If there is no buffer, no sentry at the gate, then you are leaving your soul, the most precious thing about you, unprotected and open to foreign invaders. Most people are leaving this door to darkness open.

Idols, false gods, demons and fallen desires of the heart lead to soul fragmentation instead of soul revival.

New age spiritual practices and any fallen spiritual practice outside of the Holy Trinity, opens the doors of your heart to foreign invaders. Even things we don't typically label as spiritual like listening to music, is spiritual. When your mind is awakened to how awake the spiritual world is, it can't be unseen. That's why anything, whether music or otherwise, must honor God and not the fallen culture. The open doors, that are opened through sinful living, become the legal foothold for demons and idols to come in, put up their stinky feet, and take up shop, and lay claim to the seat on the throne of your heart.

The devil is after your heart, mind and soul. That's what he wants dominion over. The enemy wants to have an invisible hand of influence over your life and life decisions in ways you are not even aware of. The enemy will do anything possible to get in and tamper with your subconscious mind. He is invisibly getting into billions of people through music, videos, symbols, and world culture.

What you cherish in your heart, what you are passionate about, and what you focus on each day is what sets the spiritual tone for the rest of your life. Does the world culture have your heart or does Jesus?

God is also after your heart, mind, and soul, but He goes about it in a gentleman's way.

You must give your life to Jesus by your own accord, by your own free will decision. If God manipulated you into accepting Him, then He would be operating in witchcraft, and God can never fall short of holiness.

The enemy is constantly prowling. When demons see that Jesus has not taken up your heart, beliefs and behavior then they rush in and set up shop without your conscious permission. This is how subtle the spiritual world is. You may have opened doors to they/them through sinful living in the new age, through fallen world culture, and through creating soul ties with boyfriends and girlfriends. That's why sinful living can get you into a spiritual kerfuffle in no time.

When an individual involves themselves with new age practices like Eastern meditation or yoga for an extended period, they are not merely emptying themselves and releasing stress; instead, they are, in fact, filling themselves with something far more detrimental. The absence of a protective spiritual shield allows the power vacuum to take hold, paving the way for the infiltration of idols and demons. Any spiritual path that does not align with the worship of the Holy God of the Bible and Jesus opens one up to the influence of demonic entities and inanimate idols. It is essential to understand that the unseen spiritual realm is consistently bustling with activity. If you could wear glasses that could show you the whole spectrum of the spiritual world you would see angels and demons and things that would shock you. It's more active than the human realm. The lesson to be learned is clear: if you offer the enemy an inch, he will unhesitatingly seize a mile.

In an Alcoholics Anonymous meeting years ago in Austin, I once heard a participant in a young people's meeting say something that stuck out like a sore thumb – I ended up finding freedom through Jesus more than the 12-step program, but that's aside from the story.

He said on the microphone if I don't get my two hours of yoga in, in the morning, then "I want to kill someone." That's a harsh stance for not doing some yoga, don't you think? The yoga demons he was yoked with had control over him and if they didn't harvest his energy each day, then they made him very irritated. If they don't get fed, then they make him feel more than not okay. That's no way to live. That's a person stuck inside of a negative feedback loop of bondage no different than a severe alcoholic.

Jesus would never do that to this individual I speak of.

If you do sin, involve yourself in new age practices, run towards occultism, mysticism, astrology, hermeticism, divination, wicca and witchcraft, participate in yogic or Eastern meditation traditions, practice witchcraft or paganism, prioritize distractions, or elevate material possessions, individuals, or activities above God in your life, you provide a foothold for the enemy. The adversary thrives on chaos and disorder, which deviates from God's intended order and design.

By placing anyone or anything above your relationship with God, whether knowingly or unknowingly, you end up opening doors to demonic influences and man-made idols.

Put simply, prioritizing your relationship with fallen spiritual practices, false gods, pets, pleasures, celebrities, politicians, bank accounts, television shows, food obsession, partying, drinking, spending excessive time on phone screens, or any other aspect of life that distracts and takes away from keeping your relationship with God as number one in your life corrupts, disrupts, and dulls the divine order and brings delight to the evil one and his demons.

Hosea 4:6 KJV

*My people are destroyed for lack of knowledge*

Many people mostly agree in the existence of demons. Regardless of if you think they are real or not, they can influence someone against their inner sense of right and wrong. This inner voice, often called the conscience, starts speaking to us from a young age. We can choose to listen to it and do what's right or ignore it and do what we want. This is tied in with the age of accountability from chapter 3.

When we ignore this inner voice, no matter what age we are, and go against what we know is right, we are likely to be opening ourselves up to negative spiritual influences. It's important to pay attention to our conscience and make choices that align with what we know is good and true.

The word conscience translates to the Greek word "suneidésis," (/soon-i'-day-sis/) which means a proper joint-knowing of what is moral and good. Starting from when we were young, a person's conscience becomes accessible, which means there is a moral and spiritual consciousness as part of being created in the divine image of God (Genesis 1:27), that's the joint, innate, general knowing of right from wrong. It can be embraced or rejected, just like the image of God inside can be embraced or rejected.

All people no matter what age have this God-given capacity to hear the little voice inside to know right from wrong, each person can abide or ignore. Ignoring that inner morality baked into us will open an individual up to demonic oppression.

This inner voice that everyone has from a young age is like Holy Spirit lite. As discuss in chapter 6, the Holy Spirit will enhance these abilities in an individual to know right from wrong and holy from unholy.

I have attended many deliverance services where I have observed demons leaving individuals when they are commanded to come out in Jesus name. Only Jesus' name makes the demons tremble (Mark 5:7). It's nothing that can be faked. It is indeed a supernatural move of God to see the sick healed and demons cast out of people. One encounter with Jesus can undo and overcome a power vacuum that's been building in a person for decades. When that pressure is undone, a person experiences great relief and newfound freedom. Only Jesus can set the captives free (Isaiah 61:1-2).

These miracles are visible proof that God loves us. God can love us by telling us, but God can also love us by showing us His power, presence, authority, and dominion over demons and sickness.

As discussed in the previous chapter, when they are commanded through the authority of Jesus to come out then they are discovered. The light of Jesus shines on them and they must "come up and out."

They get irritated, manifest, flare up and then bend to the authority of Jesus and leave the person. Deliverance is done at the identity level because Jesus paid for His children with His blood. They are His property so they are under His authority.

That's the importance of being covered under the blood of Jesus each day, that's the importance of belonging to Jesus. You can't serve two masters (Matthew 6:24). So, you either belong to and are serving satan's demons (knowingly or unknowingly) or you belong to and are serving Jesus. There's no middle ground, that's why when a believer is saved but still caught in demonic oppression its not a comfortable place to be, that is until Jesus sets them free – but they must realize they need deliverance. If you have the nudge from the Holy Spirit you might need deliverance then look into it. There is a deliverance location map at https://www.isaiahsaldivar.com/deliverance

Serving Jesus has a lot more Heavenly benefits at the end of your life. Serving the demons have hellish benefits at the end of your life.

That's the importance of putting on the full armor of God, so your shields are up, and you are buffered against the unclean spirits and schemes of the enemy. Again, here is the defense system. The armor.

Ephesians 6:10-17 KJV

*Finally, my brethren, be strong in the Lord, and in the power of his might. Put on the whole armour of God, that ye may be able to stand against the wiles of the devil. For we wrestle not against flesh and blood, but against principalities, against powers, against the rulers of the darkness of this world, against spiritual wickedness in high places. Wherefore take unto you the whole armour of God, that ye may be able to withstand in the evil day, and having done all, to*

---

*stand. Stand therefore, having your loins girt about with truth, and
having on the breastplate of righteousness; And your feet shod with
the preparation of the gospel of peace; Above all, taking the shield of
faith, wherewith ye shall be able to quench all the fiery darts of the
wicked. And take the helmet of salvation, and the sword of the Spirit,
which is the word of God: Praying always with all prayer and
supplication in the Spirit, and watching thereunto with all
perseverance and supplication for all saints.*

When you belong to Jesus He will not let you become an open target
for the enemy. That's why we have these spiritual weapons to equip
us. The weapons of our warfare are not carnal (2 Corinthians 10:4)
they are spiritual and the spiritual always has precedent over the
natural world.

God will send entire armies of angels to protect one of His children.
The armor of God is real – the favor, protection, and provision of the
Lord is real – it all must be embraced at the level of deeply knowing.

In the Bible story of the Prophet Elisha, God sends an angelic army to
protect Elisha (2 Kings 6:1-23) – when you belong to God He knows
about you and what you are going through, whether you are a prophet
or not. He sees you. He will kick down doors to save you and
preserve your life and calling. Grow in faith and seek Him, and before
you know it your identity shifts and you have a strong identity as a
child of God, rooted in truth. The old identity, whatever that may look
like, and its imperfections, has been discarded like old wineskins.

2 Corinthians 5:17 ASV

*Wherefore if any man is in Christ, he is a new creature: the old things
are passed away; behold, they are become new.*

---

186

As you walk through the valley of the shadow of death, rest assured that He walks alongside you. Referred to as the shadow of death in the Bible (Psalm 23:4), this valley symbolizes the enemy's constant presence, seeking to steal, kill, and destroy. Yet, through Jesus' victory over death, there is no need to fear, for as a new creation in Christ, you are shielded from the enemy's schemes through the blood of Jesus and the full armor of God.

As you are transformed into a new creation, you stand upon an unshakable and solid foundation found in Christ. This foundation is pure and untainted, akin to constructing with high-quality concrete rather than inferior concrete riddled with impurities. The promised process of purification within Christianity is genuine and transformative. In contrast, the purification process advocated in the new age realm can leave one vulnerable to the power vacuum.

Take rest in the knowledge when you are saved, born again and are baptized in the Holy Spirit you are sealed with the Holy Spirit. God seals those that are His children away from the demons and schemes of the enemy. The proof is also in the book of Ephesians.

Ephesians 1:13-14 KJV

*In whom ye also trusted, after that ye heard the word of truth, the gospel of your salvation: in whom also after that ye believed, ye were sealed with that holy Spirit of promise, which is the earnest of our inheritance until the redemption of the purchased possession, unto the praise of his glory.*

Once you expel any demons that were sitting in your flesh from your pre-saved lifestyle you are then protected by the armor of God and the seal of the Holy Spirit. If you are tempted to tiptoe into sin, turn the temptation over to Jesus and He will spare you. As mentioned, once demons are dealt with the Adam nature, the vile flesh baked into the human body, can still rage and must be crucified daily through intentional consecration (Galatians 5:24). The takeaway is it's not always a demon. The flesh is vile on it's own. That's why we inherit glorified bodies in Heaven.

1 Corinthians 10:13 KJV

*There hath no temptation taken you but such as is common to man: but God is faithful, who will not suffer you to be tempted above that ye are able; but will with the temptation also make a way to escape, that ye may be able to bear it.*

If you continue to surrender what is unholy you will be kept in the Spirit. He wants your obedience. His manual, the Bible, clearly explains how to be an obedient child of God and a part of His eternal family. In essence, it's about seeking Him, seeking righteous living, and staying away from sin. Believers are obedient because they love God and are saved and want to stay in right standing with Him. Obedient because you are saved, not the other way around.

He doesn't require us to do spiritual gymnastics in order for Him to care about us, love us, protect us, and provide for us. God comes in to protect through surrender to His Lordship.

The deep rest in our soul that we are all looking for is only found under the blood of Jesus.

The lowercase "g" gods have no authority, and they only come to steal, kill, and destroy. They want to rush in, live rent free, and trash the place.

John 10:10 KJV

*The thief cometh not, but for to steal, and to kill, and to destroy: I am come that they might have life, and that they might have it more abundantly.*

Demonic influence is all across modern society. On the billboards you see on the road, on social media feeds, in the movies, music, politics, everywhere. Most of what is called "entertainment" is watching people sin.

The demons want to cause harm, distort, distract, and ultimately destroy humanity, but instead books like this are being written by myself and other Christian authors so more demons, idols, and false gods are exposed and ultimately purged. Demonic oppression comes at an individual in a lot of different ways and categorically lowers one's quality of life.

A quick prayer you can say now, *"Heavenly Father, in Jesus name, I renounce any oaths taken to polytheism, false lowercase "g" gods, and other spiritual traditions outside of the Holy Trinity, they are now bound and broken in the mighty name of Jesus. I am covered under the blood of Jesus. I belong to Jesus."*

It's also in your favor to start listing and renouncing all the fallen new age practices you were involved in. Scan your memory and recall all of the things you were involved in.

*"I renounce any connection to X, Y, Z"*

Come out of agreement with what you formerly were complying with and in agreement with.

---

Now this is extremely important so you are free from the charges against you in the Courtroom of Heaven: go inside of prayer and repent and plead the blood of Jesus over all of those past sins. Allow the Holy Spirit to bring those past sins up one by one so you know the charges against you in the Courtroom of Heaven. Be patient and see what bubbles up and is revealed to you. Plead the blood of Jesus over each one of these charges so you are set free from all of them. It could be any sin under the sun – including generational sin you know your parents and grandparents dealt with that you have also dealt with, drug use, pornography, masturbation, gluttony, pride, disobedience, anger, lying, swearing, stealing, manipulating, having allegiance to false gods and false belief systems, mistreating others, mishandling past relationships, it could be anything… Jesus will tell what the charges are. Plead the blood over each one to clear the scoreboard and set yourself free before your final breath, because tomorrow is never guaranteed.

After you have done that then sincerely forgive anyone you either don't want to forgive or know you need to forgive.

Do it because your eternity is at stake and you do not want to be found guilty. As John the baptizer said, "Repent. The Kingdom of Heaven is at hand!" (Matthew 3:2). It really is because after the rapture, the saints will find themselves in Heaven, and then after the tribulation we are commissioned to reign on earth with Jesus in the literal Kingdom of Heaven millennial reign on earth.

Jesus loves you abundantly and desires for you to be free you from the chains of sin and negative patterns that may be hindering you. Once those chains are broken and sins are cleared you can keep growing. He wants to see you blameless, spotless, and set free so you can be with Him after your last day on earth.

He cleared you completely of the charges with His alive and available blood, but you must personally know what to repent about and plead the blood of Jesus over. Plead it while you still have time and keep doing it as often as needed through allowing the Holy Spirit to convict you of any new sins you committed. This will transform into a lifestyle of repentance and humility.

He offers a renewed mind and heart all through His precious blood. It infuses your life instantly with His grace and truth, leading you to a new place of freedom and peace in this life and the next. Trust in His love and God-sized power to break the chains of oppression to bring you complete healing to your soul. You must let Him set you free by pleading the blood.

Seeking the guidance of the Holy Spirit always creates a buffer against sin. Place all your faith in Jesus as your commander in chief and wonderful counselor and He will never steer you wrong. He will quickly slay any of the negative attachments that have already invaded your flesh, and He will prevent any new invaders from entering. He promises you are sealed with the Holy Spirit upon truly accepting your salvation. Embrace the treasures He has given you.

The core of being a Christian means you have a lot of help on your side in order to eternally set you free and remove the blemishes from your life.

James 4:7 KJV

*Submit yourselves therefore to God. Resist the devil, and he will flee from you.*

If you know for sure you have been involved heavily with the new age and other fallen spiritual practices or there are generational curses here is a deeper prayer for deliverance from dark spirits:

*Heavenly Father, I belong to Jesus. I am a son/daughter of the King. I am a child of God. Armed with this knowledge, I command any demons, negative spirits, and idols influencing my life to no longer have any hold on my heart, money, time, or resources. I am covered under the blood of Jesus completely. Any curses since the fall of Adam were reversed at Calvary through the work and the blood of the Son of God, Jesus, on the cross. Satan, you are my sworn enemy, and all your demons, known or unknown, must manifest and go in the mighty name of Jesus. I belong to Jesus. I am covered under the blood of Jesus. They have no legal authority to be here. Any unclean spirit must come up and out right now in the mighty name of Jesus. You have no choice but to bend to the will, blood, power, and supreme authority in the name of Jesus. Amen.*

Keep pleading the blood over yourself, over and over, until you get results and you feel some "stuckness" start to move.

Before I attended a formal deliverance service, I had the sense I needed deliverance, so I started to frequently declare over my life, "I belong to Jesus" or "I am covered under the blood of Jesus." Doing this would create instances where I was intensely dry heaving. This was the start of my deliverance. It was like I was throwing up in the spiritual, and allowing the deliverance to occur, it was intense, I could barely catch my breath when this occurred. This is all important because Jesus is looking for a spotless bride – saints without blemish.

I felt a little freedom from the rounds of dry heaves, but I could still sense there was more there to uncover and get free from so I attended a formal deliverance service. This is where me and a deliverance minister would identify the spirit that was agitated by the authority of Jesus and thus on its way out, when this deeper clean occurred actual throw up would be produced. That is common when dark spirits leave a person. I went through several rounds of supernatural deliverance services that cleaned me and provided freedom from bondage.

Some of the unclean spirits that came out of me were as follows: the spirit of rejection, spirit of anger, spirit of fear, spirit of trauma, spirit of santeria (death), and the seven headed spirit of leviathan (pride, overly critical of myself and others, alcohol and confusion, impatience, a lying tongue, contention, and hate). There were many demonic assignments to end my life starting from birth. Some of the assignments were generational curses and some started early on around three or four years old, such as spirit of rejection.

I was freed from all of these dark spirits because the blood, power, and authority are all in the name of Jesus and the work of Jesus. He has the total authority over someone who has an identity in Christ.

It's always been out identity.

The demons can't stay because they do not have the legal authority to do so. The blood of Jesus paid the fine for the removal of all sin, death, and demonic oppression. All the curses, all the generational curses, all the trauma, all the addiction, all the sickness, all the unforgiveness, all of it was paid for and nailed to the cross through Jesus' obedience to the Father. He took all the pain on. He paid the ultimate price, so we didn't have to. That is John 3:16. God loves us.

Our Father in Heaven desired for us to be spotless and liberated from the bondage of demonic oppression, therefore sparing us from hell. If we are blessed enough to realize the truth of Jesus and His blood and what it does then we are given the extremely graceful chance to repent, experience healing, claim deliverance, be cleaned and be further transformed into the likeness and image of God. This is the version of you God has always seen and has always wanted to come forth.

Once you are cleaned and set free know that you are holy and set apart from the world and you must create a distance between yourself and the world as well as those who carry the antichrist spirit.

2 Corinthians 6:14 KJV

*Be ye not unequally yoked together with unbelievers: for what fellowship hath righteousness with unrighteousness? and what communion hath light with darkness?*

One of the most subtle agendas of satan is saying we must "coexist" and all the world religions are equal, and they all lead to salvation, when eternally speaking, they are not equal and do not all lead to Heaven. Only Jesus died for you. There is only the Holy Trinity in Heaven, on the other side of the earthly realm.

His book is the Word of God, the Holy Bible. The only way to eternal life in Heaven is through Jesus.

There is a push in the west for the ecumenical agenda, which says polytheistic and monotheistic traditions, are created equal, and every "faith" carries equal truth and leads you to Heaven. This is one of the most evil and dangerous agendas because not all faiths are created equal. That's a lie created by the evil one. There is only one faith, one Jesus, and one way to Heaven (Ephesians 4:4-6).

Atheists, new agers, soccer moms with coexist bumper stickers, and religious leaders alike all push the ecumenical agenda. The evil one is using them all to spread lies. Satan is the author of lies. Can you believe satanic evil witchcraft is being equated to the holiness and truth found in Christianity? It's absolute madness.

Many atheists or agnostics often follow the belief that by doing good deeds, they will be in good standing with any potential God if one exists.

If you are trying to enter Heaven upon death by saying you are a good person and you did a lot of good deeds, and you should be let in because you are "good enough" it won't satisfy the sin debt. There is sin debt you were born with and there is sin debt you added to. The blood of Jesus is the only thing that can clear these charges against you.

The fines, the sins, must be paid for, for each human to enter heaven. The only way to clear the fine is to accept the blood of Jesus and to have a relationship with Him. Nothing else can set you free from the sin debt.

For example, if you go up to the door of a big mansion in Beverly Hills and say you should be let in and allowed to stay there because you are a good person and you do good deeds the mansion owner will not care. They will require you to vacate the premises immediately because they do not know you and they have no reason to trust you. You just showed up at the door and demanded to be let in. No matter how much you beg or say please they won't care. Now, if you were the son of the mansion owner, then he would instantly recognize your face or your voice, greet you with love, let you in, let you eat from the fridge, and let you sleep in a beautiful room.

John 14:2-3 KJV

*In my Father's house are many mansions: if it were not so, I would have told you. I go to prepare a place for you. And if I go and prepare a place for you, I will come again, and receive you unto myself; that where I am, there ye may be also.*

Jesus is saying in the book of John that there is a mansion and a place for you in Heaven if you follow Him, repent, plead the blood, and take up having an honest relationship with Him while you are here. You get to borrow His authority, His Sonship, so God recognizes you the same way He recognizes Jesus. He needs to see the Jesus in you in order to receive you at Heaven's gate. If you harden your heart to Him and His truth and reject the only blood that atones, He won't recognize you. If He let you into Heaven without clearing the sin debt with the blood of Jesus, He would be letting sin into Heaven, and that would be a transgression in itself, and God can't create transgressions. He wrote the law and judges extremely fairly.

Jesus is the Son of the mansion owner, the Father, and if you accept Jesus and His blood it is promised that you are then yoked with Jesus and therefore co-heir to the Father's mansion (Matthew 11:28-30). You also become a holy son or daughter in the eyes of the Father. Jesus, through His blood and work on the cross, shares this exclusive access to the Father with you, whether you are man or woman, young or old, skinny or fat, rich or poor, healthy or unhealthy, you can become a son or daughter in the Father's house through accepting Jesus' blood and work on the cross. Plead the blood now where there is still time.

Having faith in the one and true God is binary, not "non-binary." Meaning, you are either in allegiance and surrendered to the one true

God and His blood that sets you free, or you are not. It's a daily choice to pick up your cross and live as Jesus lived. It is a daily choice to not sin and intentionally develop a relationship with Jesus. It's a daily choice to crucify your flesh and live from the Holy Spirit and not the flesh. It's a daily choice to repent when you have done wrong.

When Paul, the writer of Ephesians and thirteen other books in the Bible, says there is one faith, that means there is one faith. The faith in the only Son of God, Jesus, that loved us and died for us (Ephesians 4:4-6).

When people say, "Oh, I'm of a different faith." It means they don't believe the Bible, which proclaims there is only one faith.

For example, Baptists and Pentecostals are different denominations but they are the same faith. The denominations are a product of man and not God.

Other world religions such as Islam, Hinduism, Buddhism, Shamanism, Shintoism, Taoism, Gnosticism, Zoroastrianism, Baha'i and Scientology and numerous others represent diverse belief systems very different than Christianity. These other faiths often emphasize works-based salvation, they promote the idea that by performing good deeds and adhering to human-made regulations, one may eventually attain divine enlightenment, personal godhood, or approval in the eyes of the most high.

However, these approaches can be seen as manipulation at the highest level, leading individuals to labor tirelessly and become even more lost only to discover at the end of their life that the promised rewards never existed, the faith they chose was false, and the salvation that was sold was never of God and therefore false. The swath of religions and spiritual traditions out there is an absolute minefield.

Such deception programs align with the tactics of the adversary, as satan seeks to deceive individuals into pursuing false paths that ultimately lead away from the truth. Deception when it comes to matters of faith is often wrapped the appearance of tradition, a fuzzy feel good message that God loves everyone equally and everyone gets into paradise, and there is no requirement for repentance or holiness.

Christianity says you can't do good on your own without Jesus dying in your place, without Him you are a slave to sin, the world, and the flesh, the Adam nature of man, and until you accept the blood of Jesus you are condemned because you're a sin machine. In God's grace He sought you out when you weren't even looking for Him. He sent Jesus to find you and only Jesus is the one that can make you something that you could not be in and of yourself, set free and innocent.

All have sinned and come short of the glory of God (Romans 3:23).

Every individual falls short of holiness, a state intrinsically connected to the divine glory of God, and we all must look to Jesus as the only faith and the only Savior that sets the captives free.

Jesus said there is only one faith, so there's only one faith.

Authentic Christianity is the one and only faith based on the grace and goodness of the Gospel of Jesus Christ: the death, burial, and resurrection of the Son of God that fully redeems.

Until you seek for the one and true Father each day, you will be walking around in a fog which is what the enemy wants. You may be convinced you found the truth, but the most dangerous lie is the one you believe.

Any other "faith" outside of the Jesus of the Bible is demonic, and you're lost, wandering in the dark, and vulnerable to the effects of the power vacuum.

Yes, it really is this black and white. Many things in life are not this black and white, we can become addicted to complexity, but Jesus is simple. You are either truly saved and born again, made new under the blood or you are not. There is no middle ground. There is no in between. Your blood and the blood of Jesus have fully mixed, or they haven't.

Christianity is the spiritual special forces in the sense that it is the only faith that seeks to liberate the oppressed. The captives are set free through elevating Jesus to His rightful position, the King of kings, the King of your heart, the commander, the wonderful counselor, and the Lord of lords.

Taking up your cross (Matthew 16:24) is the highest and hardest spiritual path but also the most meaningful. It's the only faith that understands Jesus is the one that unlocked repentance, salvation, deliverance, and healing for anyone through grace and not works. He opened Heaven's gate for you. He opened His great mansion for you.

If you are not walking around with Jesus on your heart and in your mind then you are lost in the fog of war, which is a real thing to get lost in. There is a massive spiritual war that is visible and invisible here on earth, as mentioned. The war in the Heavens is beginning to manifest more on earth (Revelation 12:7-9).

The enemy desperately wants you walking around in self-doubt, confusion, self-concern, fear, pain, and uncertainty. He wants to condemn you and forsake you. He wants to accuse you. Sometimes overtly and sometimes in subtle ways. He is the voice of the accuser. He wants to place you back in your past and not into your future in Christ.

Colossians 1:27 KJV

*To whom God would make known what is the riches of the glory of this mystery among the Gentiles; which is Christ in you, the hope of glory.*

Romans 8:38-39 KJV

*For I am persuaded, that neither death, nor life, nor angels, nor principalities, nor powers, nor things present, nor things to come, Nor height, nor depth, nor any other creature, shall be able to separate us from the love of God, which is in Christ Jesus our Lord.*

Protect your heart and be on the lookout for people who harbor fear, spread division, and have control issues emanating from underlying insecurities, as their "operating system." They can be transformed through the love of Christ, but they must be receptive to the truth of who God says they are – loved by Him to the point where He laid down His life for them.

It's very hard for an individual to switch operating systems, only the operation of God, not man, can do it, so once you have identified those that have these tools of the enemy inside them, just be aware they will most likely pull out and use those tools against you when you least expect it thereby inflicting maximum damage.

Chaos, derision, division, fear, guilt, shame and uncertainty are the tools of the enemy. The good news is those are all the tools in the enemy's limited tool belt. Not even death can separate you from the love of Christ. When the accuser is coming against you be patient and forgive them because there is a blindness in them.

Again, this may be people you barely know, but its more than likely to be friends or family member that use the tools of the enemy against you because they have proximity to you. If your family sows seeds of fear and doubt into you once you are saved then they are employed by the enemy, desperately trying to hold you back, so it's your job to be a living testimony that can show them the love of Christ and hopefully one day they will be receptive to the truth of Christ. If they have hard hearts and continually spit out the truth and kindness shown to them, you can protect yourself and create distance, so you aren't pulled down with them. Misery loves company.

The enemy inside of people will attempt to get you to doubt your new identity as a son or daughter of the King and they will attempt to get you to doubt who God is and how deep His unlimited wonder working power goes. In essence they want to gaslight you into thinking faith isn't real, isn't worth it, or is an escape. They will attempt to get you to believe the Bible is just a book, but they fail to see the pen is mightier than the sword, and the Bible is the most important book humanity has ever seen. That's why when the antichrist reigns during the seven year tribulation it will immediately be put out of print and banned. That's the antichrist's day one agenda.

If you see people in your life using these tools of darkness, then the enemy is in their head. Say to yourself, "Father forgive them because they know not what they do."

Always remember justice belongs to the Lord, no matter how heinous, the desire for revenge is, it isn't worth it because the battle belongs to the Lord (1 Samuel 17:47).

Additionally, have a lot of caution for Christians who proclaim Christ, they might even wear a cross and Christian clothing, they might talk a good game, but they don't walk in kindness, don't walk in humility, aren't patient, and are more fascinated by the things of the world like the pride of life, the lust of the eyes and the lust of the flesh. They may seek pleasure and greed more than they are seeking to know and share Jesus. It's an unfortunate fact that many Christians do not make it their mission to carry Christ and the subsequent nine fruit of the Holy Spirit (Galatians 5:22-23).

They may claim the title Christian, but they may not have truly been saved or truly received the Holy Spirit.

99% saved is still 100% lost.

The intention of this book is to be a guidebook to spark the fire inside of you to seek God like there is no tomorrow, to live from the knowledge of your salvation, and to walk by the Holy Spirit everyday.

Many ministries have been sheepish to admit Christians can be saved but still dealing with demonic oppressions operating in their flesh. For the believer it's an uncomfortable chasm because their spirit has been lit by the fire of God, but their flesh is still trying to hold them back. The process of becoming a usable saint for God is surrendering to this information so you are also set free, sanctified, and majority Holy Spirit led instead of majority flesh led. The good news is being holy and sanctified through the operation of Jesus is very attainable and not something that may or may not happen way down the line.

1 Thessalonians 5:23 ASV

*And the God of peace himself sanctify you wholly; and may your*
*spirit and soul and body be preserved entire, without blame at the*
*coming of our Lord Jesus Christ.*

The Bible promises Jesus sanctifies you wholly in an instant and sets
you free to walk the walk as a saint. Demons do hide in the flesh and
can be cast out but never forget the Adam nature is baked into the
flesh. The Adam nature in the flesh is the master sin, as discussed, it's
from the fall of Adam and Eve from grace and every human is up
against the Adam nature. It must be placed at bay through the Holy
Spirit's all consuming fire. Fallen human nature is to follow the flesh.
That comes naturally. You can be a saint in an instant but what takes
time is for the fallen beliefs and values to exit a believer as the
resurrected beliefs and values are installed through the Holy Spirit as
the new holy operating system of the mind. Get discipled, get trained,
immerse yourself into Bible studies so the absolute truths come forth
and integrate all the way into your being. All of this together is what
creates a substantial defense against the power vacuum and the flesh.

1 John 3:8 KJV

*He that committeth sin is of the devil; for the devil sinneth from the*
*beginning. For this purpose the Son of God was manifested, that he*
*might destroy the works of the devil.*

Jesus, the Son of God, loves us so much that He passionately wants as
many of us as possible to be cleaned, set free from demonic activity,
and set free from sin and idolatry so we are on the road to Heaven.
Time is short, the end of the Church Age is rapidly approaching.

Being set free from the power vacuum will always equal new freedom, deep peace, no new pains or problems, and a new hope for the future. If you have new pains or problems after deliverance, you did not receive authentic, biblical deliverance. You received something else that was not from God. After the authentic operation of God takes place, you will always feel new freedom and never new problems.

If you think you went through deliverance but it left you feeling confused, less free, and with new body pains it was not done properly and was done from the flesh, the operation of man.

Deliverance is as simple as having a member of the ministry team sitting in front of the suffering individual and calmly commanding the spirits come up and out in the name of Jesus, and that they are not welcome. A child of the King belongs to the King and therefore the demons are placed on notice, they have lost the custody battle and must go because they have no authority over the King's property. Deliverance is about identity first and foremost, who you are and whose you are.

Sometimes the dark spirits go quickly, sometimes they are stubborn and go slowly. You will never see a properly trained minister angrily yelling at a person, laughing at a person, or physically hitting a person. They will be composed no matter how much the unclean spirit manifests and protests.

The enemy wants the people of God to become angry and frustrated with the demons. Why? Because the fact of the matter is Jesus has title to the ultimate authority, and if you belong to the King, which you do, it is written, deliverance from all demons is the children of God's portion. If you belong to the King as a son or daughter of God, if you have accepted, received, and believed the blood of Jesus still saves, then you belong to Him at a deep identity level. He will chop down hell by the acre to rescue you and make sure you are set free.

Deliverance from demons and idols is being done from a place of victory, not from a place of wishing for victory. The blood of Jesus that flowed on Calvary assured this.

1 Corinthians 15:57 KJV

*But thanks be to God, which giveth us the victory through our Lord Jesus Christ.*

When the chains are broken by Jesus you will instantly feel ten times lighter, like a heavy weight was just lifted off your shoulders, because it was!

People are most susceptible to dark spirits taking hold when they are in a reactionary state of fear or hate rather than a stable state of love and peace provided by Jesus.

He was and is the nine fruit of the Spirit. It's the saint's goal to embody more of the nine aspects of God each day to become purer in heart. Growing deeper in the faith means these nine aspects of God are growing inside and creating a bigger buffer against the demonic.

Galatians 5:22-23 KJV

*But the fruit of the Spirit is love, joy, peace, long-suffering, gentleness, goodness, faith, meekness, temperance.*

Jesus is with you at all times and He will never fail you. The humans in your life have been consistent at failing you because they fall short of the glory of God, every one of them. We have to have enough grace in our hearts, to know that we can only expect so much from others, because they are human and will always fall short.

Jesus is perfection. He walked a perfect life. He never sinned.

Hebrews 4:15 KJV

*For we have not an high priest which cannot be touched with the feeling of our infirmities; but was in all points tempted like as we are, yet without sin.*

Humans are far from perfect and are terrible at creating peace. The only peace a human can create is by allow His peace, His joy, His righteousness to cover them.

If you had very good parents and role models that embodied the love of Jesus then you are blessed. That may be a generational blessing in your bloodline sown by your grandparents or great grandparents. The only good you see in a person is from Jesus.

If there is any bold promise I can give to you in this book, it's this: place all your faith and trust in Him, acknowledge Him in all your ways and He will protect you. He will never leave you. He is a wonderful friend. His leadership and guidance will never fail you. He's never lost a battle.

Proverbs 3:6 KJV

*In all thy ways acknowledge him, and he shall direct thy paths.*

Do you know why these entities like to attach to humans so much?

It's because we are powerful beings of love created directly by God. We are God's highest form of creation on earth, one notch below angels, and when we embrace the blood of Jesus we are spiritually higher than angels and demons through Jesus' authority that He provides us access to.

We are not artificial. We are not AI. We have souls directly from the God of the universe. Our souls are the most valuable part of us. God is in the business of souls and so is the evil one.

We are entirely organic beings. There is nothing fake about us. That's why part of mRNA vaccine agendas was to turn us into artificial, genetically modified humans with modified mRNA. If you have resisted all the mind control agendas here on earth that have been deployed thus far, God bless you.

That agenda was a test agenda, a precursor, to the real mark of the beast which will sell a soul to the devil and change someone's DNA.

No matter what, keep your blood and your DNA pure, as God intended. If you didn't resist the vaccines, nothing is impossible with God. That was the pre-mark not the real mark. God can remove the various heavy metals and poisons from a believer's body through the power of prayer.

We are incredibly powerful vessels for the goodness of God and our DNA programming is superhuman. It's likely scientists will never truly understand the intricacy of DNA and how it interacts with the other Kingdom where Jesus and God are always living.

We are temples of the Holy Spirit of God. The children of darkness on their way to hell do not like us, so they want to taunt us, mock us, and steal our peace. It's entirely our choice to be offended or distracted.

The spirit of death, which is one of the negative spirits out there, likes to see death and destruction in the people of God.

You can decree and declare out loud right now. *"I bind and break the spirit of death, the spirit of fear, and the spirit of heaviness over my life in the mighty name of Jesus!"* Try it on and say it confidently. Recognize within yourself who you are and who you belong to. It's who you have always been, a child of God. A son or daughter of the King.

You can take authority through Jesus' blood over any dark emotion because it could actually be an unclean spirit. You belong to Jesus, He paid for you with His blood, He sets the captives free. He knows you because He created your soul prior to the creation of the physical world.

Command out loud who you are as a son or daughter of the King, and with authority!

This will get your juices flowing and give permission to the loving, life force energies of God, Jesus, and the Holy Spirit. Remember, God is a gentleman. He respects your free will; you must allow Him to enter and move on your behalf and into your life. He will never subvert your free will.

God is patient with us, and generous. He gave His only Son to the world for humanity's redemption and restoration (John 3:16). Mental health, physical health, emotional health, spiritual health, love, joy, peace, and right standing with God – every single area of your life can be redeemed when you give your soul back to God, He made your soul. Everything already belongs to Him. Wisdom is relinquishing your free will and turning it over to Him, trusting He knows better because He is the one and true Almighty God.

Proverbs 3:5-6 KJV

*Trust in the Lord with all thine heart; and lean not unto thine own understanding. In all thy ways acknowledge him, and he shall direct thy paths.*

Philippians 2:10-11 KJV

*That at the name of Jesus every knee should bow, of things in Heaven, and things in earth, and things under the earth; and that every tongue should confess that Jesus Christ is Lord, to the glory of God the Father.*

Luke 10:19 KJV

*Behold, I give unto you power to tread on serpents and scorpions, and over all the power of the enemy: and nothing shall by any means hurt you.*

I know it sounds too good to be true but His love and care for us is supernatural. It's good news. It's better than we were ever taught or told. You may have been brought up in a society where God was put in a box or not talked about at all.

He is way beyond what we can even put into human words... His ability, His grace, and His eternal power is bigger and better than we were ever told. He made us. We belong to Him.

This is why the demonic world of the evil one wants us. He is angry that we belong to the Holy God of the universe, therefore He wants us maimed, injured, or destroyed.

We have been given a big gift through the blood of our Savior Jesus so that we don't have to stay in separation and isolation from God. The Spirit of God is still on earth, and according to the New Testament it won't be that way forever here on earth, so we must accept the blood of Jesus while the door is still open. Upon the first seal of Revelation, the Holy Spirit leaves the earth with the Church and the seven year tribulation begins (2 Thessalonians 2:7). We live in perilous times, so the time is short, and the door is closing. After you are done with this book, pass it along so more people can enter the Ark before the next "flood" this time around it will be hellfire from the sky (Revelation 8:5).

Jesus came to supply redemption to the weary, to the meekest and weakest among the earth, the poor, the decrepit, and the downtrodden. Anyone who has the simple faith and wonder of a child can accept the blessing waiting for them. He did not come for the haughty, those are the ones that believe because they have digital dollars or coins, and a boat in the marina, they don't need anyone or anything else. That's the pride of life (1 John 2:16) and pride always comes before destruction.

The blessing of accepting Jesus is an entry into supernatural living and a direct partnership with the sovereign God of the universe. It's a lifestyle realignment to begin the walk with God, instead of independently from Him.

When you earnestly partner, He will restore and repair you to spiritual wellness. There are countless people who have all the riches that the world has to offer, but they are in-fact miserable Scrooge-like individuals, without kindness in their heart, and often underneath the surface they have shoddy relationships with their spouses and children, if they are blessed enough to have a spouse or children at all.

The fact is you don't have unlimited time to restore and repair your soul. You want your soul and your life to honor the greatness of God while you are still here, living and breathing. While you are still alive you have a blessed opportunity to change course and turn hard right toward righteous living (2 Chronicles 7:14).

Jesus agreed to be completely obedient to His Father's instructions while on earth because He knew how deeply the love of the Father was burning for humanity to be reconciled unto Him.

The Father is the eternal flame of life and love. God loves Himself, and thereby He loves us, as His creation. It's our job to embody and return the love that was shown to us first.

1 John 1:5 KJV

*This then is the message which we have heard of him, and declare unto you, that God is light, and in him is no darkness at all.*

1 John 4:20 ASV

*If a man say, I love God, and hateth his brother, he is a liar: for he that loveth not his brother whom he hath seen, cannot love God whom he hath not seen.*

1 John 4:8 KJV

*He that loveth not knoweth not God; for God is love.*

1 John 4:19 KJV

*We love him, because he first loved us.*

2 Thessalonians 2:16-17 KJV

*Now our Lord Jesus Christ himself, and God, even our Father, which hath loved us, and hath given us everlasting consolation and good hope through grace, Comfort your hearts, and stablish you in every good word and work.*

God saw the need for redemption, salvation, and restoration for all of humanity, so He sent to the earth a worthy Lamb, the Messiah, the one and only worthy and willing sacrifice, to bleed, to pay the fine for sin, and to provide eternal redemption for all that have ears to hear the eternal truths of the Holy God through the Bible.

Heaven is the eternal palace where the souls of believers will find rest forever, made accessible by the redemptive work of Jesus. The concept of consciousness extending into the afterlife occurs through the soul, for those who have received salvation. While our physical bodies have limits, the soul, when saved, is understood to be infinite and destined for an everlasting existence in the presence of God in Heaven. This belief offers hope and assurance of a timeless existence in communion with God for those who have accepted His gift of salvation through Jesus. Communion with God here, equals communion with God there.

If you miss the mark and live a life of sin that opposes God then your soul goes to hell for pain, turmoil and destruction. The American church lately has been telling their congregations hell isn't as bad as you think. No, it's worse than you think. The wages of sin are death. You reap what you sow. It's basic cause and effect, not karma.

If you hit the mark and live a life of purity that honors God, then your soul goes to Heaven for eternal life with the Father. Walk with him now, carry the cross now, and walk with Him for eternity. It's a fantastic deal, assuredly the best deal I have ever stumbled upon. I hope you are seeing the value of Jesus and what He did for you by this point in the book.

If you are not pure you will be denied entry into Heaven. We have an extremely merciful God, we have been given time to change course and turn to the Father, but He will not let you through the pearly gates if you are not prepared for entry. He won't compromise. It is essential to keep Heaven a pure place for everyone that's already there, that's understandable. He won't stand for mixture with darkness and neither should we.

2 Corinthians 6:14 KJV

*Be ye not unequally yoked together with unbelievers: for what fellowship hath righteousness with unrighteousness? and what communion hath light with darkness?*

The eternal reward for living a life of righteousness while on earth is Heaven. It's not possible to tarnish the perfect community of the ones that washed themself clean while they were on earth. They laid down personal pride and surrendered to Jesus and righteous living. God is fair and just. The innocent ones that are holy and blameless are only holy and blameless because they have accepted the blood of Christ. They have allowed His blood to wash them clean from the inside out.

The righteous, God's remnant on the earth, claimed the truth of who they are, children of God, who God always saw them to be, and thus also saw God as who He is: a good and loving Father that has always been there for them, especially in the hardest and trying of times.

Jesus holds the keys to Heaven and hell and he will not allow sinful living and impurity into Heaven. It's the same expectation you have when you purchase fine gold or silver.

You expect the highest of purity, and if it's impure, also known as fool's gold, then you won't purchase it, and if you already did you will vehemently do your best to get a refund.

You will keep waiting and searching until you find the authentic, pure gold. The reason you are hearing the Gospel explained many times over in various ways is to impress your identity in Christ into your mind so that the Holy fire process of the refinement is engaged.

Only Jesus knows at the time of someone's death who has been purified into fine gold and who hasn't. He knows who you really are.

We can speculate all we want on if someone is going to Heaven or hell but it's not a good use of time to speculate. Only Jesus knows at the hour of someone's death what the truth about that soul. Only He knows if that soul honored God or rejected God.

He knows if they belong to Him at an identity level through the Holy fire process of embracing the Gospel, authentic repentance, Holy Spirit and fire baptism, and deliverance from all demons, idols, and false gods. He knows who has been after His heart, covered in His blood, and seeking communion with Him, and who hasn't.

Repentance can feel like a form of judgement in our culture. However, that is far from the truth, it's God's mercy. Surrender and humility is the admission ticket to let God show you where you are missing the mark, where your worldly programming was getting in the way, and where you were disobeying God's commandments across the New Testament. Repentance is receiving a fresh touch of God's grace, mercy, and forgiveness and a complete return home.

If it's your sincere intention to return to Jesus, to come home and be in communion with the Father, and you repent, then the repentance is indeed authentic and the Father acknowledges it, honors it, and blesses it. Whenever you feel stuck, repentance can bring a fresh touch of God's anointing and blessing back on your life.

Since He sees everything you can never deny the "three O's." Omniscience, omnipresence, and omnipotence. He loves when you return back to Him and sincerely, deeply, plead the blood over your sins, and turn away from those sins. He can forgive you of anything (yes anything) and transform you into a new creation. But you must be intentional, and not just for one day either, you must stay surrendered and keep surrendering your old life and old ways to the cross as you enter into His courts with praise and thanksgiving.

John 8:11 KJV

*She said, No man, Lord. And Jesus said unto her, Neither do I condemn thee: go, and sin no more.*

You must become good at allowing the Holy Spirit to convict you of when you fall short and think about sin or commit sin. The Holy Spirit helps you with this tremendously when He is inside.

If you keep praising and showing up for Him day after day, He will then in return keep on proving the reality of Himself to you. He wants you to see that it's not a fad, not a phase, and you are with Him for the long-haul. He knows who is faithful and who is running the race with perseverance with Him until their final breath (Hebrews 12:1).

The Father of all creation cares about us, knows about us, wants a face to face, honest, and authentic relationship with us.

We are blessed that this is the reality among us, not luck, not chance, not the work of randomness. Blessed!

As your discernment and sensitivity to the Holy Spirit grows you will become better at knowing which people are Heaven sent and which people are sent by the enemy.

When God wants to bless you, He sends people into your life. When the enemy wants to distract or oppress you, he sends people into your life. Your discernment abilities will heighten as you walk with Jesus. You will clearly see what people and what things are meant for you, and just as importantly what people and what things are not meant for you. One of the gifts of the Holy Spirit dwelling inside you, when you step in to belonging to Him, is the discerning of spirits.

1 Corinthians 12:10 KJV

*To another the working of miracles; to another prophecy; to another discerning of spirits; to another divers kinds of tongues; to another the interpretation of tongues.*

With allowing the Holy Spirit, the Spirit of God, to dwell inside, you will discern what internal thoughts are from God, as well as which people are Heaven sent: positive, uplifting, kind, loving, truthful, humble and encouraging. On the flip side, you will see which ones have a knack for chopping you down and sowing seeds of doubt, because they themself are suffering.

Once again, hurt people, hurt people and healed people, heal people.

You will discern with greater levels of awareness what thoughts inside you are aligned with God's will and not only that, which people in your life are healthy and oriented towards God's will for you. Those are the thoughts and people that God sent to help you. Even people in a good church can be from the enemy, that's how necessary spiritual discernment is. The right people can bless your life, and the wrong people can ruin your life.

Thoughts or people from the enemy's camp are generally trying to inject fear, doubt, division, drama, gossip, lies, and anxiety. Sometimes blatantly, but most often subtly.

Your thoughts as well as the people in your life are either helping expand you into holiness or they are taking you away. If you and others around you are truly walking in the Holy Spirit each day then you are destined to be expanding and growing. If others are constantly complaining and being negative and creating drama, then they are not really walking in the Holy Spirit. It really is that simple.

Remember, your checklist is the nine fruit of the Spirit (Galatians 5:22-23). Part of your identity as a child of God is to be a fruit inspector. You will be able to spot authentic fruit, imitation fruit, and the absence of fruit in others quite easily.

As a believer navigating this treacherous earth plane, your goal is to be surrounded by the Holy Spirit, inside and around you. You can do a lot to protect your eyes, ears, and social circles.

Do note that if you are authentically seeking the Holy Spirit, but the enemy is still surrounding you, attempting to take your peace and condemn you, know that in many ways you are on the right track. It means the enemy can't stand your growth in the Lord and he wants to throw you off. When this happens pause and pray and see if you have any open doors to the enemy, if the Lord shows you, then close those doors and then do your best to take rest in your identity in Christ. Jesus loves you and your identity in Him is fixed and eternal.

Worship is your weapon. Praise, pray, worship, and stay focused on Jesus and the enemy will have no choice but to flee. If you don't make yourself low hanging fruit for the devourer, the evil one, he will move on. The enemy can manifest in the form of people, but he can also flare up a spiritual war in your own mind, that's why observing your own thought stream is wise. The negative thoughts are taken captive to the sound mind of Christ. The enemy inside is simple the flesh, the Adam nature, and it must be crucified each day. Taking those negative thoughts captive and then surrendered to Christ is one of the benefits of belonging to God. God gave you many tools to help.

2 Corinthians 10:5 KJV

*Casting down imaginations, and every high thing that exalteth itself against the knowledge of God, and bringing into captivity every thought to the obedience of Christ.*

2 Timothy 1:7 KJV

*For God hath not given us the spirit of fear; but of power, and of love, and of a sound mind.*

When you accept your eternal identity in Christ you have an entire toolbelt to keep your peace, after all it's His peace being bestowed upon you. Jesus came back and shed His blood for you because He wanted to see you expanding, growing in your soul's authentic expression designed by God, filled with joy, and filled with peace.

He paid the ultimate sacrifice, He was blameless and sinless, He was and is God's only Son, God the Son, and He laid His life down for your freedom in all aspects. The blotting out of sin was just the start.

What Jesus did for you is the best gift in the world. It's irreplaceable. It gets better and better with time, no plateaus necessary. Backsliding can happen, but it's generally a result of not giving due attention to your faith, your prayer life, and your fellowship with Him and other people that have the Holy Spirit inside. Keep on your armor of God.

Jesus and His blood has the power to break you free of bondage and restore your mind to God's Holy blueprint specific to you. Your creativity, your thoughts, your emotions, and your identity can all be enhanced by His love and His truth.

He can do all of this because He has known you since the beginning of time. He knows your DNA better than any scientist in the world. He is nearer to you than your own DNA. Think about that.

As you get to know Him and hear His voice it will surprise you how well He knows you. It's a real relationship, not an imaginary friend. He is not a fairy tale; historical records document that the tomb where He was laid was found empty, and He indeed rose and visited the disciples in His glorified body after His resurrection.

He knows how to love you, how to make you feel hopeful again, He knows the exact way to deliver you, to heal you, and save you from any snare the enemy has set for your ruin. Where you don't see a way, He can always see a way. He is the waymaker. He isn't asking you to figure it all out, He's asking you to trust that He already has.

He will do this all gently, calmly, patiently, without judgement, without condemnation, and with the pure kindness and compassion of a righteous and loving Father.

He sees the best version of you at all times, your purest potential. He often wants you to win more than you do, so He's your best encourager. He can see your redeemed identity in Christ and wants you to be cleansed of oppression, set free, and walking with Him each day into eternity.

His grace is sufficient, always, and forever (2 Corinthians 12:9).

Jesus returned with the blueprint of redemption through His supernatural blood. That's why the followers of Jesus Christ are called sons and daughters of God; this the new identity. The Church is referred to as the bride. The Church is righteous men and woman and she, the Church, is awaiting a Holy marriage that is fast approaching, with Him, Jesus, the bridegroom. Jesus comes back on the clouds to snatch up His bride, the faithful that are hot and on fire for Him, totally surrendered, for the end of the Church Age, and then the tribulation ensues.

The more you embrace Sonship, being a son or daughter of the King, at the identity level, the holier your life becomes. It is your true identity, your resurrected identity, that has been waiting for you all along, and all significant breakthroughs and transformations in one's life originate at the identity level. A healthy, Holy Spirit filled identity will serve you best and bring glory to God because it was designed by Him for you to embody.

One of the most powerful guiding forces in human psychology is the self-image, which is the identity. Your identity is intricately woven into the concept of the "operating system" that I mentioned earlier.

Subconscious psychology operates twenty-four hours a day. Even when you are asleep the subconscious mind remains active. It is where the identity, along with your most cherished beliefs and values, are embedded. The subconscious mind is primarily emotional and closely linked to the physical body, every interaction between the external world and the body is recorded by the subconscious mind.

Believe it or not, humans are extremely good at maintaining consistency with their identity. The identity functions like the GPS of one's life. Once behaviors, beliefs, values and actions are deeply embedded into a person's subconscious mind, a person will consistently align and act in accordance with the presently programmed identity. When they drift off course from that identity they will automatically revert back to it. That's called the automatic success mechanism, but it can also be the automatic failure mechanism if it's programmed with a fallen identity. That's why having a Bible mentor to disciple you and audit your identity is so important. If you have been in the world or the new age for decades, which you most likely have, then your identity will have unbiblical mixture inside that needs to be refined through Jesus fanning the flames, to get a pure and golden identity that serves you and God. The new identity in Christ will be able to flip the automatic failure mechanism inside into the automatic success mechanism.

The firm foundation of a golden identity lives in who you believe you are, who you belong to, and what you stand for. Believing that you are a child of the King, that you belong to Jesus, and that you stand for the truths outlined in the Bible forms the basis of an authentic, God-fearing, blood bought, Bible-believing Jesus following identity. A God-fearing Christian understands that Heaven and hell are real destinations at the end of life and the healthy fear of missing the mark fosters spiritual fortitude and provides refuge in times of temptation.

The world is riddled with pitfalls and potential follies, so seeking refuge in God provides stability and safety in an unstable world.

To explain automatic success or automatic failure another way: a fallen identity that an unsaved person automatically snaps back to is automatic failure. A resurrected identity that a saint snaps back to is automatic success. It works like a thermostat. If you set a thermostat to seventy-two degrees and then the room temperature starts to drift above that temperature, then the air conditioning will kick on and the room temperature will cool back down to seventy-two degrees and stop. The set state will always be the target of return because the mechanism always returns back to what it was programmed to return back to, in other words, the baseline. The baseline identity of a righteous Holy Spirit filled Christian is a state of Godly awareness, never denying the omnipresence of God, and having a holy fear of missing out on eternal life in Heaven. If the resurrected identity is firmly set in the mind, then automatically a saint will recorrect course back to holiness and God's will.

The crucial question is, what is your "identity thermostat" currently set to? Is it your resurrected identity in Christ or is it a blended mixture of the world and the world's fallen beliefs and values?

Is it tuned into the death, destruction, perversion, idolatry and unworthiness of the world, or is it aligned with your Holy embodiment and emulation of King Jesus? This is the life and character Jesus. He provided the blueprint for the risen identity that God designed for you. He's always wanted to see you as a Spirit filled child of God, belonging to Him instead of belonging to the fallen world culture.

You are a child of the loving Father in Heaven and a co-heir with His wonderful Son, Jesus. When you belong to Jesus, He will never let you stray from the path He wrote for you. He will ensure that you undergo a full transformation so you fulfill God's will for you, the purpose encoded in your soul written by Jesus.

We have been given a new template of redemption, a second chance, and a new lease on life. This is what this book, and truly what Jesus, is offering you while you still have breath in your lungs – the chance to finally be alive in Christ.

The life of Jesus was marked by compassion, kindness, strength under persecution, boldness, courage, and God-given confidence. Jesus is often referred to as "the rock" because He provides a solid foundation on which to build your personality, identity, business, ministry, marriage, parental skills and your entire life upon. He's more real than life itself.

In every life situation, ask yourself, "How would Jesus respond here?" Would He lose His temper and become angry quickly, or would He exhibit temperance and self-control regardless of the circumstances? The Bible reveals that Jesus maintained a sense of coolness and composure no matter what chaos ensued around Him. He walked in alignment with the Father's will for Him and was fully aware of it.

When you enter into God's Kingdom, you will be capable of achieving great things in ministry, business, or marriage with others who are equally yoked – being equally yoked means that the person you are with is also embodying their Christ-given identity rather than the fragmented, broken identity the world placed on them.

If you and your ministry partners, business partners, family, and spouse are aligned on Kingdom principles and Kingdom identity then God-ordained blessings will unfold. Isn't God's design beautiful? Again, perplexing on why so many reject it.

If you feel the thermostat of your faith faltering, and your sense of identity slipping away from holiness, causing doubt to seep, drawing you back towards the fallen world and the Adam nature, remember that you have the chance to pause and express gratitude to God for His ongoing work in your life, and the victories He has already won. Surrender the challenges to Jesus. Consistently lay them at His feet and never deny the omnipresence of the Holy Spirit. Sometimes, a recollection of past triumphs and the realization that you fight from a position of victory is all it takes. He is much bigger than any situation you may be up against.

You must stay in the fight while in His Holy Kingdom, because if you don't belong to His Kingdom then by default, you are in the kingdom of darkness and He is looking for saints that are married to Him.

Turn over the challenges to Jesus because the Heavenly tool belt is always more effective. The battle belongs to Him as prior mentioned (1 Samuel 17:47), no matter the circumstance, justice belongs to the Lord. He is the ultimate judge and jury.

When you are facing a challenge or temptation, be mindful of your words, as the words you speak are like a sword that can either avert destruction or bring about destruction. The choice is always yours.

Proverbs 18:21 KJV

*Death and life are in the power of the tongue: and they that love it shall eat the fruit thereof.*

Pause and consider this before speaking curses over others, especially your own children, who belong to God. The tongue, the mouth, and the words you utter hold the power of life and death. That's how crucial your choice of words is in every situation. Negative words can create curses, while positive words, such as invoking the name of Jesus, can bring people back to life, both literally and metaphorically. Kind and Godly word choice pleases others in your life and God, alike.

Proverbs 16:24 KJV

*Pleasant words are as an honeycomb, sweet to the soul, and health to the bones.*

Psalm 119:103 KJV

*How sweet are thy words unto my taste! yea, sweeter than honey to my mouth!*

As Jesus becomes more integrated into your identity, gradually and gently, you will improve at pausing and sincerely asking yourself what Jesus would do in each situation rather than react through the flesh.

He would never lose His cool, instead He would pause and entrust the challenge to the Father for breakthrough and intercession. He consistently sought the wisdom from the Father and surrendered it to the Father for transformation. He never drifted from His identity as the Son of God. He methodically sought guidance directly from the Father for a clear path of action moving forward. That's why He went and prayed each morning with the Father.

Mark 1:35 KJV

*And in the morning, rising up a great while before day, he went out, and departed into a solitary place, and there prayed.*

We can embody the same identity as a son of God that Jesus did while on earth. Don't forget Jesus said greater things we will do.

John 14:12 KJV

*Verily, verily, I say unto you, He that believeth on me, the works that I do shall he do also; and greater works than these shall he do; because I go unto my Father.*

Jesus is the most famous person that ever walked the earth, the predominant focus point of all human history didn't do it for likes, blue check marks, riches or fame, never for ego enrichment.

He lived for saving souls, delivering souls, and healing bodies. He came to provide access to peace, joy, righteousness, faith, hope, and love for anyone that had ears to hear. He came to glorify the Father.

He came from Heaven for you.

1 Corinthians 13:13 ASV

*But now abideth faith, hope, love, these three; and the greatest of these is love.*

The identity is the learned habit pattern of the mind, the collection of the most dominant thoughts that strengthen over time. The identity you adopt is a choice, and because it's a choice, you can be transformed into Christ's image at any moment through surrender to His Lordship. This is why born again Christians are a new creation in Christ. You truly do become a completely new individual in Christ at the identity, mind, body and soul level.

One of the most effective ways to reprogram the subconscious mind is through two things: books and repetition, that's why reading the Bible and studying it often is essential to remarking the identity.

You will see every area of your life gently heal. Anything the enemy stole or ruined can be redeemed thousands of times over.

We have a miracle working God!

2 Corinthians 5:17 KJV

*Therefore, if any man be in Christ, he is a new creature: old things are passed away; behold, all things are become new.*

Deuteronomy 1:11 KJV

*The Lord God of your fathers make you a thousand times so many more as ye are, and bless you, as he hath promised you!*

Some identities hinder blessings, while the identity in Christ enables blessings. We do not serve a God with a clenched fist; rather, we serve a wise God who does not endorse unrighteousness.

An identity is like an internal garment that we wear whether we want to wear it or not.

The garment inside can be a beautiful coat of many colors (Genesis 37:3) that is full of God's promises and glory. Or it can be a dirty drab and worn out coat that looks just like the darkness of the world. The coat of many colors will be inside of someone that had an open enough mind to accept Christ and therefore they have a growth mindset – they keep transforming and becoming better. The worn out coat checkered with darkness belongs to someone with a closed mind and a fixed mindset unable to accept the blessings and promises of God, stuck in the false identity and automatic failure.

The book of Revelation also shows what a new garment inside can look like. This is referencing tribulation saints that washed themselves with the blood during the seven year tribulation.

Revelation 7:14 KJV

*And I said unto him, Sir, thou knowest. And he said to me, These are they which came out of great tribulation, and have washed their robes, and made them white in the blood of the Lamb.*

If you step into a life of salvation and live with the Holy Spirit on board, your identity is seated in Heavenly places. How amazing is that? It's like becoming a truly out of this world human, holy and set apart from the world and seated in Heavenly places.

Ephesians 2:6 KJV

*And hath raised us up together, and made us sit together in heavenly places in Christ Jesus.*

You have to be able to discern for yourself which identity you want to plug into. The fallen identity of Adam, who did not obey God, or Jesus who obeyed God no matter what the cost. He never lived for pleasure or vainglory, He only lived for the Father's will.

Issues like addiction often stem from one's identity. The mind aligns with this identity, leading individuals to remain trapped in a cycle, believing they are defined by their addiction. Through Jesus, the chains of bondage are broken, allowing for a new narrative to be written and a path to freedom to be embraced.

If you frequently are looking backward at your past stumbles, which is what satan will attempt to do through your own mind or people in your proximity, it may keep your identity stuck in the past and trapped in past pain. The evil one loves this dynamic, so instead, look forward to the blessed hope, embrace Christ in you the hope of glory, and your eternal and secured future as a new creation in Christ.

Your new identity in Christ is a newly received wineskin, as mentioned, in ancient Hebrew times people would place fresh wine into fresh wineskins for storage. If they tried to put the new wine into old wineskins they would burst. The identity in Christ is like the container of your mind and when you are discipled and study the Bible, you also embrace the new identity then God can personally pour in the new wine, the new wisdom, the new truths for you.

Mark 2:22 ASV

*And no man putteth new wine into old wine-skins; else the wine will burst the skins, and the wine perisheth, and the skins: but they put new wine into fresh wine-skins.*

Choose the new identity because you only have this lifetime to align your soul and spirit fully toward God. When you embrace the faith of following Jesus, your wineskin will supernaturally change.

Basic logic dictates that you should embody the true identity that leads to life, blessings from God, fulfillment of God's will for you, lasting satisfaction, and a deep purpose in Christ.

Romans 8:28 KJV

*And we know that all things work together for good to them that love God, to them who are the called according to his purpose.*

So many people in modern times are searching for meaning in all the wrong places. They are infatuated with the idea of love, not knowing it's nothing like the love of God. They are captivated by the notion of becoming wealthy. They are enamored with the idea of achieving social media fame. They are fixated on their egos. They are indulging themselves to the fullest extent with worldly pleasures, quite literally.

Many are stuffing themself with food, drugs, alcohol, sex, "doom" scrolling, binge watching, shopping, fornicating, and chasing after their next dopamine hit. This is because we live in a consumer culture more than a producer culture. About 80% of people are professional consumers leaving 20% of the population to be the producers: the ones producing the infrastructure, goods, services, and media.

Most people go into the lifestyle of looking for meaning through consumption because they want to fit in with what the culture is already doing. They want to be accepted so they pick up a cocktail or the latest luxury good.

Many are seeking worldly validation and acceptance rather than the acceptance of the Savior, who already bled and died for them. Why seek validation from a world that crucified a perfect man?

I have had powerful encounters with Jesus where I see His face and He has told me "I receive and accept you" and "welcome home my son." Words of encouragement like that make my heart melt and I am completely full and satisfied. He is more than enough and will always be enough.

You don't know how meaningful and satisfying encounters like that are until you have similar encounters with Jesus, and you certainly will if you step deeper into the offer to give your whole heart over to Jesus. These encounters typically happen during worship or prayer, or when I am intentionally thanking Him and meditating on all the things that He has done for me and for humanity.

Many are looking for something beyond themself, yearning for something beyond the apparent level of work, food, social life, entertainment, sedation, and sleep. One of the deepest human cravings is to get lost in a purpose larger than themselves, this leads people to the spiritual. They want to know why they feel so alone.

Regrettably, many individuals seeking spiritual fulfillment may explore various avenues such as yoga studios, meditation halls, crystal sound bath meetups, or even stumble into drug dens, where they may encounter polytheistic beliefs, spiritual dangers, unsettling psychedelic experiences, and misleading promises of well-being and healing.

How did we get to modern spirituality? It's a convoluted answer but what I am sure of is it's a minefield. What people identify as "spiritual" is largely demonically influenced. The current spiritual landscape is a mess of gurus, life coaches, yoga teachers, courses, retreats, and hallucinogenic trips.

Once again, how did the modern landscape get here?

It could be because it's entirely too easy to become a spiritual junkie that is starving for relief while going from healing to healing, tradition to tradition, and trip to trip; never truly getting spiritually fed.

People go on new age goose chases because they just want to feel meaning and relief. They desperately want to know their purpose. They want to know the plan for their individuated soul. They want to know why they feel alone no matter what they do. They think perhaps a tarot reader, or a psychic medium will tell them, or at least clue them in on the hidden self-knowledge they are desperately in need of.

Often, spiritual seekers become consumed by a quest for information, much like I once was. The consumer culture fuels this hunger for seminars, documentaries, and media, all in pursuit of meaning and fulfillment. However, true growth comes from applying and living out even a small portion of God's Word, rather than merely accumulating knowledge without action. The Bible serves as a living guide, a love letter from the Creator, offering a path back to Him and to one's true self. As His children dwell in Him, He, in turn, dwells in them, fostering a deep connection and a journey towards wholeness.

Romans 8:1 ASV

*There is therefore now no condemnation to them that are in Christ Jesus.*

John 15:4-5 ASV

*Abide in me, and I in you. As the branch cannot bear fruit of itself, except it abide in the vine; so neither can ye, except ye abide in me. I am the vine, ye are the branches: He that abideth in me, and I in him, the same beareth much fruit: for apart from me ye can do nothing.*

If someone memorizes every single chapter of the Bible, all 1,189 chapters, its meaningless without any daily and personal application. Implementing what you have learned is incredibly important.

To know and not to do, is not to know.

The world has countless spiritual traditions and practices, over 4,200 to be more specific, but they were not all created equal as mentioned in the previous chapter. They are not all connecting to the same source. The true growth is going to come from actually having traction.

All the 4,000+ traditions, except Christianity, are plugging into a fallen energy source, or signature. All of the fallen traditions have a common origin, the fall of man, the original curse and fall from grace that occurred in the garden of Adam and Eve. That placed a separation between man and God. This leads to no traction.

Are you starting to see why globally the world is a mess in many ways? The broad majority is plugged into fallen energetic signatures.

Only Christianity leads the pack and creates meaningful traction because it's a direct relationship with the source. The source is the one and true Almighty God. If you are not plugged into the source of God Himself, the source of love, the source of truth, the source of life, then you are not going to get any results. There will be no lasting fruit.

The fact is, there's only one empty tomb. There is only one man who conquered sin, death, and hell forever. There's only one way to Heaven and His name is Jesus.

Traditions missing out on an authentic relationship with Jesus will always look light and innocent, that is until you look under the hood, and you realize there's no engine, rather the engine is the demonic realm, meant to take you further away from healing and further away from truth.

Jesus is the only one worthy to open the seals of Revelation (Revelation 5:5-7).

Jesus is the light, the truth, and the way (John 14:6).

4,000+ traditions outside of Jesus can never bring you closer to a meaningful life and God's will for you, because they have no authority here. This is God's green earth. He created it.

New age thought leaders are the blind leading the blind. However, it's worse than that, it's the sinister (that likely do not believe they are ill intentioned) leading the blind.

If you can get millions or billions of people to believe in a lineage of buddhas, ascended masters, the aspiration of personal enlightenment, and becoming a buddha or a god, then they will seek nirvana endlessly, and will never find the source, the life, the truth, and the way. Those that have found the traditions of man, not the tradition of God, have found humanism. It sounds good, it seems esteemed, noble, and mature, but it's a giant distraction trap to place all the focus on self rather than the Savior of the world.

Many embark on the death of their own personal ego in spiritual traditions and Christianity has parallels with that, but if you white knuckle it through traditions teaching you to focus on "self" hours at a time then the only rational outcome is the enhancement of "self" also known as ego, rather than the reduction of ego.

The new age community is riddled with those individuals that have a giant "spiritual ego" where they feel superior to others. Jesus blasts past these pop psychology concepts of ego and superego and goes right to the meaningful simplicity of "less of me, more of you Jesus."

The only way you can have God fill you with His wonder and clarity is through humility, which is the loss of self-importance and pride. When we meet our Maker, His deepest joy is to see us overflowing with the nine fruit of the Spirit (Galatians 5:22-23), which is the character of God, He wants to see His image in you, He does not want your book report on how full of yourself and how special you are. Pride blocks God and humility allows Him in.

Jesus is the only one waiting for you on the other side in the Courtroom of Heaven. He is a fair judge. He is very interested in those interested in Him and He can't recognize His image in those uninterested ones that are devoid of the nine fruit.

There is a social media channel called "Beyond Death" (found at https://www.youtube.com/@beyonddeath22) and on the channel are many real, medically documented near-death experiences, where people visit the other side, are given a second chance, and come back to earth, and go back into their bodies for one last chance. They come back from the "other side" with a clear memory of what occurred beyond the veil.

There is an extremely consistent theme across these documented experiences: they meet Jesus for their life review in the Courtroom of Heaven. He often gives them a fresh dose of conviction about the way they have been living and are given a second chance to glorify Him and start living right before their final death.

Again, no other "religion" or spiritual tradition has evidence this consistent. I put religion in air quotes because Christianity is more about following Jesus and the Bible and developing a real relationship with Him, more than following man's religion. Going through the motions and checking the box of attending church once or twice a year is not what Jesus died for, that's what I mean by playing games of religion. If people go to church here and there, or even daily, they could still be entirely missing the point of developing a relationship with God more than a relationship with religion. The Bible is an instruction booklet to help you develop that relationship with Jesus directly. If a church is more about intramurals or dogmatic rituals (that the Bible never prescribes), then you probably found religion but missed Jesus.

He is a man, not a series of rituals or rites of passage. An easy way to tell if you have found religion or a sideshow instead of a direct relationship with God is through objective observation. By examining oneself or others, one can assess the manifestation of the nine fruit of the Spirit. Among the fruit is love for fellow humans, reflecting a genuine reflection of the character of God rather than mere religious appearance. You should see a culture of peace, joy, love, and miracles.

John 13:35 KJV

*By this shall all men know that ye are my disciples, if ye have love one to another.*

When you observe how others treat each other, a lot is revealed. For example, you can easily see those who embrace self-importance, their own personal celebrity and separation from others, compared to those who embrace humility. If you have been humbled enough to accept Jesus then you can then share the love of Jesus with anyone regardless of their place and position in life. Following Jesus is much more about the relationship that compounds across time rather than following any one religious version of Christianity. The meaning comes from the relationship and not the appearance of a relationship with Him.

Do your best to not confuse having a relationship with God and religious indoctrination, often found at less than perfect local churches. Local churches can easily fall into the trap of man worship and placing the pastor or priest on a pedestal. One is a local church with a lowercase c. The other is the Church with a capital C. The Church belongs to Jesus. He is God and He paid for it with His blood (Acts 20:28).

He already died for His Church and accomplished the work, and at the end of the age He is coming back for His Church to spend eternity with them, the chosen ones (Ephesians 1:4-5). The rest are not included. It's above yours or my paygrade to speculate on why this is the design of things – many will enter few will win. The difference here is "winning" is defined by our relationship with Jesus and our free-will choice to live His will, surrender to Him daily, plead the blood, resist the temptations of the flesh inside of all of us (the fallen Adam nature) and live in a way that glorifies God, rather than grieves God.

The people that are not a part of His Church have all been given the free-will opportunity to place their faith in Jesus at some point across their life. Jesus is the most famous man in the world, so there is no excuse for not having heard of Him, however, some local churches and religious types have done a terrible job at representing Jesus and explaining to the public what the Gospel is and what Jesus did. They quickly overcomplicate it or mask the truth and go beyond the death, burial, and resurrection rather than embrace it. This is THE GOSPEL.

1 Corinthians 15:1-4 KJV

*Moreover, brethren, I declare unto you the gospel which I preached unto you, which also ye have received, and wherein ye stand; By which also ye are saved, if ye keep in memory what I preached unto you, unless ye have believed in vain. For I delivered unto you first of all that which I also received, how that Christ died for our sins according to the scriptures; And that he was buried, and that he rose again the third day according to the scriptures.*

The primary focus on the Gospel to the Church is what Jesus did. The churches that missed what the Gospel is are trying to gain meaning through anything other than the relationship with Jesus.

The New Testament takes account of the different archetypes local churches fall into. Those archetypes either honor God, or not. In the book of Revelation the seven types are mentioned, and Jesus only approves of two of them, Philadelphia and Smyrna. That's only 28.5% of the churched world seeking authentic intimate relationship with Jesus. As mentioned, many will enter few will win.

Jesus labels the other five as lukewarm, and He would rather spit them out (Revelation 3:16). You are either on fire for the relationship with God or you are not, there is no halfway measure with surrendering your life to Jesus, you must die do your old life.

Many religious churches are mixing religious rituals and Jewish law which was based on works with the pure message of the Gospel which is the Grace Covenant, thus watering down the purity of the Gospel message being taught. The Gospel of grace is red hot. Anything else mixed in with it is ice cold. The result is lukewarm. In Revelation 3, Jesus is talking about the churched world – and not even the unchurched world. If the churched world has this high risk of being spit out by Jesus Himself, imagine where the unchurched world stands with Him.

The book of Revelation is one giant prophecy about the tribulation, the time the world is quickly approaching. Currently, it's hard to tell if we are watching the evening news or witnessing prophecy from Scripture. As mentioned, the wars and the rumors of wars, plagues, natural disasters, the elevation of untruth and mass civil unrest are all mere foreshadowing of the seven year tribulation and it's playing out right before our eyes. Bible prophecy is unfolding daily so time is short to be on fire and ready for the rapture. The warnings and signs to look for are clearly given in the Bible, many interject with "we don't know the day and the hour stop looking" but they forget we can observe the season, the confluence of signs, and the extreme warnings through the weather. Quite simply the evidence of the rapture being nearby is rapidly mounting. All the signs are there to the point where it could be any day.

We will remain in the build up to the tribulation until the end of the Church Age ends and Jesus comes back for His Church, the spotless bride that is on fire for Him, the remnant around the world that He has embraced the Gospel, the Holy Spirit, and has remained faithful. God always keeps a faithful remnant (Romans 11:4-5).

In these end times Jesus will only approve of 28.5% of the church body. That's not the same as who His Church is. He has people in His Church that don't attend a local church at all and they are indeed righteous, justified, and on their way to Heaven, rapture ready. For the sake of a thought experiment, it's estimated there are 2 billion local church attendees around the world. Using these figures, we can make a very rough estimate that 570 million people are approved by Jesus and part of the authentic remnant, His Church.

It could be much more or much less but just based on these rough figures that's 7% of the global population of 7.9 billion.

I know God wishes that 100% of the global population was on their way to Heaven, He lovingly gave His only Son to redeem the whole world (John 3:16). But the world at large is up against the flesh (the fallen nature from the curse of the fall of Adam caused by satan), their own free-will, distractions, fallen cultural programming (including new age modalities), self-importance, pride, religion and ignorance.

To be direct, it's a gigantic spiritual war of epic proportions, and in war there are winners and losers. It's a war for souls that's why satan has worked so hard to inject religious indoctrination into the churches. Regardless, of your circumstances you are inside the war, and whether austerity or abundance surrounds you, you always have the conscious free-will choice to focus on faith, hope, and love (1 Corinthians 13:13), or you slip through the cracks into the fallen ways and patterns of the world.

You are blessed to be learning more about Jesus. Some might go as far as to say chosen (Ephesians 1:4-5). The path is narrow (Matthew 7:13-14) and those who find the narrow path also find the deepest fulfillment out of life and do not look back. They have already surrendered their life and every area of their life to the perfect will of God. They have not complicated or mixed up the Gospel message. The way we become victors are through surrendering to the Lord in all ways and embracing the Holy identity, then we are the victors.

Joel 2:25-26 KJV

*And I will restore to you the years that the locust hath eaten, the cankerworm, and the caterpiller, and the palmerworm, my great army which I sent among you. And ye shall eat in plenty, and be satisfied, and praise the name of the Lord your God, that hath dealt wondrously with you: and my people shall never be ashamed.*

These verses convey the promise of restoration and abundance that God offers to His people after a long lonely road of devastation and loss.

By submitting to His Lordship, the global Church advances, pushing back the forces of darkness without falter. This is because the gates of hell will never prevail against the Church (Matthew 16:18).

Rather than retreating, they stand firm with Jesus in their hearts, equipped, on their shield of faith, ready for any challenge, as they are united with God in faithfulness and obedience through any challenge.

Picture a soldier "full of oil" meaning charged up with the anointing of the Lord, full of confidence from God and consistently ready for growth and challenge. That soldier is unstoppable. Not even death can stop that soldier. Being equipped like that can allow you to serve in an extreme scenario like actual kinetic war, thankfully that is not a reality for most of us currently, but our daily lives can often feel like a battlefield, and we want to stay on top of the challenges rather than retreating. That way we grow instead of shrink.

People that have meaning and fulfillment in their life, categorically, have a growth mindset and keep growing especially in the face of any adversity or adversary.

Deuteronomy 7:6 KJV

*For thou art an holy people unto the Lord thy God: the Lord thy God hath chosen thee to be a special people unto himself, above all people that are upon the face of the earth.*

The enemy knows Jesus is real and wants you focused on anything or anyone other than Him. That's the power in His name. Say "Jesus is Lord!" out loud, try His name out. Say it a few times. See if you feel "life" from saying that.

You can use the name to remove demonic spirits from people and places, you can bring a dead baby or an elderly person back to life, this is all through His mighty name. He can supernaturally restore and redeem those that hear the call to follow Him. You can claim true freedom and healing in every area of your life through Jesus – that's deep meaning.

His capacity for mercy outweighs your ability to be a sinner. The sins of your past are not as powerful as Jesus, so please know that if you accept Jesus then backslide and run back to eating your vomit like a dog (Proverbs 26:11) you can stop, drop the sin, and repent. Go back to the Father with genuine remorse for screwing up, have a change of heart, plead the blood over the sin, and have a real desire to turn from your fallen ways. Only God can recognize true repentance. Not a spouse, not a friend, not a priest, not a pastor.

The only way to Biblically repent and return to right standing with the Father is by dealing with the Father directly, and not through human intermediaries, no matter how well-intentioned they may be. Some of the religious factions of Christianity like Catholicism teach that you can't deal with the Father directly; they would rather sell their supposedly anointed authority and instruction rather than allowing you to use the anointing Jesus places on you for repentance and growth. He has already given us the direct route. The Bible tells us this: the direct way engages the operation of God in your life.

Some local churches really do want to help set you free and yet others want to play games of religion and want revolving customers that never truly find Jesus, heal, and become holy.

The operation of God is so essential and needed in your life because stop, drop, and roll doesn't work in hell. I don't want to "Bible bang" and say you are doomed if you don't believe but the truth is hell is a hellacious "resting" place for the unbelievers (Revelation 21:8). During some eulogies when a priest or pastor says the deceased have moved onto a better place are not telling the truth. The truth is the path is narrow and few find Heaven. What could be more meaningful than entrance into Heaven?

Hell is worse than you could ever fathom, far beyond the worst you can imagine. The closest picture that comes to mind is linked to a scene from a WW2 movie where bombs have been dropped on a quaint country village. It was peaceful and calm one moment. Business as usual. Children riding their bikes. Farmers tending to their field. This is akin to your everyday life. Then boom, something happens, and you take your last breath. Then the next moment people are on fire, screaming for their life, getting tortured by extreme pain and destruction, it's like that; just 1000x worse. It's the resting place for the souls that did not accept their get out of hell free card, Jesus' blood. God needed to provide humanity a way out from satan's influence on the earth and He lovingly did, however through free will rejection of Jesus, many miss their ticket to Heaven.

If you do claim the name and the blood of Jesus, then carry Him without shame, because you are likely to be the only Bible people ever read. When we say the name of Jesus unashamedly and out loud, we become a vital connection in the Great Commission that He needs filled here on earth. He wants more souls in Heaven and less in hell, and He needs all the help He can do – so we as humans step in to be the conduit for the power and authority of Jesus to come through us, that is the anointing. That's the access He gives us. When there is a miracle healing it's all Jesus. When there is a salvation it's all Jesus.

We as humans are a vital link in the circuit to bring in more of the operation of God on earth.

We become His mouthpiece, His eyes, His ears, His hands, and His feet. The Bible would have never been written without humans, attentively listening to the Holy Spirit, and writing down what was heard. When we write or when we speak, we are using the language of God: speech. He spoke all into existence (Genesis 1:3). As we learned in the last chapter, speak as Jesus would speak.

Proverbs 15:1 KJV

*A soft answer turneth away wrath: but grievous words stir up anger.*

Proverbs 18:21 KJV

*Death and life are in the power of the tongue: and they that love it shall eat the fruit thereof.*

My hope is that the words in this book encourage you to run into the arms of Jesus. It was blood, sweat, tears, several near death experiences, and years of pain and suffering to find out everything I am sharing is true. You too can be a servant of God.

The truths being shared with you are battle tested. They did not arrive in a nicely wrapped envelope like this book, it took years of toiling and getting lost in the new age to come to the realization that only Jesus is real. It is only through the grace of God that Jesus reached me at the right time, in the right way, and in a way where beyond a shadow of a doubt I knew it was Him entering into my life, for good. That was through a girl that was a willing conduit of His operation.

I'm writing this book so you too can receive the good news about God without needing to go to hell and back and if you are a tribulation saint reading this, God bless you, you are in my prayers, prayers that are not constrained by time or space.

Embracing Jesus regardless of your standing in life can be as easy as drinking water for you. He can quench the cries for help emanating from inside, and instantly He can provide supernatural provision and protection. All you need to do is deal honestly and directly with Jesus, and He will return the favor and start doing the same with you. He is a good God.

Proverbs 25:25 KJV

*As cold waters to a thirsty soul, so is good news from a far country.*

In the new age, yogis, pagans, and witches all worship the material world of water, fire, air, and earth. The four elements. The four elements are there to serve us and not to be worshiped otherwise they become idols; items worshiped instead of God.

It's just like how money is there to serve us as a tool and not to be worshipped. It's a brutal master.

Christians worship the creator, the Father. The protector, provider, owner of everything. It's already all His anyways.

We do not worship the created. We do not find deep meaning in the created. We find deep meaning in the Lord and Savior. A relationship with Him is by grace through faith. He is not of the physical world and its been proven that the non-physical world is more real than the so-called real world. Even the human to human relationships in your life are non-physical when you think about it. Matter in the form of people, places, and things is vibrating in and out of existence trillions of times a second to create the illusion of solid objects in space, in the world around us, however, the permanent and eternal world that never dies is non-physical, and goes way beyond the constraints of the 3D world.

Romans 1:25 ASV

*For that they exchanged the truth of God for a lie, and worshipped and served the creature rather than the Creator, who is blessed forever. Amen.*

Once you take the Christ pill you can see even deeper behind the veil and into the nature of reality. You are even more aware of mass deception and propaganda programs because the Spirit of Truth resides inside of you, and greater is He that is in you, than any false lying spirit of the world (1 John 4:4).

The true freedom through Christ starts to come in and add color to your entire life.

Jesus comes in like a wrecking ball and before you know it you are experiencing a consistent river of joy and meaning that wasn't there previously. This is the right version of joy and meaning, not artificial euphoria. He is the meaning we have been craving for our entire lives.

If you start to walk with the Lord, you will see exactly what I mean. You can only experience this for yourself, nobody else can experience it for you.

The world is chock full of distractions and consumer pleasures, all devoid of God.

People, especially men, think that one of the keys to meaning and fulfillment is having an expensive car. Men can ogle at an exotic sports car and think it's beautiful or even spiritually alive. This is a continuation of the deception of the fall in the created world. The matter in the world is ephemeral, meaning it is going in and out of existence faster than we can discern with everyday cognition. The 3D world isn't even "real" so how can we place our faith in it? We can't.

What most perceive as beautiful is simply what aligns with Fibonacci ratios. People, cars, corporate logos, paintings, plants, animals, and seashells all have ratios and curves in all the right places that is pleasing to the eye, but the Fibonacci ratio is only present in those things with a finite lifespan. A beginning, middle, and end of life.

You can see why so many in the new age look to the beauty of a Nautilus shell as a divine code of life, when ironically, it's a code of death. This is why Christians learn to fall in love with the permanent and non-physical relationship with God and place all their faith in that. It's not based on the created world at all and by default not based on the accumulation of money, things, or stuff for fulfillment, a void that can never be satisfied.

Christian thinking becomes less dialed into the already dying, finite, fleshly world and more focused on Heaven, the Kingdom of God, the Bible, and the eternal.

Having deep relationships with friends or family is a positive aspect of the nonphysical world. Those covenantal extremely close relationships will never fail based on outward circumstances, such as a child's newfound disability or a spouse's fading beauty. It's about attuning your mind to God's perspective.

Romans 12:2 ASV

*And be not fashioned according to this world: but be ye transformed by the renewing of your mind, that ye may prove what is the good and acceptable and perfect will of God.*

Anything that is in the physical world is not from the other Kingdom that Jesus spoke of. The Fibonacci ratio in a car's design, a seashell, or a human face is made of finite energy signatures. The human body is just a limited, finite temple that happens to have the God-given blessing of being able to carry the Holy flame of eternal life through Jesus. The body will pass away and then the non-physical soul that has been redeemed by Jesus will enter into eternal life, as God promises, and God will never let you down. He is the only one that will never let you down.

Only God, Jesus, and the Holy Spirit are waiting for you on the other side. Thor isn't waiting for you on the other side, Hercules isn't waiting for you on the other side, Apollo isn't waiting for you on the other side. There isn't a road to Valhalla. All your digital dollars and coins are not waiting for you on the other side. All your money, things, and stuff is not waiting for you on the other side. You have never seen a U-Haul on the back of a hearse, for a good reason.

What is waiting for you is your spiritual bank account and your residence in Heaven.

What you can deposit into is your eternal bank account in Heaven while still on earth. A Christian is someone recruited by God to live their life with an unashamed faith in Jesus (Romans 1:16). Glorifying God and making deposits into the Heavenly bank account is accomplished through producing fruit. The fruit is proof someone has been saved, the fruit is not the source of their salvation.

Productive Christians assure deposits through sharing testimony of what Jesus did for them as well as sharing the ultimate testimony of what Jesus did for humanity, the Gospel.

Some of the ways deposits are made is through worship, praying for others whether believers or not, praying for wide scale situations to resolve, praying for others to be saved, praying for Christians under persecution, praying against potential disasters that God's prophets have been shown, serving the less fortunate, setting captives free, sharing the Gospel on a wide scale and on a small scale, and through loving and forgiving others even when it's hard to do so, that's the nine fruit in action.

Considering what fills up a spiritual bank account in Heaven… do you really think those ayahuasca trips with hours of nausea, those mushroom trips with leftover paranoia, those self-focused meditation retreats, the expensive crystal collection, the sound bath sessions you attended, tarot card readings you paid for, and psychic readings that left you with more questions than answers were filling up God's eternal and Holy bank account? You can see how the Christian approach is largely about the welfare of others, whereas the new age approach is largely about only focusing on the self and nobody else.

The ultimate template for a human to model is Jesus. He was a servant of the Father that selflessly died for all of humanity. Let that sink in. The highest calling in His Church is be a servant.

Thats why the war for dominion over humans is so drawn out and dramatic. The devil wants human energy. Our energy is either used to glorify God and add to the eternal bank account or it's used to ignore God and live for the fallen whims of the world.

People are also looking for meaning and happiness in their marriage partner too. God's purpose for marriage is two imperfect people coming together to honor God and be a model of the love of Christ. Jesus is the bridegroom, and He loves His Church, the bride, that He sacrificially gave His life for, in the most brutal death the world has ever seen.

The bridegroom and the bride are the model of Jesus and His Church.

The world's strange version of marriage is two people, maybe of the same gender, looking for their ideal perfect partner to help them with career, to help them with status, to help them with finances, or to help them feel good about themself.

After that person is no longer gratifying the personal needs of the other, then one side or both sides begin to look at why the other person isn't the right pick, and a divorce is needed. How sad.

The Jesus way is to look for the best in others, to see their identity and destiny in Christ, to see them as worthy of forgiveness, love, and grace, just as Jesus died to supply us with His forgiveness, His love, and His grace. Mutually growing in His holiness, peace, joy, and righteousness is the goal. The world says the goal is happiness, but that's much harder to quantify than are you at peace in your soul or not.

The byproduct of a steady marriage should of course be happiness, there was a reason you married to begin with, you enjoy being with each other, but that's not the purpose. The meaningful purpose behind marrying a spouse of the opposite gender in the Kingdom is to glorify God, for the man to love his wife just as Christ loved the Church, with His entire life, and for the wife to submit to his leadership. He is the servant leader; she is the servant helper. They each have their respective identities in Jesus as a servant. They are both bought into serving the mission, to serving the family, and to serving God and growing closer to God, together. It's beautiful. It's Christ's design.

Ephesians 5:22-33 ASV

*Wives, be in subjection unto your own husbands, as unto the Lord. For the husband is the head of the wife, as Christ also is the head of the church, being himself the saviour of the body. But as the church is subject to Christ, so let the wives also be to their husbands in everything. Husbands, love your wives, even as Christ also loved the church, and gave himself up for it; that he might sanctify it, having cleansed it by the washing of water with the Word, that he might present the church to himself a glorious church, not having spot or wrinkle or any such thing; but that it should be holy and without blemish. Even so ought husbands also to love their own wives as their own bodies. He that loveth his own wife loveth himself: for no man ever hated his own flesh; but nourisheth and cherisheth it, even as Christ also the church; because we are members of his body. For this cause shall a man leave his father and mother, and shall cleave to his wife; and the two shall become one flesh. This mystery is great: but I speak in regard of Christ and of the church. Nevertheless do ye also severally love each one his own wife even as himself; and let the wife see that she fear her husband.*

This passage from Ephesians highlights the relationship between husbands and wives, comparing it to the relationship between Christ and the Church. It emphasizes the importance of mutual love, respect, and mutual submission in marriage, mirroring the sacrificial love that Christ has for the Church. It's deeply meaningful and not based in the world. It's based on the non-physical primarily, just like Jesus and His Church.

A man and a woman will come together to fulfill a Kingdom mission, an assignment ordained by God, and through that mission you can receive deep meaning together. It's His will, it always has been, and it's always going to be better than our limited imaginations.

Proverbs 16:9 KJV

*A man's heart deviseth his way: but the Lord directeth his steps.*

Many go into relationships to find peace, joy, happiness, and life purpose, but you can only find that in a direct relationship with Jesus.

That's why two people need to come together while independently yet simultaneously chasing nearness with God. A marriage is not a requirement for holiness in the Bible, but it can be seen as a once in a lifetime opportunity for each spouse to be molded more into the likeness of Jesus through their relationship that reflects more and more of the love that Jesus has for His Church each day. It's a beautiful model. That's why brides wear white wedding garments, the bridegroom is accepting a spotless bride (Ephesians 5:27).

Humanity across the board is mindlessly seeking satisfaction, satiation, fulfillment, peace, joy, purpose, contentment, and meaning… worthy ideals to aim for, but in all the wrong places. It's a

God sized hole in each person's heart and it's there because of the fall in the garden, the Adam nature. Considering it's a God-sized hole, it sounds like a job for Jesus. That void can never be filled by the fallen culture and the fallen world. Many have died trying.

Through going inside, into radical acceptance, surrender, repentance and not only that, forgiving yourself and others, you can allow God in to partner with you on your life so that you can find long-lasting joy.

You will be able to tell what comes from the Holy Spirit and just as importantly what doesn't come from the Holy Spirit based on its energetic signature. This concept applies to people as well as inanimate things.

Your ability to read the energetic signature, which is seen as a spiritual gift, the discerning of spirits, will enhance as you grow in the Holy Spirit. The new age community thinks they are reading a person or an item's energy through vibes, intuition, chakras, or auras.

The Holy Spirit reads energy just by telling or showing you the truth rather than having you guess if your "vibes" are accurate. When you receive a word of divine knowledge about someone or something through the gift of the Holy Spirit, you are accessing the guiding abilities of the Holy Spirit.

John 16:13 KJV

*Howbeit when he, the Spirit of truth, is come, he will guide you into all truth: for he shall not speak of himself; but whatsoever he shall hear, that shall he speak: and he will shew you things to come.*

Having a healthy discernment of people, places, and things that are meant for you, and just as importantly, not meant for you, will come through the Holy Spirit. Not intuition, vibes, psychic precognition, telepathy, clairvoyance, or any of those things.

The Holy Spirit is a vital component to the "operating system" God wishes for you to be depending on every day. As you get synced up with the Holy Spirit, He will become even more helpful to you.

The Holy Spirit will tell you with laser focus who you can trust, what people said about you behind your back, and He can even help you remember where your keys are or even assist you in recalling that memory or thought on the tip of your tongue.

This knowledge does not come from so-called psychic gifts like "channeling" either. It comes from the Holy Helper himself. The Holy Helper is a He because the triune God is all male, the fruit of life starts with a seed, and without seed there is no life.

Growing in the Holy Spirit means that He starts to flow through you and give your mind a Holy nature - a natural inclination towards righteousness instead of sinfulness. The process of sanctification allowing God to work on your mind, body, and soul so you become "good soil" for the Holy Spirit to dwell in.

Sanctification doesn't have to be a laborious life long process, it's a process of letting go of your old life to make room for the new "energetic operating system" to come in. The Father, Son, and Holy Spirit was always meant to be flowing through us. Some people let go of their old life and lifestyle quickly, others are more stubborn and like to hang on because it's how they learned to cope for decades.

If you desire to be filled with the Holy Spirit, then seek His presence through prayer and worship, and through seeking His presence, the power of God will flow into your life, over your life, and into your marriage, ministry, or business.

Since allowing fruit of the Holy Spirit to dwell inside comes with ease rather than strenuous effort, you will thereby be able to navigate challenging life decisions with greater ease.

You will be able to see people for their underlying energetic signature as the Holy Spirit takes over. You will be able to see people for who they really are. You will be able to see the energetic signature of food and what it really is. You will be able to see the energetic signature of alcohol and what it really is. You will be able to see the energetic signature of music and what it really is. You will be able to see the situations and offers that come your way for what they really are. You will be able to see books and media for what they really are.

You will discern whether people, resources, messages and media are coming to you in the name of the Lord, or not. The energetic signature reveals the energy behind the person or thing, especially with money. With the Holy Spirit dwelling inside you will be able to discern the intention, or reasoning behind it, and you will see if its coming from a place of love and gratitude, or if its coming from a darker place like manipulation and control. You will be able to see with laser focus if the thing being offered is with strings attached to continue a pattern of slavery or not.

The Bible promises we are no longer slaves. The slavery program is an energetic chord they wish to either install or maintain, but when you have the Holy Spirit inside you become awakened to the devil's subtle schemes.

Galatians 4:7 KJV

*Wherefore thou art no more a servant, but a son; and if a son, then an heir of God through Christ.*

Romans 8:15 KJV

*For ye have not received the spirit of bondage again to fear; but ye have received the Spirit of adoption, whereby we cry, Abba, Father.*

Being offered $5,000 from a source with dark intentions will bring no joy; instead, it exposes the plans of the enemy to ensnare, that's blood money and no joy comes with it. On the contrary, receiving $50 from a fellow brother or sister in Christ as a sincere act, a love offering, always fills with joy and gratitude from God and for God.

A Holy filter will come upon your mind, and again, it feels surprisingly natural like an ability we are supposed to have onboard, inside of us, working with us, and helping us to see the truth – the Holy Spirit is the Spirit of Truth (John 16:13).

As you start to make the correct daily decisions that lead you closer to God, your life will begin to heal and beautify; purpose will come in. Your mind, your thoughts, and your actions will begin to edify God rather than grieve Him. You will have more consistent joy.

Think back to Philippians 4:8, about focusing on what is good. God will gently come in and heal your life as you plug into Him as the source. Focus on Him, what honors Him and how to serve Him.

Joshua 24:15 KJV

*And if it seem evil unto you to serve the Lord, choose you this day whom ye will serve; whether the gods which your fathers served that were on the other side of the flood, or the gods of the Amorites, in whose land ye dwell: but as for me and my house, we will serve the Lord.*

God will not come into your life like a "bat out of hell." Getting saved by Jesus may bring a wrecking ball into your life, but that means your life was loaded with unholy structures, false altars, fake people, and activities that needed to be removed.

This next Scripture is an Old Testament story about King Josiah, he arrived a few hundred years after King David in the Holy lineage that eventually led to Jesus. He sought after God and God convicted him about the false alters, false gods, and idols in his country. He then enacted a purge of all the false religion, the false energetic structures.

2 Chronicles 34:3-7 KJV

*For in the eighth year of his reign, while he was yet young, he began to seek after the God of David his father: and in the twelfth year he began to purge Judah and Jerusalem from the high places, and the groves, and the carved images, and the molten images. And they brake down the altars of Baalim in his presence; and the images, that were on high above them, he cut down; and the groves, and the carved images, and the molten images, he brake in pieces, and made dust of them, and strowed it upon the graves of them that had sacrificed unto them.*

God wants you to let Him in so He is with you at all times, and in all situations. He just requires the false altars, the false religion and false idols to be demolished first. The false energetic signatures need to be forsaken and turned away from so you are not committing spiritual adultery.

Judges 6:12

*The Lord is with thee, thou mighty man of valour.*

---

He wants to be a partner with you on everything in your life so that it's transformed into its highest and best nature including your life purpose.

As more of God is inside of you, the enemy's footsteps will become more obvious.

Your awareness will become heightened around the enemy's signature, and the enemy doesn't have a large playbook either. He uses the same signature each time. There is nothing new under the sun.

Ecclesiastes 1:9 KJV

*And that which is done is that which shall be done: and there is no new thing under the sun.*

Here is what to look for in the world and in other people: if it's sinful, unrighteous, impure, deceitful, degenerate, prideful, rebellious, generating envy, generating strife, counterfeit, inauthentic, dangerous, harmful, laced with anger, and riddled with fear, doubt, and unbelief then it's from the enemy.

As you will recall from the prior Scripture John 10:10, the enemy wants to distract, steal, kill, and destroy anything that is good and pure, such as an preborn baby in the womb. The enemy wants to stop life in its tracks, create lies, and distort truth to sow division and confusion, and then sell a solution to create control.

God, however, wants to heal your life; and not only that, every area of your life. He wants to put you back in the driver's seat, paradoxically, through putting Him in the driver's seat. This works because He wrote your will before you were born. He wants you to attain your destiny He wrote, that's your legacy!

The wicked ways of the enemy will become more obvious with time as the Holy Spirit gently flows through you more each day. More of Him will flow through you each day as you choose Him, crucify your flesh, pray for wisdom, praise God, and stay focused on the face of Jesus. Focus on the face more than what He can do for you.

Your discernment and self-control abilities will grow. All of these things are within the promises of having the Lord by your side. He wants to give you a sound mind, a mind at peace, not at war.

2 Timothy 1:7 KJV

*For God hath not given us the spirit of fear; but of power, and of love, and of a sound mind.*

He wants you to have harmony in your mind so that you aren't distracted by fear, worry, poverty, anxiety, depression, cravings, uncertainties or your past. He wants to supply you a sound mind through the supernatural Holy fire process of transformation.

The Holy fire process equates to powerful prayer, praise, and worship with other Christians at church and outside of church.

You can certainly go it by yourself, and those prayers will always be heard, but there is something about including other Christians that moves the heart of God further. Your intentions synchronize, harmonize, and you obtain God's full attention faster, because you are together on the same "energetic operating system" and creating a unified and new sound (Psalm 33:3, Psalm 40:3, Psalm 96:1).

The same Holy Spirit is flowing inside of each authentic believer in Christ. The Holy Spirit is very consistent.

Matthew 18:20 KJV

*For where two or three are gathered together in my name, there am I in the midst of them.*

For example, I will be in a prayer room praising God and one person will walk up to me with a prophetic word from the Lord. Five minutes later a new person will walk up to me with a near identical prophetic word. That's all through the power of the Holy Spirit; the Spirit of God that God was sent to help His Church.

Your spiritual supernatural faculties of creativity, perception, prayer, truth, and imagination also improve with the Holy Spirit.

Not only does your perception and creativity get stronger, but God also starts to speak His creativity, His perception, His ideas, His blueprints, and His truth into your life. If you think your imagination is advanced, think about God's imagination abilities.

As your perception and creativity strengthen with God's influence in your life, it is essential to consider the source and purpose behind your imaginative pursuits. The key lives in discerning what glorifies God, as this discernment is crucial in navigating the spiritual realm. In contrast, individuals in the occult and new age often unknowingly compromise their soul's integrity through giving into the fallen desires of the heart in their quest for personal elevation, risking life and limb in the pursuit of worldly recognition and status. Just look to some of the most famous politicians and celebrities. They inherited the worldly riches and fame but their life is publicly a chaotic mess.

This is where your discernment is key. Many people in the occult and new age fall victim to selling their souls, whether they know it or not. They do this in pursuit of becoming greater than they were previously. They desire to be a somebody.

That's the gateway lie from the enemy, to build up someone's future state of self-importance and self-pride. What to look for is this: the enemy tells someone they aren't enough, and they need to become someone greater than themself. The new age movement gets an individual to imagine that future state of bliss when everything is perfect. God says comes as you are, you are enough.

The enemy says: you want to become a buddha, don't you? You want to become famous, don't you? You want all the riches of the world, don't you? You want to become powerful, don't you? You want to become important, don't you? You can clearly see the manipulation involved.

The Christian approach goes like this: realize you are a sinner because of original sin, the Adam nature, and you have also fallen short of the holiness of God many times, you are a regular nobody, and a somebody named Jesus saved your life and made you somebody through helping you see the truth that was always there: you have always been a child of God. Your soul and body were stitched together by Him. He granted you life. You have a wonderfully designed will for you to step into and claim. Any life you try to build outside of your God-given will will add unneeded chaos and stress in your life. The Holy Spirit is a treasure granted to you on what energetic signatures to follow or avoid. You are worthy of receiving His love and transferring that into everything you do. Come as you are, allow in the operation of God, and let go of your old life of sin.

Through the operation of God, not by human effort, commit to consistent study of the Bible and the cultivation of your relationship with Jesus. As you do so, you will naturally grow in significance without the need to seek recognition. Often, individuals strive to be someone they are not or seek to be more than themselves due to low self-esteem, lacking the understanding of their true identity as a child of God. A child of God does not need to beg or sell themself.

The Lord goes before them, the anointing ordained by God goes before them.

God values humble hearts that seek to bring glory to Him rather than themselves. When He observes this humility and desire for His glory, He will elevate and promote according to His divine plan.

People ignore the truth of God, the Bible, and step into things they think glorify their life, but they really are just guessing and walking around in a cloud of darkness, without a the light of the world, Jesus.

Walking in communion with the Holy Spirit is akin to journeying through the shadows of life with a divine light guiding your way. Just as navigating in complete darkness is challenging without illumination, the world we inhabit presents many obstacles and uncertainties that require the guiding light of the Holy Spirit to navigate effectively.

Colossians 1:13 KJV

*Who hath delivered us from the power of darkness, and hath translated us into the kingdom of his dear Son.*

If a Christian that has the Holy Spirit inside has a sense they are doing something that doesn't glorify God, they will feel convicted right away and sense that it's disobedient and therefore sinful.

It is prudent to consider the placement of your focus, always keeping in awareness the limitedness of our time on earth. While some Christians view staying informed on political news as a way to uphold God's principles, Ephesians 5:11-12 cautions against involvement in unproductive deeds of darkness and advocates for their exposure. This exposure should not lead to an unhealthy fixation on the negative aspects of society. The verse highlights the importance of avoiding an excessive preoccupation with dark and hidden actions, emphasizing the need to reprove and distance oneself from ungodly behaviors rather than dwelling on them. It is crucial to remember that attention fuels one's identity and energetic signature and therefore growth. Once again, it's Godly to confront evil but the key is to not glorify or become consumed by it.

Instead, believers are encouraged all throughout Scripture to focus on what is good, pure, and pleasing to God, promoting righteousness and virtue in their thoughts and actions (Philippians 4:8). By shifting focus away from darkness and towards the light of Christ, believers can uphold the values of God's kingdom and live in a manner that honors Him.

A large swath of political voices, even Christian voices, are caught up in the death energies of the world through us vs. them thinking.

Us vs. them thinking is manifesting in extreme ways on both sides of the political aisle. There already is a uniparty authored by satan.

The hope of America and all people groups around the world are not presidents, prime ministers, or popes. The only hope is Christ Jesus. The entire political system in an institution of satan. Christians must place their faith only in Jesus.

He is the same always and forever (Hebrews 13:8). Anything less than placing all of your faith and allegiance in Jesus is idolatry.

The wars of man create supposed winners and losers, but there are no winners when death and destruction tortures humanity. An eye for an eye leaves the whole world blind.

Matthew 5:9 KJV

*Blessed are the peacemakers: for they shall be called the children of God.*

The enemy wants individuals or entire nations lusting after pride, money, power, territory, vainglory and so on, in other words the spoils of war. The slogans and messaging behind political campaigns is always for purposes of social engineering and never the advancement of the common man. The middle class gets smaller every year, that trend is not going to change.

Instead surrender all to Jesus. Let go and let God be your protector and provider.

Psalm 37:25 KJV

*I have been young, and now am old; yet have I not seen the righteous forsaken, nor his seed begging bread.*

Increase your faith, increase your reliance on God, and take rest in Him. God ultimately pulls the levers on which countries rise, and which countries fall. Some countries deserve grace, and some countries deserve judgement (2 Chronicles 7:14). God can see the energetic signature of each country, people group, or person. He can always see who is heavy on righteousness and who is overweight on the world.

God promises, "I will transform you, heal you, deliver you, uplift you, and usher you into a supernatural life that stands in stark contrast to the fallen energies of death prevalent in the world."

Jesus promises a supernatural life just like He had. You can participate in the continuation of the same exact ministry of Jesus through offering salvation, healing, and deliverance, all through the blood, power, and authority of Jesus.

Just like Jesus when the anointing comes upon you, you can discover and cast demons out of believers. You have the ability to love just like Jesus does. You can heal sickness in others and even raise the dead. You have all the spiritual abilities He has. You are granted co-access through the acceptance of His blood.

When you heal others in the future, bring the dead back to life, or deliver someone from evil spirits, you are being an obedient conduit for God, Jesus, and the Holy Spirit to flow through. At the end of the day, He did it through you, He gets all the glory and the honor, the battle belongs to Him the glory belongs to Him and He couldn't have done it without you. We are anointed servants of God, no more, no less.

All Holy Spirit filled believers have various supernatural gifts, such as the discerning of spirits which is the capacity to perceive energetic signatures, akin to latent DNA being activated.

These supernatural abilities waiting for you may in fact be your dormant DNA being activated by the Holy Spirit. The scientific community has labeled a section of human DNA as "junk." We know DNA was ornately programmed by God, He didn't screw up and provide junk. We don't know what transformation our DNA goes through once we become a born again new creation, only God does, but reason would have it the extra abilities of a born again believer are also occurring at the DNA level.

Your DNA whether used or not, is never junk. It is divine programming and barely understood, even despite all of the advancements in technology and health care. In many ways health care has become hellish care, working against the design of DNA and the body's biological systems. That trend will continue.

The scientific community on earth tends to play God and mock God. This is out of their own inflated egos, pride, and self-importance. They think they are smarter than believing in the concept of a "sky daddy" so they just say, "God is dead." They are playing into the lies and the death energies of the world. They are making a liar out of God and God's Word, and that won't end well for them. They have a bone to pick with God, but the fact they hate God confirms He is there.

They fail to see that.

God is superior to us in all ways and is ultra-intelligent.

As you accept your supernatural lineage as a blood bought born again believer following Jesus, then you step into your new life with Jesus and the Holy Spirit dwelling within.

Acts 20:28 KJV

*Take heed therefore unto yourselves, and to all the flock, over the which the Holy Ghost hath made you overseers, to feed the church of God, which he hath purchased with his own blood.*

When allow yourself to be washed with the blood, you do indeed change "eidos" (/ee-dos/). This is the Greek word for form, shape, or appearance. God sees you as an entirely new being. Spiritually dead to spiritually reborn.

We most likely will never understand this at the level of biology because His operation is supernatural. Doctors can't explain when miracle healings occur. Some have realized God can do these things.

You do become a new creation with a brand-new life. In essence you have changed teams from team death to team life. People are kinder and more genuine on team life.

The most used term for the phenomenon of switching teams *all the way* from the kingdom of the world to the Kingdom of Jesus, is "born again." Another way of describing this is "truly saved." Only God knows who is truly saved. There are many Christians that think they are saved but are not truly saved in the eyes of God. 99% saved is still 100% lost. So many Christians found religion but missed Jesus.

If you are still reading and following along, it signifies a hopeful future in Christ – a genuine chance to be born again to study His character and His divine plan for your life.

His will is always way bigger and way more creative than anything our non born again minds could ever discover.

His ways and His thinking are much larger, vastly larger. God can see across all dimensions of time and space. He can see what you can't. Each human's largest risk in life is they don't know what they don't know. His design is assuredly better than the life plans you were planning on when you were on team death.

When you are reborn as a new creation, you start operating in the radiant energy of His light. This divine essence becomes your distinct signature, equipping you to positively impact the world instead of letting the world dictate your energy and influence. Just as Jesus dined with sinners without being influenced by them, He touched them with His presence and love. It is invigorating to begin making a positive impact on the world, rather than allowing the world to sway and corrupt you.

His warmth, faith, hope, and love will guide you on the straight and narrow path. The overflow of love and truth from Jesus spills over into others, leading you down a trajectory of loving God and loving others. A holy fear is generated because it gets good, really good while serving Jesus and the carnal mind tiptoes in and make you question when will glory slow down? You genuinely hope He continues to keeps keeping you in His anointing, and the good news is as long as you keep showing up, repenting for stumbles, praying, and praising He keeps proving and you do go from glory to glory.

Once truly saved you will begin to see His grace and His mercy decorated all over your life. You will even be able to have gratitude for the shortcomings of the past, because all of the events in your life have connected and led you to the most valuable gift in the world. Jesus. In a short amount of time you will see the fruit of being reborn.

He is a good God, and He wants to bless you as His son or His daughter. As His son or His daughter, you become heir to supernatural royalty. Through His grace you inherit the riches of the Kingdom of God, well before you even arrive in Heaven.

Ephesians 3:16 KJV

*That he would grant you, according to the riches of his glory, to be strengthened with might by his Spirit in the inner man.*

I wish I knew all of this sooner. Now, I know it's my duty to tell more souls, especially those lost in the new age fog about the Gospel of Jesus Christ and what He did. I just pray the Lord makes me the evangelist and teacher He has always wanted me to be, so that I hit the mark He intended for me in this lifetime.

God bless you for making it through these lessons on energetic signatures, understanding the differences between the two kingdoms, and what your identity in Christ can look like.

Thank God you found this book just in [His] time.

Literally, take a second and thank God.

God very much wanted you to find this book to give you the supernatural opportunity to switch teams, to leave team death and enter the lineup on team eternal life.

You are chosen.

You are blessed.

God bless you.

Numbers 6:24-26 KJV

*The Lord bless thee, and keep thee: The Lord make his face shine upon thee, and be gracious unto thee: The Lord lift up his countenance upon thee, and give thee peace.*

Abide and acknowledge Him in all your ways (Proverbs 3:6) and steward Him intentionally like the unquenchable fire He is, and He will uphold you through every trial and deflect every fiery dart away from you.

Ephesians 6:16 KJV

*Above all, taking the shield of faith, wherewith ye shall be able to quench all the fiery darts of the wicked.*

# Ch. 13 APPRECIATION OVER EXPECTATION

Appreciation is a two-way street.

God wants you to appreciate what He has done for you, He gave you His only Son to give you freedom and blot out your sins. He gave you a remarkable body and an advanced immune system. Your brain is the finest instrument the world has ever seen. Like DNA, its barely understood how the brain truly functions. The divine creator mapped Himself onto us.

The human mind is more advanced than any AI. God's image on a human will always reign supreme when the Holy Spirit in accepted and embraced. AI is man-made in the image of the beast, so it can never be holy or righteous, it will take humanity down a bad road. It will be used in the "beast system" to control and enslave.

God birthed your soul ages ago and the intelligence encoded into your soul gives you a meaningful will written by Jesus Himself. He knew you while you were being stitched together in the womb.

Psalm 139:13-16 KJV

*For thou hast possessed my reins: thou hast covered me in my mother's womb. I will praise thee; for I am fearfully and wonderfully made: marvellous are thy works; and that my soul knoweth right well. My substance was not hid from thee, when I was made in secret, and curiously wrought in the lowest parts of the earth. Thine eyes did see my substance, yet being unperfect; and in thy book all my members were written, which in continuance were fashioned, when as yet there was none of them.*

Isaiah 43:1 KJV

*But now thus saith the Lord that created thee, O Jacob, and he that formed thee, O Israel, Fear not: for I have redeemed thee, I have called thee by thy name; thou art mine.*

Jeremiah 1:5 KJV

*Before I formed thee in the belly I knew thee; and before thou camest forth out of the womb I sanctified thee, and I ordained thee a prophet unto the nations.*

Galatians 1:15-16 KJV

*But when it pleased God, who separated me from my mother's womb, and called me by his grace, To reveal his Son in me, that I might preach him among the heathen; immediately I conferred not with flesh and blood.*

The more appreciation you have for God's eternal involvement in your life, the more He will manifest Himself to you. You will start to perceive Him in various aspects of your life — peace, joy, signs, wonders, dreams, numbers, songs, and moments of synchronicity where you know it's Him quietly and joyfully stitching your life together. You will observe your life is beautifully coming together according to His plan and timing.

Praising and worshiping Him creates a continuous cycle of you loving on Him, and Him loving on you. He is extremely effective at loving us when we let Him in. He just wants our worship and full attention, in other words, your whole heart. For where your treasure is, there will your heart also be (Matthew 6:21).

Take a moment to remember all the ways God has shown up for you. Pause and reflect on that. Consider how He rescued you from life's destructive fires, most likely before you even sought Him out.

He sought you and kept you safe when you weren't even seeking Him, and now, if you have accepted the blood of the Lamb, He can transform you into something and someone that you could have never been on your own through your own self-will and self-striving (flesh).

Worship Him through Holy Spirit filled church services and on your own, or with other Spirit filled brothers and sisters, and He will show up every time. You will feel His presence in a way that's unique to you, but you will know its Him each time. He's a good Father so He always shows up for His children.

He kept you safe over the years so that you could remain alive and able to embrace the truth of Him. Personally, there have been several occasions where I should have died, or at the very least, been seriously injured, yet through His grace He supernaturally kept me alive and safe. This all occurred before I knew Jesus, I was still in His thoughts because He always saw the greater destiny of me in Christ.

If you are still reading, the same must be true for you. He truly desires for you to have a beautiful life that brings honor to Him and magnifies His Son.

If you wish to enter a feedback loop of love, a "love-loop" with God, simply set the intention to get into the relationship. God is so powerful that He can perceive not only your thoughts but also the underlying intentions and what you are really going through. If you fear Him, He will have mercy on you (Psalm 103). He will discern if you are aiming to establish an honest relationship with Him with fear and trembling (Philippians 2:12).

In relationship God will always love you with His cosmic agape love more than you can humanly love Him. Furthermore, the more you prioritize Him, the more He will prioritize you. If you have been seeking a shortcut to a fulfilling life, the bad news is that there is none. The good news is that a supernatural culture of miracles is what you have been searching for.

Many new age and law of attraction teachings offer promises of miracles in various forms. However, you can cease your search and turn to the truth of God, Jesus, and the Holy Spirit for the culture of miracles you have been seeking for.

We have a miracle working God.

Let the triune God of everything begin to love you, heal you, cleanse you, and deliver you from all evils from word curses spoken over you, negative soul ties, demons, hindering spirits, monitoring spirits, familiar spirits, witchcraft, yoga, polytheism, paganism, hexes, vexes, divination, tarot, psychics, mediums, mystics, sorcerers, astrologers, secret society generational curses, trauma, pain, sadness and other generational curses, also known as bloodline curses.

Those individuals that were trying to get you to "open" your third eye and chakras were not of God. You know which of those things you have been involved in, and you must consciously renounce each one of those you know you have previously been involved in. Stop and take a few minutes to do that. "I renounce any involvement with…"

Always remember, the biggest deliverance needed is from the Adam nature, the flesh, and it's baked into the human body. The Apostle Paul writes most about how to keep the flesh at bay in the book of Galatians. I highly suggest reading the whole book so you start be discipled by the Bible, and hopefully become a student of the Bible, so you have a fighting chance at staying on top of the battles that will come your way.

Romans 8:13 ASV

*For if ye live after the flesh, ye must die; but if by the Spirit ye put to death the deeds of the body, ye shall live.*

Galatians 5:16 KJV

*This I say then, Walk in the Spirit, and ye shall not fulfil the lust of the flesh.*

Galatians 5:24 KJV

*And they that are Christ's have crucified the flesh with the affections and lusts.*

Galatians 5:25 KJV

*If we live in the Spirit, let us also walk in the Spirit.*

Colossians 3:5 ASV

*Put to death therefore your members which are upon the earth: fornication, uncleanness, passion, evil desire, and covetousness, which is idolatry.*

1 John 2:16 KJV

*For all that is in the world, the lust of the flesh, and the lust of the eyes, and the pride of life, is not of the Father, but is of the world.*

Upon reflecting on 1 John 2:16 and considering the allure of worldly temptations, it becomes crucial to acknowledge that God desires our genuine gratitude and obedience, giving Him both will always be reciprocated by God many times over. When we yield to Him and surrender all and steadfastly acknowledge the omnipresence of the Holy Spirit, we demonstrate our appreciation for God. Actions that are out of order and perverted grieve Him.

This is not about adhering to a religious version of Christianity or conforming to rigid behavior modification standards. We are not dogs; we are humans designed for an intimate and direct relationship with our Creator, and you don't want to grieve Him and take Him for granted. Disobedience is sin.

Romans 5:19 KJV

*For as by one man's disobedience many were made sinners, so by the obedience of one shall many be made righteous.*

Romans 6:16 KJV

*Know ye not, that to whom ye yield yourselves servants to obey, his servants ye are to whom ye obey; whether of sin unto death, or of obedience unto righteousness.*

A born again believer who is captivated by God's love responds with holiness and righteousness as a natural outpouring, rather than viewing it as a burdensome duty. Such a believer walks in alignment with God's will because of a deep understanding of the knowledge of Christ, the truth of reality, and takes pleasure in living holy knowing it's a pleasing aroma to God. The identity of a saint of God stays consistent with the identity of a saint.

Ephesians 5:2 KJV

*And walk in love, as Christ also hath loved us, and hath given himself for us an offering and a sacrifice to God for a sweetsmelling savour.*

He longs for us to truly experience freedom through Christ and to take significant steps towards deliverance from any influences of the enemy. It saddens Him to witness His children being tormented and manipulated by the flesh, idols, demons, and evil people.

After pondering the previous verses and the power of Christ, it is evident that Jesus longs for you and His bride, the Church, to be pure, cleansed, and protected by His blood, otherwise He died in vain.

The authority of Jesus compels demons and flesh alike to flee at the sound of His name. When you pray and keep an attitude of gratitude, He will not allow you to remain in bondage. As you walk in fellowship with Jesus as your Savior, you are His precious possession (1 Peter 2:9

God desires to act on your behalf and to reveal His greatness to you.

He wants to show you that as you follow and commit to Him, stay committed to His Word and His gentle whispers, your life will start to expand into new airspace and improve. If you are patient and persistent in your study, prayer, and worship, He will certainly keep His manifest presence in your life.

He tends to the needs of His hungriest children right away. Those that wish to ignore Him and do their own thing, He tends to them last. He is characterized in the nine fruit of the Spirit (Galatians 5:22-23) as generous, but it's a two-way street, just as any real relationship is.

Sometimes, new believers in the faith become discouraged because they don't see immediate results. Jesus is not a genie; He is not there to bestow blessings at your every request. He is there for you to appreciate Him and what He accomplished on the cross for you. He opened the way to Heaven and provided a path for you to walk in a way that reflects His holy identity. He has forgiven your sins and healed the wounds of the past through His blood. Because of His work on the cross the Kingdom of God can dwell inside of you. The Kingdom of God is peace, joy and righteousness (Romans 14:17). The Hebrew word for peace is "shalom" (/sha-lohm/) which means nothing broken. In Israel, "shalom shalom" is a common phrase for greeting or farewell and it means "perfect peace."

Certain churches missing the presence of God and God appointed and anointed leadership may inadvertently (or intentionally) promote a distorted version of Jesus to cater to what they believe their audience desires to hear.

The false portrayal of Jesus is a hippie genie that doesn't call for true repentance. This massively distorts the Bible. This misrepresentation depicts Him as a chilled out hippie who merely grants wishes and affirms sinful desires, catering to human whims without regard for righteousness or holiness – a travesty. The "love is love" crowd says that Jesus accepts them as they are and they can live how they want. You mostly find this false version of Christ inside of the Methodist and the Unitarian Universalist denominations. They missed the death, burial, resurrection and the resulting supernatural blood.

They missed Jesus.

The distorted image of Jesus undermines His sacrificial love, His call to repentance, and His desire for us to walk in obedience and alignment with God's will.

Embracing the hyper grace version of Jesus means there is no gratitude for His sacrifice, no gratitude for the faith, and a perverted preference for the flesh and hedonism instead of the Spirit. The result is the lust of the eyes, the lust of the flesh, and the pride of life instead of genuine spiritual growth and transformation. "Affirming" churches do teach this false version of the faith and it deeply grieves the Holy Spirit. Judgement upon the ministries that seriously blaspheme the Holy Spirit belongs to the Lord. Judgement day is coming soon.

To access the real Jesus, start by seeking His face, entering into His courts with praise and thanks, adhering to the commands in the New Testament, receiving the Holy Spirit, praying and worshipping, giving money, food, or clothes to others when you see a need, and staying consistent and committed to bible study and spiritual growth. This produces lasting and authentic fruit.

This involves responsibly managing the gifts bestowed upon you, stewarding the eternal flame the faith, honoring the presence of the Holy Spirit within you (avoiding actions that grieve God), and diligently safeguarding your own salvation (Philippians 2:12). When you don't give Jesus lip service but actually live for Him like a committed spouse, you open the gateway to receiving more of God's will, blessings that align with His purpose for you, and healing and freedom in every aspect of your life.

Walking with boldness and conviction on the initial steps to Heaven it shows God your commitment, your faith, even when there may be no evidence of your commitment to Him yet.

Surrender, repentance and pleading the blood over your sins is a great place to start.

Humbly and sincerely seek God to reveal those sins and plead the blood over those sins. Remember, sin is sin. In God's eyes any and all sin creates separation. It's important to remember that everyone has sinned because nobody is perfect, and all fall short of His glory.

We are not equal to God and cannot become God or a god. Those who believe they are God or have attained godhood are ensnared in a deception and are likely under demonic oppression.

If you don't know what you need to renounce and repent of, then ask Jesus, wait on Him, and observe what bubbles up in your mind. Ask Him what He thinks of you. Ask Him what you need to know when it comes to your repentance. As Him what the charges are against you in the Courtroom of Heaven. Through your conscience (suneidésis) you will know what you need to seek reconciliation for. Once you have received the Holy Ghost and fire baptism then you will have an even more pronounced still small voice inside. The voice of the Holy Spirit inside is quickly offended by sin and will help you stay the course.

When the Holy Spirit fills you, you begin to take on some of the burdens that God shares. What pains Him in the world also starts to pain you. That's why one of the requirements for walking with Him in brokenness. You will start to empathize deeply with what grieves God. When you see others getting drunk for example, you will feel how the Spirit inside of you is grieved. You will see how when you or others lie or swear the Holy Spirit inside is grieved. The instant conviction you feel from sinning against yourself or others becomes a gift you are grateful for because it keeps you on track, a new GPS inside to keep you on the road home to Heaven.

God sees you are either living holy or you are not. It's a hardline that should not be crossed. You can't pick and choose what commands in the New Testament you will follow and which ones you won't. It's either all of the New Testament is believed and behaved or its not. It's Jesus' words, not man's words.

The concept of repentance encompasses more than mere remorse for past actions; it involves acknowledging one's wrongdoings, pleading the blood of Jesus, and expressing genuine sorrow for the harm that was caused to yourself or others. True repentance prompts a heartfelt desire to change course and realign with God's intended will for you. Drifting off course will always lead to unneeded pain and trials.

It is essential to prioritize addressing one's own sins before focusing on the faults of others, as attempting to point out the speck in another's eye while ignoring the log in one's own leads to hypocrisy and a double life. Many Christians today are unfortunately living a double standard, they bully others about their sin but never address their own.

Matthew 7:3-5 ASV

*And why beholdest thou the mote that is in thy brother's eye, but considerest not the beam that is in thine own eye? Or how wilt thou say to thy brother, Let me cast out the mote out of thine eye; and lo, the beam is in thine own eye? Thou hypocrite, cast out first the beam out of thine own eye; and then shalt thou see clearly to cast out the mote out of thy brother's eye.*

As you repent and seek His presence, you will start to see Him heal every area of your life. Stay patient, persistent, and consistent. He will reveal Himself in ways that will make it clear it is Him.

God thinks in grand ways, and He desires for you to think on a larger scale too. His imagination knows no bounds. He wants you to experience an extraordinary and supernatural life, not a small, impoverished existence restricted by sin and narrow thinking. The Gospels are synoptic, not myopic.

The term "synoptic" refers to the three Gospels of Matthew, Mark, and Luke in the Bible, which share a similar perspective and often parallel accounts of Jesus' life, teachings, and miracles. These Gospels provide a harmonious view of the life and ministry of Jesus Christ. After the Gospels of Jesus are the Epistles, also known as the Gospels of Paul. These are love letters to the Church that provide guidance, instruction, and wisdom for the Church to be sound believers to keep them focused on grace and not works. It must always be remembered Matthew, Mark, and Luke was Jesus ministering to the lost sheep of Israel so the Kingdom of Heaven would come down and meet the earth right there. They crucified Him, a perfect man, and opened the faith to all people groups. The Epistles are the main Gospels for the Church because Jesus gave the Gospels written by the Apostle Paul to the Church. Jesus said to the lost sheep who He was, the Messiah, and that's all they needed to believe. Paul says to the Gentiles what Jesus the Messiah did for the Gentiles to give them access God's Kingdom.

The term "myopic" refers to a narrow or short-sighted perspective, often focusing on a limited view lacking in foresight or a broader understanding. It can suggest a limited or restricted point of view that fails to consider the bigger picture. Rightly dividing the Gospel (2

Timothy 2:15) means seeing the whole picture, the context, and knowing who it was written to.

If you are a small thinker, it indicates that you are thinking from a place of fear. Fear is one of the primary weapons of the enemy. The Bible refers to fear as a spirit. The spirit of fear can hinder individuals in various ways. When fear arises and you sense yourself withdrawing and regressing, return to thankfulness for God through prayer and praise. This will help shift you back into a mindset of gratitude. Keep on the armor of God and take the negative thoughts captive so they are submitted to the sound mind of Christ (2 Timothy 1:7), which is one of the parts of your new holy operation system.

He longs for you to dwell in a state of peace, joy, and love regardless of external circumstances, all the while embodying boldness without fear and humility without pride.

Romans 12:12 ASV

*Rejoicing in hope; patient in tribulation; continuing stedfastly in prayer.*

This is known as the joy of the Lord, regardless of how the circumstances around you appear. Steadfast joy will flow into your relationships with others, your workspace, and the atmosphere of your home. Joy will beautify your environment and enhance the most important relationships in your life, including those with your spouse, children, and friends. Joy will infuse every aspect of your life with a touch of God, and each activity you engage in will begin to honor Him.

The Christian journey involves the transformation of your heart and mind so that Jesus reigns on the throne of your heart above all else.

When God is rightfully seated on the throne of your heart, things that are not of God no longer hold sway over your heart and mind. God deeply desires to be with you and within you at all times. He deserves to hold the highest place in your heart above anyone or anything else because He created you, loves you, and blesses you in more ways than you can imagine. He deserves this position, sitting "first chair" on your heart, so He can be the focal point of your appreciation, adoration, and love, more than anything or anyone else, including a spouse, children, parents, and friends.

He has kept you alive and breathing for this many years already. He didn't bring you this far to only bring you this far. He has done far more for you than you could ever imagine. He has kept you safe countless times, preserving your mind and body to give you the opportunity to seek Him.

This is a crucial point for former new agers, as many of them have a history with drugs, psychedelics, and other shamanic substances in their quest for self-knowledge and healing. The reality is that psychedelic drugs can have a chaotic impact on the body and mind, leading individuals into the realm of negative spirits and sometimes perilously close to death or to death.

More commonly accepted drugs have tragically resulted in the deaths of many individuals, particularly pharmaceuticals (spirit of pharmakeia) and alcohol.

"Pharmakeia" (/far-mah-kay-uh/) is a Greek word found in the New Testament that can encompass the practice of sorcery, witchcraft, or the use of drugs, potions, or magical arts.

In America alone, approximately 150,000 people die suddenly each year from overdosing on alcohol, which is about three times the number of deaths from motor vehicle crashes, and about 100,000 people die suddenly from pharmaceuticals. The enemy comes to steal, kill, and destroy (John 10:10).

Psychedelics, drugs, and alcohol can never provide true satisfaction or peace like Jesus does. I can attest from personal experience that only Jesus can truly satisfy. Any substitute for the God-sized void within us will always fall short. If you have experienced severe trauma or rejection at a young age, your God-sized void may feel even larger. The beauty of this is that when you do encounter God, His presence and love will impact and restore you even more.

If you have been fortunate (through generational blessing) to have a childhood free from significant trials and trauma, experiencing God's love will certainly bring about a sense of improvement and blessings in your life. However, the transformation and impact may not feel as monumental compared to someone who has endured a traumatic upbringing filled with deep depression, shame and chaos. The contrast between the before and after experiences can be more profound and remarkable for those who have faced significant challenges and hardships, in other words, all of a sudden, they have a Father that loves them into the depths of their soul without any strings attached, a very new experience of deep appreciation and healing, a type and depth of love that was not previously known before.

All God asks for is your allegiance and your heart. Once He sees your commitment, He will begin the work of healing your soul, mind, emotions, and body. He will give you a new life and a new calling to follow. He wants you to have dreams and goals, not to be aimless, distracted, or addicted. He desires your freedom and values you immensely.

The lower nature of humanity, the Adam nature, inclines towards self-centeredness, pride, and ego. It is often suggested that the acronym for ego can be interpreted as "easing God out." A bloated ego can foster feelings of isolation from both others and God. When the ego emphasizes division, it hinders our ability to thrive in today's interconnected world. To be impactful in our personal lives and in sharing the Gospel, it is crucial to foster a spirit of cooperation and collaboration with those around us. The ego often operates from outdated instincts, viewing others through a lens of threat rather than potential partnership.

God deserves the highest place in your life because He is the Creator of all things and has authority over your life. He gives you life and serves as the ultimate judge in your life, both now and in eternity. Remember, God is on your side, desiring to guide you on the right path (Proverbs 3:5-6).

When you know you need to repent, do your best to avoid falling into self-condemnation and shame. We all come from a background of being flawed sinners who have made many mistakes. God provides second chances through the blood of Jesus so He welcomes us home with open arms to be purified saints in our identity instead of sinners. His willingness to forgive always surpasses our ability to sin; we just need to persistently run back to Him when we know we did stray.

The storyline of loss to redemption in the Bible finds its ultimate expression in Jesus' sacrificial journey, where He not only offers redemption but also restores what was lost, including time but more importantly the innocence and purity that sin had sullied. Through His death and resurrection, Jesus provides a holy and transformative path from despair into hope, from brokenness and wholeness. His unparalleled sacrifice not only redeems but also brings color back into our life. This renews us and brings us back to child-like wonder and joy and a profound soul level restoration that transcends all loss that were incurred and ushers in a new beginning filled with grace and hope.

Joel 2:25 KJV

*And I will restore to you the years that the locust hath eaten, the cankerworm, and the caterpiller, and the palmerworm, my great army which I sent among you.*

We are blessed to have the opportunity to be born again and accept His love. Through Jesus, we transition from broken individuals heading towards death to a new and purposeful life filled with vitality. When you become a new creation in Christ, the river of life (Jeremiah 2:13) flows from your heart, impacting the world around you.

This new lease on life will impact every relationship and interaction, whether with a spouse, friends, acquaintances, or strangers. Jesus set a powerful example of patience and kindness towards everyone, irrespective of how they treated Him. The Jesus in you starts to shine through into everything else.

John 13:35 KJV

*By this shall all men know that ye are my disciples, if ye have love one to another.*

If Christians are not walking in love and appreciation towards others, then they are not walking with the fruit of the Spirit which means they have not been cultivating their relationship with the Holy Spirit.

When Jesus is living inside He shows love to anyone including the outcasts and the forgotten ones, the ones the rest of society has labeled as trash. Born again people do not look and act like the world, instead they are patient and self-controlled in affliction, this is through God's operation and not through an operation of the flesh.

Galatians 5:22-23 KJV

*But the fruit of the Spirit is love, joy, peace, long-suffering, gentleness, goodness, faith, meekness, temperance.*

With the nine aspects of God, we are "fully on." We are activated, and we always prioritize love in every interaction, just as Jesus did when He walked the earth among humanity 2,000 years ago, even in the face of torture and ridicule.

Luke 23:34 KJV

*Then said Jesus, Father, forgive them; for they know not what they do. And they parted his raiment, and cast lots.*

As Jesus was being tortured, He asked His Father in Heaven to forgive them because they did not truly understand who He was. The Jews tore apart His expensive tunic and held a luck of the draw contest for sections of His garment.

The more I appreciate what God has done for me, the more I sense His appreciation for me. This forms a sustainable, long-lasting, loving, and rejuvenating relationship. The "love-loop." He is the redeemer, the master restoration artist, the healer, the Savior, the defender, and the arbitrator of your redemption. It is your choice to fully claim your redemption.

Many people expect God to fulfill their needs, yet they overlook the importance of intentionally having prayer time and communion with Him. He will provide for your needs provided they align with His will for you; His plan holds far greater significance than your own. Trusting in His ways, which are higher and more intelligent, is the way because His plan is best suited to your purpose and skills.

In my experience, as you seek Him, you will go through layers of surrendering to Him and letting go of self-importance, haughtiness, arrogance, and pride. His ways are superior and His plans are meticulously well thought out.

Human-made plans can be tainted with pride and desires that do not align with His will, sometimes without our own awareness. He shields you from these plots, protects you and keeps you away from the pitfalls of sin. Remember, sin is missing the mark, and straying from His will is also considered sin. Any form of disobedience against His will for you is considered sin (James 4:17). He wants us growing.

Previously, you were depending on the fallen desires of the heart, which is a recipe for disappointment, that's why so many modern pop and country music songs are about lust, drunkenness and the consequential breakups that follow those things. Culture has made idols of just about everything including hookup and breakup culture.

As you deepen your relationship with the Lord, you will come to realize that prayer, worship and gratitude are key elements that pave the way forward and buffer you against chaos and worry. Entrusting Him to supply your needs, offer protection, bestow blessings, and guide you towards a purpose aligned with His will constitutes most aspects of your role as a child of the King.

A simple way to start praising Him is by expressing gratitude and recognizing that the Father sacrificed His only Son to redeem humanity from sinful, selfish, lustful, and destructive ways. This act demonstrates immense love from the Father and the Son, an overflow of Heavenly love. Jesus endured immense suffering on behalf of humanity so that you may be free, not to sin, but to live righteously and walk in God's will and God's Spirit.

His grace is not a license to sin. That's referred to as riding the line of "greasy grace." Some Christians do attempt to live that way and entertain a double life. Do you really think God is not omnipresent?

Just as He could heal others, He could have healed Himself on the cross. However, He chose not to because it was not God's will for Him. Being God in the flesh, it was part of God's well-thought-out plan to defeat the devil. If Jesus took short cuts and walked in disobedience He would have failed the mission, and nobody would have access to salvation and eternal life. But instead, He was fully obedient and took no half measures. This resulted in the greatest victory the world has ever seen.

Checkmate, devil. The checkmate occurred 2,000 years ago.

God graciously provided a worthy Lamb on behalf of humanity so that individuals could be liberated from sin, pain, and self-destruction. This demonstrates immense grace, appreciation, and mercy for each person.

God has always seen your true identity as a son or daughter of the King, rather than a sinful and destructive individual. Some may call you reckless, God sees you as relentless. We serve and appreciate a good God who desires the best for us and sees the best in us. He longs to have a relationship with us and offer guidance through Jesus, the wonderful counselor and the prince of peace. Jesus still speaks, all you need to do is quiet your mind, quiet your environment and listen.

You can cultivate the voice of Jesus through intentional prayer with Him. When you pray in a quiet place of your home, close the door behind you, ensure it is silent, so you aren't distracted, and inquire, "Jesus, what do you think of me?" Wait on the Lord, remaining calm and addressing Him by various names such as Father, Jesus, Holy Spirit, Jehovah Jireh, Jehovah Rapha, Abba, the God of Israel, the God of Abraham, Isaac and Jacob. Make it very clear your intention is to call upon the one and true Holy God of the Bible.

Jehovah Jireh signifies the Lord our provider, while Jehovah Rapha means the Lord our healer. Wait patiently on the Lord without rushing, keeping your mind silent and tranquil, finding the space between your thoughts. This is not meditation time, it's a time for intentional communication and communion with the Father, that's what prayer is.

Initiate the two-way communication with Jesus and persist in it. Over time, you will begin to discern between your thoughts and His voice. Remember, it is written, His sheep know His voice, and this has aligned with my personal experience (John 10:27). Through the power of the Holy Spirit you will become better at discerning your thoughts from His words. His words will begin to feel like a key going into a lock. The becomes your secret place where you communicate.

Receiving direct counsel from the King on any topic, down to planning each day, is a significant gift. It will change your life!

He will impart insights that you would not have known or seen without seeking Him. His ways are so much higher. He can see through space and time, so He can see things you can't.

293

He wants you to seek daily bread and receive daily fresh oil. While these are culinary terms, they hold spiritual significance. Receiving daily manna, or daily bread from God, entails studying the Word of God each day (Matthew 4:4). Pressing and yielding fresh oil signifies implementing the teachings of the Lord, engaging in biblical prayer, and offering your worship, which allows the daily bread of God's Word to be spiritually transformed into fresh oil. This pressing in process is akin to the refining fire that Jesus fans the flames of to turn you into His image, which is the best version of yourself.

The Bible talks about manna in the Old Testament as one of the most remarkable and longest occurring miracles in the Bible. God supernaturally provided for His Hebrew sheep for forty consecutive years while they were in the desert. This extraordinary display of provision stands as a testament to His unwavering faithfulness, this is found in the book of Lamentations, where His mercies are described as new every day.

Lamentations 3:22-23 KJV

*It is of the Lord's mercies that we are not consumed, because his compassions fail not. They are new every morning: great is thy faithfulness.*

Exodus 16:35 KJV

*And the children of Israel did eat manna forty years, until they came to a land inhabited; they did eat manna, until they came unto the borders of the land of Canaan.*

This forty year miracle, the longest consecutive miracle recorded in Scripture, in either the Old or New Testaments, underscores God's continuous care for His children.

The setting of the miracle starts at Horeb, also known as Mount Sinai, the place where the Israelites received the Ten Commandments and embarked on their journey from Egypt after their miraculous deliverance from slavery. Under the leadership of Moses, whom was appointed by God, the Israelites confronted Pharaoh, leading to a series of divine interventions that culminated in their liberation from Egyptian bondage. Despite Pharaoh's resistance, God's power was revealed through ten plagues, with the final plague sparing the Israelites through the blood of the Passover lamb, marking the beginning of their journey towards the Promised Land. The freedom from slavery and death through the blood of the Lamb was a shadow and a type of Jesus as the ultimate Passover Lamb.

Exodus 16:31 KJV

*And the house of Israel called the name thereof Manna: and it was like coriander seed, white; and the taste of it was like wafers made with honey.*

Numbers 11:8 KJV

*And the people went about, and gathered it, and ground it in mills, or beat it in a mortar, and baked it in pans, and made cakes of it: and the taste of it was as the taste of fresh oil.*

As you can see the bible demonstrates the transformative process of daily bread being ground, pressed and baked into new cakes tasting of fresh oil, a wonderful metaphor for taking the Word of God and applying it, living it, and allowing the Holy refinement process to take place and make fresh oil. Jesus is looking for a bride with oil in her lamp.

Focusing on appreciating he Lord underscores the significance of being grateful for the abundant blessings God has bestowed upon including His Word, His voice, His guidance, and various forms of provision and protection. It necessitates a shift in perspective from a mindset of entitlement to one of humility and thankfulness. Despite the Israelites' doubts and grumblings, God remained faithful by providing daily mercies and manna throughout their time in the desert. This serves as a reminder of the consequences of doubt and lack of trust in God, yet His kindness and patience towards His children is always there.

The Israelites journey from Horeb to Canaan should have taken eleven days (Deuteronomy 1:2) and instead was forty-years, a delay 1,327 times longer than anticipated, this shows the character of God, to be patient and graceful amidst the flock's extended time of confusion. The Israelites were so used to the slavery in Egypt that they questioned what was beyond the horizon of what they were familiar with, a life of slavery. They needed faith and obedience to move over the horizon and into the Promised Land. This is why it says it's impossible to please God without faith (Hebrews 11:6).

If the Israelites had been grateful for freedom and grateful for the daily provision provided by God, they would have operated from a place of faith rather than doubt. This shift could have led them to reach Israel sooner as faith, gratitude, and obedience pave the way for expedited progress on the journey to God's promises.

A grateful and appreciative heart towards God is a magnet for miracles and blessings. If you ever get to the point where your flow of fresh oil is stagnant then you must examine where you are complaining, being disobedient, ungrateful and desiring to go back to slavery. If you allow the Holy Spirit to recalibrate you back towards serving and appreciating God, you will get out of your own way and then Jesus can take the wheel and get you moving again.

Hebrews 7:25 KJV

*Wherefore he is able also to save them to the uttermost that come unto God by him, seeing he ever liveth to make intercession for them.*

Isaiah 9:6 KJV

*For unto us a child is born, unto us a son is given: and the government shall be upon his shoulder: and his name shall be called Wonderful, Counsellor, The mighty God, The everlasting Father, The Prince of Peace.*

"Jesus the Nazarene, the King of the Jews," is what was written on the cross that Jesus was tortured and crucified on. The cross, a cruel Roman tool of torture that Jesus was nailed to and hung on inflicted excruciating pain and resulted in a humiliating and public death, it required Jesus to push up on His nailed feet to delay suffocation.

During that era, the Jewish Pharisees, influenced by the teachings of the Oral Torah, the man-made Talmud, and the Babylon law known as the code of Hammurabi, adamantly rejected the belief that Jesus was the Messiah, they wanted to look back rather than look forward.

The actual Torah is the first five books of the Old Testament. The Pharisees, filled with man-made religion and hate in their hearts, collectively accused Him of blasphemy for claiming to be the Son of God (Psalm 2:6-7). The Roman soldiers inscribed the title on the cross as a form of mockery during His torment and crucifixion.

Unbeknownst to them, their mocking inscription was and is truth. Jesus is not only the King of the Jews but also of the Gentiles. His ministry of salvation, healing, and deliverance is open to all that can hear the call, regardless of their background or faith they come from. After the Jewish people rejected their Messiah, He became the sacrificial offering from the Father (John 3:16) to open the gates of Heaven for all people groups in the world with ears to hear.

Jesus was condemned for claiming to be the Messiah, a truth that ultimately led to His crucifixion. Jesus, aware of His impending death, willingly chose not to heal Himself or avoid the cross, as it was not the Father's will. Jesus surrendered to the Father will for Him right before His crucifixion and carrying the cross through Jerusalem (Matthew 26:39). His mission was to bring true freedom to humanity by becoming the ultimate sacrifice to defeat the devil once and for all. This exalted Jesus to the name above all names, a name that even causes demons to tremble, be bound up, and flee at the mere mention of His name to this present day.

The religious mindset and human understanding could not grasp the supernatural reality of the Messiah standing before them in the plainly human form of a man from Nazareth from the tribe of Judah. Many who claim to have faith but fail to acknowledge Jesus as Lord means their faith lies in a false belief system, rather than having the sole faith of following Jesus and accepting what He did.

The Word of God emphasizes the importance of one faith, not many faiths, the one and only faith that sets the captives free (Ephesians 4:4-6). This is part of satan's design with religious denominations. It has fooled Christians into thinking they have separate faiths.

Today, 97% of Jews still do not recognize Jesus as Lord. However, a minority within the Jewish faith, known as Messianic Jews, have embraced Jesus as the Messiah. The rest will realize who He was and is during the seven year tribulation.

Those who openly confess Jesus as Lord and have a deep recognition of what He did, discover new life, freedom, beauty, and a faithful companion. Jesus serves as a wonderful counselor and a provider of peace, offering solace and tranquility in the midst of life's storms, whether they be literal or metaphorical.

John 16:33 ASV

*These things I have spoken unto you, that in me ye may have peace. In the world ye have tribulation: but be of good cheer; I have overcome the world.*

2 Thessalonians 3:16 ASV

*Now the Lord of peace himself give you peace at all times in all ways. The Lord be with you all.*

Isaiah 26:3 ASV

*Thou wilt keep him in perfect peace, whose mind is stayed on thee: because he trusteth in thee.*

Nobody else has dominion over us like Jesus does. He is the only man that defeated the grave. Every other god is an idol. Buddha is still in the grave. Muhammed is still in the grave. Vishnu is still in the grave… but Jesus is alive!

Jesus and the Holy Spirit are freely with us until the end of the Grace Covenant, then the rapture of the Church, then tribulation for seven years for the Jews to awaken and then Jesus reigns from Jerusalem.

His blood that was shed on Calvary in Jerusalem was and is still alive today, offering salvation, healing, and deliverance to all who can accept Him with the simple and uncomplicated faith of a child.

Mark 10:15 KJV

*Verily I say unto you, Whosoever shall not receive the kingdom of God as a little child, he shall not enter therein.*

It does not matter what nationality you belong to, what skin color you have, or what social class you claim to belong to. What matters is to not overthink yourself out the acceptance of what Jesus did for you.

If you too hear the call you can accept Jesus into your heart to cover your life and sins. If you haven't already, I encourage you to declare that Jesus is Lord and to plead the blood over your life. Time is short.

He has been seeking you. He is the reason you picked up this book.

Come home and take rest in Him.

Romans 10:9-10 KJV

*That if thou shalt confess with thy mouth the Lord Jesus, and shalt believe in thine heart that God hath raised him from the dead, thou shalt be saved. For with the heart man believeth unto righteousness; and with the mouth confession is made unto salvation.*

If you would like to take the next step of embracing Jesus then say this prayer:

*Jesus, I accept that you were wounded and died on the cross and rose from the dead three days later for all of my debts, sins and iniquities. I deeply ask for your blood to cover and blot out all of my sins. I accept you as my Lord and Savior. My defender. My King. I give you all of my heart so that I may begin to heal and be delivered from all the evils in my life. Please place me Lord on the right course aligned with you and your perfect will for me. Jesus I need the Kingdom of God: your peace, your joy, and your righteousness to invade my mind and my heart. I lay down all pride. I surrender all. I no longer want chaos. I no longer want my plan. I want your plan. Holy Spirit come and live inside of me and baptize me with fire. Come and rest on me so I may turnover any and all burdens, whether known or unknown, to you for healing and transformation. I want to be a new creation in Christ that honors you. Father, I take rest in your everlasting goodness all the days of my life. I have faith that you have me in your embrace and that you are hearing my cries for a new lease on life. I want a sound mind and a beautiful life that honors you. Thank you for your work on the cross. Thank you for the blood. Thank you for keeping me alive to accept the salvation of my soul. Fortify my faith. Please permanently live inside me Holy Spirit and keep me away from any negativity or temptation the enemy may manufacture against me. I want only you as my Lord and Savior Jesus. I cast down every idol and false god I ever placed faith in. I never want to grieve you Holy Spirit. I place you Jesus on the throne of my heart. I trust you are the same always and forever. Captivate my heart. Do not allow me to backslide and go back into the sinful ways of the flesh. Give me the greatest measure of the Holy Spirit I can handle, so I am buffered away from sin. I trust you are the living Holy God of Israel and you provided me the Holy Bible so that I can turn my life around, yes even a wretch like me, I want my new identity in Christ as a son [or daughter] of the King to rewrite my mind. I am washed new into a saint of God through the blood of the Lamb. Direct me in all my ways, pointing me only towards the Son, so I never stumble, and faithfully run the race to the end of the age with persistency and perseverance. Thank you for receiving me back to you, Father. Fan the flames and form me into your image through the blood of Jesus Christ! In Jesus Holy name, Amen!*

God raised Jesus from the dead through the resurrection power of the Holy Spirit therefore He can redeem your life through the same resurrection power to greatness, a greatness you would have never known without Him.

God needs great men and great women here on earth. Now that you have read that prayer and surrendered all to Him, you are now on the path to becoming a great man or great woman in the eyes of God.

If you haven't accepted Jesus because you say to yourself you don't need restoration, your life is alright, pretty comfy, and "you're good," then just know this, you don't know what you don't know about the other side and that's a human's biggest risk. His ways are much greater. He graciously gave us His Spirit and the Bible to guide us home.

You have not seen the ways that Jesus can work in your life yet. You don't know God's will for you yet. Discovering it is not an activity based in striving either. It's a process of surrender, repentance and acceptance. I have faith that those who have ears to hear have heard the call to surrender to Jesus.

If you really still aren't sure about Jesus, give him a trial run, and surrender all, say the salvation prayer, and see what your next thirty days is like. You have nothing to lose and everything to gain. Eternity is a long time.

As mentioned, multiple times, all Jesus wants is to be on the throne of your heart above anything and anyone else. He is the only one worthy of the throne on your your heart. When the Holy Spirit in flowing inside of you and Jesus is on the throne of your heart, and you pray and seek His will, everything about your life will be more clear.

We have a very kind Father, and clarity is kindness.

I have found that along my journey my soul was fragmented and my life was chaotic until Jesus stepped in and intervened.

I accepted Jesus in 2020 and He started to heal me and transform my life right away. Even though it took me a year to enter a Holy Spirit filled church He was already inside at work gently cutting cords, gently healing, guiding my mind, guiding my decisions away from sin, and giving me an additional peace I never experienced before. About six months after being born again He brought me out of a sinful living situation and away from sinful friends. I was part of His Church through accepting salvation before I ever entered a local church, so don't confuse allow Him to purchase you with building attendance.

God stands for order not for chaos. God's goal is to bring order into your life and to remove the chaos, the toxic habits, the toxic people, the toxic food and drink, and the sexual immorality. Only He can clean you and your life up. Your own personal willpower never will be able to accomplish a job meant for Jesus. That's how kind He is to His children, that's the grace and glory of the operation of God.

1 Corinthians 6:9-10 KJV

*Do you not know that the unrighteous will not inherit the kingdom of God? Do not be deceived. Neither fornicators, nor idolaters, nor adulterers, nor homosexuals, nor sodomites, nor thieves, nor covetous, nor drunkards, nor revilers, nor extortioners will inherit the kingdom of God.*

---

1 Corinthians 6:18 KJV

*Flee fornication. Every sin that a man doeth is without the body; but he that committeth fornication sinneth against his own body.*

All the addictions that were destroying you, He will remove. He can do it in an instant rather than through hours of pagan practices, chakra chants, lengthy meditation sessions, or secular psychotherapy.

The peace I experience from a few minutes of praise or prayer surpasses any two-hour meditation sit while working hard to focus on "nothing."

He desires for you to return home and find rest in Him.

He wants all His children in the family of God to be aligned in the same direction, pointing towards Him, and He is perfect at achieving His desires. He's God after all.

This reorientation of souls back toward Him is not from a place of God having selfish ambition. He can't sin. He's perfect and can't operate in witchcraft and manipulation. He simply knows when you are focused and allegiant to Him as a loving Father in Heaven its for our benefit. Soon you will say to yourself, "It's so much better this way." God so loved the world He gave us Jesus to reconcile us back to Himself (John 3:16). It's a beautiful story of redemption because there is no greater story.

You can assess the improvements that have occurred in your life after salvation by viewing the fruits that are produced across time. If you take the time to personally audit what your life was like before and after a few months of walking with Jesus, and you see apparent improvements, apparent fruit.

The fruit is proof that Jesus is indeed who He said He was before being hung on the cross and what He did for you through His shed blood was real and is still in operation. Hindsight is 20/20 and with looking back you will see His relationship has always been for you.

Every time a lost soul turns back to God through His Son Jesus, it is like God has reclaimed one of His children from the dead. This illustrates the immense significance to God – Heaven rejoices when another individual discovers the truth of Jesus, repents, and begins to experience true freedom through Christ (Luke 15:7).

Psalm 46 KJV

*God is our refuge and strength, a very present help in trouble. Therefore will not we fear, though the earth be removed, and though the mountains be carried into the midst of the sea; Though the waters thereof roar and be troubled, though the mountains shake with the swelling thereof. Selah. There is a river, the streams whereof shall make glad the city of God, the holy place of the tabernacles of the most High. God is in the midst of her; she shall not be moved: God shall help her, and that right early. The heathen raged, the kingdoms were moved: he uttered his voice, the earth melted. The Lord of hosts is with us; the God of Jacob is our refuge. Selah. Come, behold the works of the Lord, what desolations he hath made in the earth. He maketh wars to cease unto the end of the earth; he breaketh the bow, and cutteth the spear in sunder; he burneth the chariot in the fire. Be still, and know that I am God: I will be exalted among the heathen, I will be exalted in the earth. The Lord of hosts is with us; the God of Jacob is our refuge. Selah.*

Selah is believed to be a musical notation, possibly indicating a pause or a moment of reflection in the Psalm.

Pause and reflect on everything you have learned about Jesus so far.

# Ch. 15 THE WORD OF GOD

Hebrews 4:12 KJV

*For the Word of God is quick, and powerful, and sharper than any twoedged sword, piercing even to the dividing asunder of soul and spirit, and of the joints and marrow, and is a discerner of the thoughts and intents of the heart.*

"Okay so what's up with the Bible? It doesn't make sense. It's huge." Your main requirement to understand the Bible is to have the Holy Spirit inside. Now that you have accepted the blood and work of Jesus into your heart and soul you can now be filled with the Holy Spirit so you start to understand the Bible and have the Holy tour guide inside.

*Lord, baptize me with your Holy Spirit and fire. Ignite my spirit with your divine presence and power. Fill me up all the way with your anointing to walk in your will, understand the Bible, and to spread your radiant love to those around me. In Jesus name, Amen.*

The Word of God originates from God, was divinely inspired by the Holy Spirit, and was passed down from Heaven through divine providence to forty specific writers, offering us guidance on living joyful, holy, healthy lives free from sin and aligned with God's will. It is sixty-six books, 1,189 chapters, and was finalized 1,500 years after the resurrection of Christ. We are very fortunate to have it! The writers do not contradict themselves and they largely never knew each other and was written in three languages. It's a miracle of God it all connects and confirms itself. The term for teaching from the Bible in a way where it all connects to itself is known as hermeneutics. The Greek word for this is "hermēneia" (/her-may-ni-ah/). It means interpreting the books of the Bible to understand their meaning and context to see how it all connects. It involves principles and methods for accurate understanding without private interpretation, taking into consideration factors like language, culture, and historical context and most importantly who was the book written to. "Was this book written the lost sheep of Israel or the Gentile Church?" Each book after Jesus shed His blood on the cross (Matthew 27) is written to the Church that was purchased with His blood (Acts 20:28).

The Bible is a manual for living a holy and righteous life that pleases God, it provides clarity on all of God's intentions for humanity so you can see your place in the story – we are fast approaching the end of the Church Age and the seven year wedding feast in Heaven.

The Bible features approximately 63,779 cross-references, showcasing the interconnectedness and internal harmony and integrity of its content. These cross-references, compiled by theologians display the relationship between different verses, themes, and narratives. The cross-references prove it's a unified and connected story by providing parallels between themes, words, events, and individuals. There are visual representations online of these cross references, when you see all the connections visually it appears as a rainbow the symbol of God's promise to His people. Despite being written by a diverse body authors across 3,000 years in total it connects perfectly and maintains a remarkable consistency and unity, this confluence of evidence further enhances its credibility. It's the only book I could read every single day and never stop learning about the goodness of God. No other book is this alive or supernatural.

Both the Old and New Testaments hold significance; however, we are in the grace dispensation, the Church Age, meaning we are in the grace period where Jewish people and all other people groups of the world can come to know Jesus and turn their lives to Him before the end of the age. You can personally track how many people groups have been introduced to the Gospel at https://www.joshuaproject.net.

The Old Testament should certainly be studied for the wisdom, to understand the history behind Christianity and to learn more about the character of God, but the practices of the Jewish law were written to the Jewish people. That was previous dispensation where God was dealing with humanity differently than the New Testament. The primary role of the Jewish law was to show humanity sin was a big problem in God's eyes. That's why Moses divinely wrote the Ten Commandments. The people needed to grasp that their lack of morality was causing offense to God. The Jewish law was something to be followed through willpower and flesh instead of grace.

In the current dispensation of grace, God progressed beyond the foundation laid by the Jewish law and provided a much better form of access to holiness and right standing with God through Jesus' blood. The law was to be practiced through sheer willpower, so it was a brutal master, and grace on the other hand is accomplished through faith in His blood and allowing in His peace, His joy, His righteousness and the gift of the Holy Spirit to rest on you.

The New Testament revealed to everyone that Jesus' blood is the ultimate solution to sin. Sins are charges placed against a soul. The Holy Spirit serves as a helper to convict believers of those sins, to show where Jesus needs to set believers free through the blood, this moved believers in Jesus beyond being under the law of condemnation and death through the Ten Commandments and 613 laws in total. These laws of morality are written onto a believer's heart rather than on a stone tablet (2 Corinthians 3:3).

The Word of God chronicles the narrative of humanity before, during, and after Jesus' resurrection, highlighting that Jesus was not a backup plan but always the primary plan to conquer death, defeat the devil, and eradicate sin, all through His holy blood. Love covers a multitude of sins (1 Peter 4:8) and there is no higher love than God Himself laying His life down for you. His love covers a multitude of sins.

John 15:13 KJV

*Greater love hath no man than this, that a man lay down his life for his friends.*

Building on the profound message conveyed in John 15:13, the New Testament emphasizes the significance of grace and the realization of over three hundred Old Testament prophecies that point to Jesus as the Messiah. His life, death, and resurrection fulfill these prophecies, showcasing the ultimate demonstration of sacrificial love on the cross and validating the fulfillment of the former Jewish law.

While the Old Testament provides the foundation and context for understanding who God is and His consistency in supporting His people, especially when the odds are stacked against them, the New Testament reveals the fullness of God's grace and desire for complete communion with humankind through Jesus' sacrifice on the cross. The veil was torn with Jesus and we were given direct access to the throne room and God in Heaven. The veil torn by Jesus was symbolic and indeed literal. The cloth veil of the tabernacle, the draping that was creating separation between the Ark of the Covenant and the rest of the world was supernaturally torn immediately at Jesus' final breath.

Matthew 27:51 KJV

*And, behold, the veil of the temple was rent in twain from the top to the bottom; and the earth did quake, and the rocks rent.*

The Old Covenant was initiated through Abraham, who is still considered the father of the nation of Israel and the Jewish faith. This covenant was then passed down through Isaac and Jacob, who were Abraham's descendants. Then Moses played a significant role in delivering the Israelites from slavery in Egypt, bringing them back to the Promised Land, Israel, and received the Jewish law at Mount Sinai. Later on, David and Solomon and many other kings ruled as king of Israel. The major and minor prophets came in Israel's history to call the people back to faithfulness and obedience to God – this same exact bloodline with these major fathers of the faith continued through Jesus and the spiritual focus transformed from Mount Sinai the mountain of the Jewish law to a new spiritual focus locate on Mount Zion, the mountain of grace, signifying a New Covenant through Jesus' blood and a spiritual kingdom where believers from all people groups can find salvation and redemption through Jesus' sacrificial death and resurrection.

Isaiah 61:3 KJV

*To appoint unto them that mourn in Zion, to give unto them beauty for ashes, the oil of joy for mourning, the garment of praise for the spirit of heaviness; that they might be called trees of righteousness, the planting of the Lord, that he might be glorified.*

Hebrews 12:22 KJV

*But ye are come unto mount Sion, and unto the city of the living God, the heavenly Jerusalem, and to an innumerable company of angels.*

Both the Old and New Testaments are integral parts of God's plans for humanity, with the New Testament underscoring the finalization of God's plan to defeat death and hell and bring people into full reconciliation with Him. That is evident in Jesus' words while on the cross, moments before His final breath, He declared, "it is finished."

Colossians 2:11 KJV

*In whom also ye are circumcised with the circumcision made without hands, in putting off the body of the sins of the flesh by the circumcision of Christ.*

The first Covenant between God and Jewish men was a blood Covenant through literal circumcision. The second Covenant is between God and Jesus it's a purely spiritual circumcision through the blood of Jesus for a believer in Christ to accept. Life covenants are done through blood because in the blood there is life. Life can't exist without blood. Circumcision whether literal or spiritual is symbolic the cutting away of the old man, the old form.

John 19:30 ASV

*When Jesus therefore had received the vinegar, he said, It is finished: and he bowed his head, and gave up his spirit.*

To mark the moment Jesus declared "it is finished" the Greek term the Bible uses is "tetelestai" (/teh-TEL-es-tie/). The word carries profound significance beyond a declaration of completion. This term, rooted in the world of commerce and accounting, conveys the truth of a debt fully paid and a task entirely accomplished. In the ultimate act of love and redemption on the rugged cross, Jesus fulfilled the Jewish law, defeated satan, and finalized the divine plan for salvation and eternal life in Heaven, thereby settling the sin debt once and for all. The resonance of "tetelestai" echoes throughout eternity by proclaiming the fact that Jesus ensured the victory and established the fullness of God's grace and mercy for humankind, forever.

Greek was selected for the New Testament to engage a wider audience within the diverse cultural landscape of the Roman Empire, where Greek was the dominant language. In ancient Hebrew, a language that predates Jesus, symbols resembling hieroglyphics were used. The symbol representing mark, covenant, monument, and sign is the cross. This symbol was chosen approximately 1,000 years before Christ's crucifixion on a cross.

A distinct shift occurs between the Old and New Testaments, the Old and New Covenants, occurs when Jesus' blood sheds down the cross at Calvary. Everything was unlocked through His divine blood.

Jesus still stands as the most influential figure history has ever seen or will see. His supernatural blood, name, and presence continue to cover the world today. The antichrist will put an all-out stop to this during the short window of the seven year tribulation. This is why the carnal Christians that did not make the rapture will have to become tribulation saints. Not only will the Bible be banned. Professing Jesus is Lord will be banned. His name will be banned. So now is a great time to accept His blood and His name.

God is a triune being—Father, Son, and Holy Spirit—each serving a unique role in the divine plan. He is three in one and one in three, and that's part of God's mystery.

All spirits apart from the triune God are demonic and worldly, contrasting with the all-encompassing nature of the triune God who fulfills our ever need. God's perfect creation reflects His infinite wisdom and power, deserving our highest reverence.

Our role is to accept God with childlike faith, trusting in His divine wisdom and sovereignty. Surrendering to it in humility.

Matthew 18:2-4 KJV

*And Jesus called a little child unto him, and set him in the midst of
them, And said, Verily I say unto you, Except ye be converted, and
become as little children, ye shall not enter into the kingdom of
heaven. Whosoever therefore shall humble himself as this little child,
the same is greatest in the kingdom of heaven.*

To summarize the New Testament: Jesus revealed Himself as the
Messiah, the chosen one, to the Jewish people, offering them the
chance to bring in the Kingdom of Heaven through Him. Through
their rejection of their Messiah. The New Covenant began with Jesus
shedding His blood on the cross, ushering in a new era of grace, the
Church Age. Jesus sent the Holy Spirit and fire, at Pentecost, a crucial
moment, signified to the whole world a broader recognition of what
He did and He sent His Holy Spirit. Jesus' perfect fulfillment of His
mission opened the way for all with ears to hear access to the
Kingdom of God which is peace, joy, and righteousness. The promise
of the Kingdom of Heaven will be realized after the seven-year
tribulation, when Jesus literally reigns on earth as King and there is
peace.

The Old Testament offers a rich tapestry of kings, encompassing both
the righteous and the wicked, some transitioning from righteousness
to evil, and others from evil to righteousness. Among these figures,
King David stands out as the shining example, as he experienced a
shift from righteousness to sin through his infamous affair with
Bathsheba and the subsequent murder of Uriah. David turned the
corner and marked his life by a remarkable journey back to God. He
ultimately returned to a state of righteousness through genuine
repentance and Godly sorrow.

David's journey stands out as the most prominent example in the Bible of a cycle involving righteousness, a significant fall into sin, and eventual redemption and repentance. While there are other kings in the Bible who displayed a mix of righteous and unrighteous actions during their rule, their narratives do not parallel David's journey as closely of redemption to loss back to redemption.

Paul, author of fourteen New Testament books, underwent a transformation arc similar to David's journey. He went from a zealous Pharisee persecuting Christians, and then he encountered Jesus Himself on the road to Damascus on Strait Street. God set him straight in an instant and he was completely undone, leading to a profound and immediate change of heart. Just as David went from sin to righteousness, Paul transitioned from an adversary of Jesus to a faithful and fruitful servant, showcasing God's graceful and transformative power to turn enemies into allies for His Kingdom.

The Old Testament also introduces God's major and minor prophets who paved the way for the arrival of Jesus. A prophet is someone who conveys God's declarations. These prophets did not seek their own glory but aimed to glorify God.

The Hebrew word for prophet is "nebi" (/nay-bee/) meaning "to bubble forth" like a fountain. The biblical prophets spoke the truth that originated directly from God. They were uniquely anointed by God to be His mouthpiece, called to speak authoritatively on His behalf, and make known His will, holiness, and instruction to reject idolatry and sin. They were completely accurate and trusted, unlike the countless social media prophets today that are not real prophets, there are a few prophetic voices out there today that are accurate, but they are extremely few and far between, and they usually don't have large followings.

In the account of Abraham, God tests Abraham's faith by instructing him to sacrifice his only son, Isaac. Abraham obediently prepares to carry out the sacrifice, but God intervenes at the last moment, providing a ram as a substitute for Isaac, showing the Lord provides, provided His people are obedient.

God required Abraham's obedience, regardless of how seemingly irrational the command. This event foreshadowed and prepared the way for God's ultimate sacrifice of His only Son, Jesus, on the cross. It allowed God to understand the concept of sacrificing His own son through Abraham, providing insight into the significance and implications of such an act. This event may have served as a preparatory step for God to plan and strategize the sacrificial act that would later be fulfilled through Jesus.

During His earthly ministry, Jesus had one opportunity to fulfill His mission correctly.
Since Jesus walked in God's will for Him perfectly, Jesus executed God's instructions perfectly and always stayed ten steps ahead of satan. The adversary thought he successfully and swiftly killed the Messiah, but in reality, Jesus' death opened Christianity to the world.

After Abraham obeyed God, the people of Israel were blessed by God for generations. If Abraham had returned to Egypt, as his pagan wife Sarah wanted, then he would not have embarked on the journey with Isaac to Mount Moriah in present day Jerusalem. Human history would have unfolded entirely differently without the obedience of these men.

The faith of Abraham paved the way for the faith of Jesus.

The book of Matthew explains the genealogy of Jesus.

Matthew 1:16-21 KJV

*And Jacob begat Joseph the husband of Mary, of whom was born Jesus, who is called Christ. So all the generations from Abraham to David are fourteen generations; and from David until the carrying away into Babylon are fourteen generations; and from the carrying away into Babylon unto Christ are fourteen generations. Now the birth of Jesus Christ was on this wise: When as his mother Mary was espoused to Joseph, before they came together, she was found with child of the Holy Ghost. Then Joseph her husband, being a just man, and not willing to make her a publick example, was minded to put her away privily. But while he thought on these things, behold, the angel of the Lord appeared unto him in a dream, saying, Joseph, thou son of David, fear not to take unto thee Mary thy wife: for that which is conceived in her is of the Holy Ghost. And she shall bring forth a son, and thou shalt call his name JESUS: for he shall save his people from their sins.*

Jesus grew up with Mary and Joseph as His parents and He was water baptized by John the baptizer, not the same person and writer of the book of John. The latter John was one of the original twelve disciples, he was supernaturally kept alive after being thrown into boiling oil and went on to write the book of Revelation after being brought into Heaven.

John 3:16-17 KJV

*For God so loved the world, that he gave his only begotten Son, that whosoever believeth in him should not perish, but have everlasting life. For God sent not his Son into the world to condemn the world; but that the world through him might be saved.*

*And lo a voice from heaven, saying, This is my beloved Son, in whom I am well pleased.*

After Jesus was baptized by John the Baptist in the Jordan River, the Holy Spirit descended on Him in the form of a dove, and He heard the voice of God the Father affirming Him as His Son (Matthew 3:16-17).

Following His baptism, Jesus was led by the Holy Spirit into the wilderness, where He fasted for forty days and nights and was tempted by the devil (Matthew 4:1-10). This testing in the wilderness marked the beginning of Jesus' public ministry and demonstrated His victory over temptation and the power of the enemy.

Matthew 4:5-10 KJV

*Then the devil taketh him up into the holy city, and setteth him on a pinnacle of the temple, And saith unto him, If thou be the Son of God, cast thyself down: for it is written, He shall give his angels charge concerning thee: and in their hands they shall bear thee up, lest at any time thou dash thy foot against a stone. Jesus said unto him, It is written again, Thou shalt not tempt the Lord thy God. Again, the devil taketh him up into an exceeding high mountain, and sheweth him all the kingdoms of the world, and the glory of them; And saith unto him, All these things will I give thee, if thou wilt fall down and worship me. Then saith Jesus unto him, Get thee hence, Satan: for it is written, Thou shalt worship the Lord thy God, and him only shalt thou serve.*

The key point from this Scripture is that Jesus was a real man; He was tempted, but His faith and identity as the Son of God was much stronger than any of the enemy's temptations and offers. Remember, Jesus is Adam 2.0, the last Adam (1 Corinthians 15:45). He wasn't going to fall for the devil's lies this time around, and He didn't.

The enemy questioned the identity of Jesus. He said, "If you are the Son of God." One of the main ways the enemy will attack the innocent is by making them question their identity. Why do you think there is such a large identity crisis among young people today?

The enemy targets the young and their identities. That's why young people in the world need some of the most prayers. The enemy goes after the young because the sooner you gain someone's allegiance, the longer you have their hearts and minds. This is also why it is even more crucial to train young people on where their identity lives – in Jesus and not the world.

If someone's identity is corrupted, they will miss out on Jesus and miss out on the identity God wants for them as a child of God. When someone has a corrupted identity, first they are ineffective for the Gospel, and second they are weak and vulnerable to demonic attacks and attachments.

A strong identity as a child of God is the best defense against cultural programming that aims to confuse and corrupt. The identity of a child of God, a son or daughter of the King, is for believers in Christ at any age as their best defense. They know who they are whose they are.

A child of God studies Jesus, the Bible, worships God, prays, and aims to embody more of the qualities of Jesus each day. Jesus had no problem handling the spiritual attacks from the enemy because He knew who He was and what He was all about. He wasn't going to let the enemy chip away at His identity and who He was and still is.

God was pleased when Jesus resisted the identity attack from the evil one, so He sent angels to minister to Him (Matthew 4:11).

The core message of Jesus to the lost sheep of Israel is found in Matthew 5.

This sermon is called the Sermon on the Mount. Please note this was directed toward the lost sheep of Israel, the Jewish people only. We can study the principles and teachings being shared but this is not a sermon to the Gentiles. He was offering the Kingdom of Heaven right then and there. His is saying all these things come to pass in the Kingdom of Heaven, but it was postponed because the Savior was rejected.

Matthew 5:1-14 KJV

*And seeing the multitudes, he went up into a mountain: and when he was set, his disciples came unto him: And he opened his mouth, and taught them, saying, Blessed are the poor in spirit: for theirs is the kingdom of heaven. Blessed are they that mourn: for they shall be comforted. Blessed are the meek: for they shall inherit the earth. Blessed are they which do hunger and thirst after righteousness: for they shall be filled. Blessed are the merciful: for they shall obtain mercy. Blessed are the pure in heart: for they shall see God. Blessed are the peacemakers: for they shall be called the children of God. Blessed are they which are persecuted for righteousness' sake: for theirs is the kingdom of heaven. Blessed are ye, when men shall revile you, and persecute you, and shall say all manner of evil against you falsely, for my sake. Rejoice, and be exceeding glad: for great is your reward in heaven: for so persecuted they the prophets which were before you. Ye are the salt of the earth: but if the salt have lost his savour, wherewith shall it be salted? It is thenceforth good for nothing, but to be cast out, and to be trodden under foot of men. Ye are the light of the world. A city that is set on an hill cannot be hid.*

This sermon was mind-blowing, revolutionary, and counter-cultural and offensive to others. It flipped the Jewish law which was based on eye for an eye and harboring wrath on its head. Jesus was instantly a very polarizing figure, gaining both followers and haters rapidly.

His message was about embracing meekness, lowliness, humility, and preferring peace and kindness towards one's enemies instead of reacting with war as a knee-jerk response. These principles are still very much alive today in the Church. During the time of Jesus, the common understanding among the Jewish people was to "love your neighbor" as commanded in the Old Testament, specifically in Leviticus 19:18, however Jesus raised the standard, He challenged this interpretation and expanded the concept of love to include loving not only neighbors but also enemies.

The statement "Blessed are the peacemakers, for they will be called children of God" highlights the importance of promoting peace and righteousness, reflecting the values of God's kingdom.

After Jesus' sacrificial death on the cross, it became clear that belief in Jesus Christ and being born again through faith are essential requirements for Gentiles becoming children of God, as stated in John 1:12. This emphasizes the centrality of faith, leaving the old life behind, and becoming crucified with Christ is essential salvation and being part of God's family.

Galatians 2:20 KJV

*I am crucified with Christ: nevertheless I live; yet not I, but Christ liveth in me: and the life which I now live in the flesh I live by the faith of the Son of God, who loved me, and gave himself for me.*

It is crucial to understand that God's love extends to all, including sinners, and the sacrifice of Jesus on the cross was intended for the redemption of all who have ears to hear and believe in Him for the remission of sins.

Overall, the teaching on being peacemakers and being called children of God underscores the importance of living out God's values of peace and righteousness in our lives as followers of Christ.

Jesus emphasized that modeling the Father in Heaven as the perfect template is best for humanity because He represents virtue and integrity, rather than propagating violence and chaos.

God doesn't desire to see anyone stumble on earth and go to hell; He loves all of His children, so He provided a way out through Jesus' blood.

God shows through Jesus that when a person is lost in sin, showing love towards them is the best approach to lead them to repentance and a return to godly behavior, rather than condemning and attacking them back. This is the divide between religion and relationship.

Relationship touches the heart; religion creates an ultimatum.

Religious condemnation and attack can lead individuals into shame and anger, causing them to become even more sinful and evil, and can push them further into their fallen identity.

God, with His all-encompassing wisdom, sees the cause and effect cycle of responding to anger with anger, thus creating a negative feedback loop where both parties end up turning out worse in the long run. Picture two neighbors at war with each other. They tend to escalate until someone calls the cops.

This same truth about temperance is found in the book of James.

James 1:19-21 KJV

*Wherefore, my beloved brethren, let every man be swift to hear, slow to speak, slow to wrath: For the wrath of man worketh not the righteousness of God. Wherefore lay apart all filthiness and superfluity of naughtiness, and receive with meekness the engrafted Word, which is able to save your souls.*

Jesus came to completely flip the fallen nature of man, which was completely natural to man. He came to reverse the curse of Adam all the way... with Him being the last Adam, He needs a wife.

His wife is the bride of Christ, the Church, the global remnant of His true followers. The Church He paid for with His blood. In ancient Jewish custom, it was common for the groom or the groom's family to pay a bride price or dowry to the bride's family as part of the marriage arrangement.

The timeless significance of the Sermon on the Mount remains relevant in today's world. In the midst of global conflicts and political divisions, including both international disputes and local disagreements among neighbors, the peacemaking principles taught by Jesus are more vital than ever. Current tensions and conflicts, like those seen in regions such as Ukraine, highlight the urgent importance of embracing the message of peace, love, and reconciliation that Jesus emphasized in His teachings.

Jesus went forward after the Sermon on the Mount with His miraculous ministry of supernatural healings, raising people from the dead multiple times, and casting out demons. His twelve disciples modeled His supernatural activities and began doing the same.

All of these supernatural activities as well as Jesus plainly stating that He is the Son of God rustled a lot of feathers. He created a lot of enemies in a small area in a short amount of time.

The religious Pharisees, the religious charlatans, ruled that His punishment must be death for being a blasphemous preacher.

Jesus died at the hand of His fellow Jews. He died at the hand of the religious spirit – the spirit that condems, accuses, and attacks. They did this to Him because He didn't fit their fleshly expectation of who and what a Messiah would look and act like. So instead, they condemned the actual Messiah to death. This was the hatred of satan moving through the spiritually blind people, demanding His blood, not knowing it was the way, the truth, and the life they truly needed.

Matt 27:25 KJV

*His blood be on us, and on our children.*

Jesus never wanted to create a religion. His intention was to create followers that embodied Him and His way, just like His dozen disciples (minus Judas) who would take His teachings, run with them, and confront the fallen world, heal the broken, deliver the demonized, and raise up the lost. This is why Jesus added Paul to His core group.

Jesus came not to establish a religion but to foster a relationship between God and humanity through grace, faith, love, and redemption. He emphasized personal transformation, repentance, and following Him for eternal life. Even though organized religion formed around His teachings later, Jesus prioritized inviting individuals into a personal relationship with God over instituting a formal religious system. It was the religious complex which ultimately led to His crucifixion.

His emphasis was on grace, mercy, faith, love, and living out the Kingdom of God here on earth: peace, joy, and righteousness.

Judas betrayed Jesus for thirty pieces of silver. In Matthew 26, Judas turned over His location to the Pharisees (he doxxed Him and gave away hidden location), then the religious leaders ran across Jerusalem and snatched up Jesus and the insanely brutal crucifixion began.

This is the proof you can have the best preacher, the best spiritual teacher the world has ever seen, God Himself in fact, and through satan's influence one can be corrupted. Judas had a direct hand in Jesus dying at thirty-three years old.

Jesus was aware that one of His disciples harbored treacherous intentions, long before the betrayal unfolded (Matthew 26:21). This revelation suggests God knew Judas never truly believed in Jesus as the Messiah. Instead, he viewed Jesus' ministry as an avenue for financial gain and selfish ambition. This was the same spirit that was initially behind Simon the Sorcerer in chapter 1, to exploit.

It stands to reason that Judas went to hell because of his betrayal of the Son of God, exchanging the divine for a mere sum of silver, leading to his subsequent remorse after seeing Jesus being tortured and then impulsively taking his own life. Scriptural evidence suggests that those who take their own lives will be facing the consequences of their actions in eternity. No matter how desperate you become it is never a way out.

John 6:70-71 KJV

*Jesus answered them, Have not I chosen you twelve, and one of you is a devil? He spake of Judas Iscariot the son of Simon: for he it was that should betray him, being one of the twelve.*

1 Corinthians 6:9-10 KJV

*Know ye not that the unrighteous shall not inherit the kingdom of God? Be not deceived: neither fornicators, nor idolaters, nor adulterers, nor effeminate, nor abusers of themselves with mankind, Nor thieves, nor covetous, nor drunkards, nor revilers, nor extortioners, shall inherit the kingdom of God.*

1 Corinthians 6:19-20 KJV

*What? know ye not that your body is the temple of the Holy Ghost which is in you, which ye have of God, and ye are not your own? For ye are bought with a price: therefore glorify God in your body, and in your spirit, which are God's.*

Romans 6:23 KJV

*For the wages of sin is death; but the gift of God is eternal life through Jesus Christ our Lord.*

Proverbs 6:16-19 KJV

*These six things doth the Lord hate: yea, seven are an abomination unto him: A proud look, a lying tongue, and hands that shed innocent blood, An heart that deviseth wicked imaginations, feet that be swift in running to mischief, A false witness that speaketh lies, and he that soweth discord among brethren.*

Judas betrayed Jesus for thirty pieces of silver, a sum typically given for a slave in the Old Testament (Exodus 21:32), revealing the low value placed on Jesus' life. After Judas saw Jesus getting tortured he became overwhelmed with remorse, instead of seeking repentance, Judas returned the silver, then took his own life. His actions from beginning to end suggest an unchanged heart hardened against God, leading to eternal separation from Him. As you see, we can either surrender to the world and things like money, a brutal master, or we can surrender to the Savior as the graceful master. Satan is extremely crafty that's why Judas, while in the presence of God Himself, still was overcome with sin.

For me, thick or thin, no matter what, Jesus will always be enough. I pray the same goes for you.

The Bible underscores God's fairness and mercy, as only He knows the hearts and destinies of individuals. While Judas' final destiny remains unspecified in Scripture, his narrative underscores the importance of genuine repentance, faith, and the repercussions of betraying God. Even though he had a surge of remorse, it wasn't enough. That's why one day in the Courtroom of Heaven you don't want to experience the same surge of remorse. Repent while you can.

It says all across the Scriptures that God terribly dislikes disobedient people that lie, get drunk, sow discord, gossip, are greedy, are sexually immoral, are homosexual, reject their God-given gender, plan the demise of others, steal, cheat, defile their God-given vessel of the Holy Spirit, and the God-given vessel of the Holy Spirit of others.

Jesus sacrificed Himself for all of these types of sinners, both for the just and the unjust. He dined with sinners to reveal His love and truth to them, igniting a transformation in their lives. Sharing the gospel with those who are lost in sin is the Great Commission. The goal as a Christian is always to build a bigger table, not a bigger wall. Big walls create religious sects and cults.

The Commission is a collaborative effort, a partnership with God, to bring about new salvations and healings and offer individuals a fresh start. Introducing others to the Kingdom of God holds eternal significance for both them and you.

Everyone with ears to hear, no matter how depraved they are, or how far gone they think they are, do have the opportunity to hear about the Gospels or read the Gospels, turn away from the path of evil they walk, be spared from the hellacious destiny that awaits them at death, and begin to walk with God's will for them – the will that's always been there, waiting.

Imagine how frustrating it must be to be God sometimes. He has excellent and beautifully written wills for everyone, their Heavenly inheritance for this life and the next, and a large swath of humanity still hasn't accepted His Son, because of spiritual blindness and idolatry with the preference to selfishly and through the feeble strength of their own flesh.

Walking under the dominion of Jesus and finding God's will is better late than never. He promises He will make up for lost time with you.

Where you are at right now, with what you have or don't have, is all you need – as long as you have breath in your lungs you can still accept Jesus now. Come as you are.

If we lived in a world where the majority of people were walking in their God-written will, think of how different the evening news would be, think of how different the internet would be, all of the media, all of the business world, and really every component of society. The peace that many of us crave in our souls won't arrive until we reach Heaven. The harmony we crave is in Heaven.

If everyone surrendered to the knowledge of Christ it would be a lot different, but we are in the realm of illusion and delusions, as Plato understood 400 years before Jesus arrived, therefore we look forward to our total redemption and entry into the Kingdom of Heaven, where our true life really starts.

It's hard to discern what's true down here, so we must look at first principles and study the evidence. The evidence is overwhelming that Jesus lived, died, was resurrected from the grave, and sent His Spirit.

If you want the truth you end up at Jesus, the embodiment of truth. Conversely, avoiding the truth and embracing spiritual blindness leads to sinful activities that grieve the Lord. The compassion of the Lord extends to those who have strayed, and He mourns daily for the lost.

Bringing more of the Kingdom of God to the earth before the end of the age is a worthy ideal, regardless of what the "realists" say. The realists say we are on a rock floating through space, by random happenstance, we evolved from rambunctious monkeys, and we share 50% of our genes with bananas. Sounds bananas, doesn't it?

I would rather take my chances and instead put the Great Commission, the great partnership with the Lord, into action. It's worth spending the time, money, and effort on helping beautify humanity through one salvation at a time while there's still time. Each salvation quite literally equals more of God's will on the earth and more entrants into Heaven.

Proverbs 11:30 KJV

*The fruit of the righteous is a tree of life, and he that winneth souls is wise.*

In the world today there are about a few hundred million to 1 billion people that have faith in the good news of Jesus and behave the Bible.

On the upper end that's one in eight and if we are optimistic its two in eight. That means there are endless opportunities to share the good news with the lost. It's an ocean of ministry opportunities if you have the eyes to see it. Only Jesus knows who and how many are in His Church. Salvation is a personal matter between each individual and God, based on their faith in Jesus and what He did.

Each person's journey of faith is unique, and it is essential for individuals to continually seek a deeper understanding of God's Word, strive to live according to biblical principles, and grow in their relationship with Christ.

On the other side when you meet Jesus, you want Him to think highly of you and hear Him say to you, "well done good and faithful servant" (Matthew 25:21) which is often taken out of context. People confuse it with equating their salvation to good works, when its more about who you are as opposed to what you do. A servant of God, with the Lord in their heart, will naturally share the love of Jesus to others. Doing good works on His behalf, for His glory, builds up your treasures in Heaven, but being a servant is in your resurrected identity.

2 Corinthians 5:10 KJV

*For we must all appear before the judgment seat of Christ; that every one may receive the things done in his body, according to that he hath done, whether it be good or bad.*

2 Timothy 4:8 KJV

*Henceforth there is laid up for me a crown of righteousness, which the Lord, the righteous judge, shall give me at that day: and not to me only, but unto all them also that love his appearing.*

After death, we face the judgment in the Courtroom of Heaven to receive our rewards. We either receive eternal life and heavenly treasures or eternal death without any treasures. Our actions are recorded in a heavenly account, and God, the righteous judge, will review them to reward our service in His Kingdom. Conversely, we will also face consequences for neglecting our responsibilities in God's Kingdom.

Mark 8:36 KJV

*For what shall it profit a man, if he shall gain the whole world, and lose his own soul?*

You can be assured that God is the best record keeper there is. His accounting is honest and fair.

Engaging in Kingdom building and ministry is not a requirement for salvation, but according to the teachings of the Bible, it does result in additional Heavenly rewards. It is likely that God's divine plans for each individual align closely with activities that contribute to building His Kingdom because He has so few servants in the world.

For those who have experienced genuine salvation, a natural response is to share the gift of salvation and the love of Jesus with others. It's coming from a place of love and compassion and not fleshly works.

The sharing of Jesus is not driven by a religious performance; it must flow from a place of love and healing that they have personally received. Understanding that they cannot conceal the gift that was shown to them, the love and grace is shared as an expression of their gratitude and devotion to Jesus. If you feel the call to start doing Kingdom work, you don't have to be in the ministry full-time, to be in the ministry full-time. I frequently hear stories of people leading others to Christ in their secular day jobs, whether they are dentists, hairdressers, landlords, firefighters, or food delivery drivers.

If you give God your yes, He can use you anywhere.

While still alive, try to keep short accounts with people, meaning have a lot of mercy with others, and be quick to forgive. That's exactly what Jesus did. He was quick to forgive the Jews and the Romans that were torturing Him on the cross (Luke 23:34). He says to forgive 70 x 7; that's a lot of times to forgive. Keeping long accounts is God's job.

Realize that the final goal you are intending for is simply being in Christ, and Him in you, and that's not in or of this world.

Finish the race strong while in the world, as the Apostle Paul instructs, your real life will begin upon entrance into Heaven when you receive your glorified body. God's design is way more grand than you could ever imagine. We are seeing a small sliver of it on earth. The lifetime we are granted here is like a vapor that appears for a little while and then vanishes away (James 4:14).

Study and cling to the Word of God as the most important part of your Christian walk while you still have breath in your lungs. It will strengthen your identity as a child of God, strengthen your awareness of the Holy Spirit, and bring you into deeper union with Jesus.

2 Timothy 4:7 KJV

*I have fought a good fight, I have finished my course, I have kept the faith.*

# Ch. 16 HOW TO IDENTIFY FALSE CHRISTIANITY

Matthew 18:20 KJV

*For where two or three are gathered together in my name, there am I in the midst of them.*

As you walk on the Christian path you will find that it's easy to connect with others who are also grounded in the teachings of Jesus and walk with a strong foundation in Him, He is all three persons of the Trinity. Not one of three, not two of three, all three persons of God dwelling inside. When you are authentically being yourself as a Holy Spirit filled child of God you can't put on a facade, God won't allow it, you can't wear a mask, and you can't live a double life.

Way too many Christians are bought into flesh based religion more than a Holy Spirit based relationship. This makes them professionals at pretending to be perfect, pretending to be someone they are not, and pretending they are walking holy, that's all the work of satan and man-made religion. If you are born again and Spirit filled it's a challenge to relate to a lot of people because the standard is high and most Christians who are supposed to be walking the same standard aren't even aiming for the standard that Jesus set. They aren't even thinking about holiness because they are bought into their flesh.

Born again people are constantly aware of the eternity that awaits and they walk in the fact that any day could be their last, so they always are doing their best to be in a state of holiness and right standing with God, to the point of a healthy obsession. Christians that are likely not saved are living for the flesh and the desires of the world and also aren't letting God seek their heart and burn away the chaff.

Truly saved people are constantly focused on their salvation and are working it out with holy fear and trembling (Philippians 2:12). Likely unsaved people are barely trying and assuming God loves them no matter how much hell they are raising. This is the same thinking as the "love is love" crowd. You must let Him purchase you fully.

A born again person is seeking God's blessing and grace over every situation, roadblock or stumble and the other is taking God's grace for granted and assuming Jesus is their homeboy.

On the rapture day it will massively reveal in one instant who was actually walking with Him and who was pretending. Many Christians that thought they were good with God because they went to Church or went on religious pilgrimages never actually allowed themselves to be washed in the blood.

There are millions if not billions of lukewarm Christians who claim to follow Jesus but do not actively live each day for Him nor embody the nine aspects of God (Galatians 5:22-23). Some may declare their willingness to die for Jesus, yet they do not consistently read the Bible, pray or praise. Without relationship there are no relations.

These lukewarm Christians often tarnish the reputation of the Church, as they claim they are a Christian out in public, and this leads many others to get the wrong idea about what a Christian person is. This is because for most people lost in the world the closest they ever get to reading a Bible is by encountering either a real Christian or a fake Christian. One way or the other they will walk away with an impression about Christianity and therefore Jesus.

One ounce of placing the Word of God into action is worth a pound of talk. In other words, you have to walk the walk more than talk the talk in authentic Christianity. There are many Christians that talk a good game, they know some Scripture, they most likely go to Church, but do they live for Jesus? Have they surrendered their old life? Have they been born again? Have they turned away from a life of sin? These are Jesus' commands, they are not suggestions.

You can't fake it until you make it, and you can't fake it in the eyes of God. He sees what everyone is doing at all times. That's the omnipresence of the Holy Spirit. Only God truly knows who each person really is. Deception is rampant and there are many people who claim Christianity, but they do the work of the devil for their day job.

To discern who is a genuine follower of Jesus, listen to their testimonies of faith and observe the fruits of their commitment to following Jesus in their daily lives. If they look like the world, talk like the world, act like the world then they are earth dwellers, they are of the world and by default in their flesh more than in the Spirit, they aren't born again. Keeping people like this close by will bring you down in your personal walk with Jesus. The titles for these types of Christians: lukewarm, carnal, worldly, and potentially unsaved.

Living in the Holy Spirit rather than the flesh is a daily choice and a lifestyle change to be embraced. The Bible has called Christians out of the world to embark on the lifelong journey of crucifying their flesh, leaving behind their old life of sin and forsaking the world. The world culture was designed by satan to bring people into a life of sin and keep people bound in sin through the normalization of it in entertainment and media.

The holy standard is high and lifted compared to the baseline of the world because satan is the prince of this world according to the Bible (John 12:31), he has a season of all out destruction during the seven year tribulation then he is defeated in the battle of Armageddon in Israel.

In the same way when Jesus said "Lazarus come out of that grave" after He raised Lazarus from the dead, Jesus is also calling you out of that world and out of your grave clothes.

John 11:43-44 KJV

*And when he thus had spoken, he cried with a loud voice, Lazarus, come forth. And he that was dead came forth, bound hand and foot with graveclothes: and his face was bound about with a napkin. Jesus saith unto them, Loose him, and let him go.*

Until a man or woman is born again they are still in the grave and the grave clothes.

When you become born again you become holy and set apart from the world, it's not something most people want or are ready for, but due to rejecting Jesus and embracing the world there will be hell to pay.

Many lukewarms want to serve two masters because they want to live their best life while they are here, which is chasing pleasure and the false identity, yet they want the benefits of Jesus without any of the commitment to the relationship. Knowing God means He knows you and has a relationship with you, if you aren't strengthening the daily walk with Jesus then you are by default grieving the Lord.

The mixing of the death programs of the world based in the flesh and the life program of Jesus based in the Holy Ghost and fire results in a grayed out lukewarmness. Most that think they have been a little lukewarm lately are in fact cold as ice, and those that are in fact on fire wonder if they are being lukewarm. Are you seeing the dynamic?

The flesh feeds on the flesh and living in the Spirit leads to more of living in the Spirit and being extra cautious about grieving the Holy Spirit, that's how much a born again believer cares about their relationship with God. It's the most important relationship in their life and they treat it that way. If you place God in any other position than the first position in your life you are out of order.

This isn't opinion either this is the standard Jesus sets.

Nibbling on the world and the flesh will always dull a believer down to the level of lukewarmness, and Jesus' requirement for His bride on wedding day is they are prayed up, oiled up, and hot in anticipation of meeting Jesus and going to Heaven.

One is tuned into the impermanent things of the world, enjoying their possessions and pleasures, and living like they will live forever and the other is tuned into their eternal life in Heaven, and not only that, is committed to Jesus like there is no tomorrow. Do you see the gap?

That gap is the state of modern Christianity to a tee. The lukewarm ones will say "come on live a little" to make themselves feel better about living from their false identity and against God's design. The on fire ones know God's design embrace their holy identity, and forsake the world, take up their cross, and crucify their flesh because the real goal is going home to Heaven for eternity, the only requirement is making it through the bootcamp on earth first.

You will witness Holy Spirit filled Christians authentically embodying the nine aspects of God, including joy, kindness, patience, humility, and self-control and their desire to elevate Jesus above themselves will be evident. God will promote those souls who seek to exalt the name of Jesus rather than their own.

He has very few faithful and consecrated servant saints on earth.

The servant saints know they are no longer their own, they were purchased by Jesus, and Jesus Himself is more than enough because they know the truth that nothing else satisfies and nothing else will ever be able to take the place of Jesus.

Engaging in friendships and worship time with other consecrated believers will bring forth the Scripture that says "iron sharpens iron." Developing these types of friendships with fellow believers will assist you in deepening your relationship with the Lord. A Bible teacher or elder than can disciple you will be one of the fastest routes towards learning the Bible and building up your identity as a Holy Spirit filled Christian.

Proverbs 27:17 KJV

*Iron sharpeneth iron; so a man sharpeneth the countenance of his friend.*

When you listen to the testimonies of other believers, your faith will be strengthened. Often, other believers become lifelong friends due to the shared commonalities in belonging to the same Kingdom.

If you want to go to a local church to find fellowship with other believers generally speaking it's a good idea, just know denominationalism and religious performance has wreaked havoc on the body of Christ.

Please steer away from Roman Catholicism, Mormonism, Jehovah's Witnesses, Christian Science, Church of Christ, 7th Day Adventist, Methodist and Unitarian Universalist because they have gone beyond the Bible and are into the false operation of man rather than the authentic operation of God. The Bible warns against going beyond what was already written by God (1 Corinthians 4:6).

Trigger warning: if you are part of the Catholic version of Christianity (or are considering the denomination) you are sowing into the part of the body of Christ that looks the most like the Roman empire that killed Jesus and the part of the body of Christ with the most idolatry and paganism baked in.

Roman Catholicism has elevated Jesus' mother Mary and the Catholic saints to an equal level to Jesus. In some denominations they believe Mary is a higher-ranking spiritual authority than Jesus, or that the only way to God is through Mary. The Bible directly states Jesus is the Savior and the only way to the Father is through Him.
It's a slight of hand to get your focus away from Jesus and onto idols.

Only God, Jesus, and Holy Spirit are real and still living. Mary, for example, was a sinner and she knew Jesus was her Savior. She was an average woman and then the anointing of the Lord came upon her. She was obedient and accepted the task to be the earthly mother of Jesus. She's likely in Heaven but she is not God. Here is the verse that proves she knew Jesus was the Savior of mankind, not her.

Luke 1:46-47 KJV

*And Mary said, My soul doth magnify the Lord, And my spirit hath rejoiced in God my Saviour.*

Roman Catholicism came on the scene hundreds of years after the early Church in the book of Acts was already formed. It rushed in to "steal the show" and unfortunately satan was somewhat successful at doing so.

It integrates teachings from various sources, including those of Jesus, the Jewish law fulfilled by Jesus, Roman polytheism, and Roman paganism. The amalgam that's created from the vegetable soup theology in many ways is a different faith and not the one faith the Bible talks about.

Ephesians 4:4-6 KJV

*There is one body, and one Spirit, even as ye are called in one hope of your calling; One Lord, one faith, one baptism, One God and Father of all, who is above all, and through all, and in you all.*

Transubstantiation, a doctrine in Roman Catholic theology, asserts that the bread and wine in the Eucharist become the literal body and blood of Jesus Christ while maintaining their physical appearance.

This belief is not in alignment with biblical Christianity, which views the bread and wine as symbols or representations of Christ's body and blood, commemorating His sacrifice on the cross, rather than literal physical items with Jesus inside. They are stuck in the physical world of the flesh, rather than the non-physical and eternal Kingdom. The Bible emphasizes the spiritual significance of the Last Supper as a remembrance of Christ's atoning work, rather than a literal transformation of Jesus into physical elements.

The operation of God is a purely spiritual transformation in a person's life, a spiritual circumcision (Romans 2:29) and is not based in the earthly world. The Kingdom of God is spiritual and not of this world (John 18:36).

How Catholicism came about was Emperor Constantine decided to embrace Christianity in the year 380 AD. This was after the Roman Empire began killing Christians starting in the year 50 AD. The

Emperor did this because of the recognition that if you couldn't overcome the Christians, then merging with them was the best answer. In other words, if you can't beat them join them.

The roots of Roman paganism included a variety of deities, rituals, and sacrifices that were important in Roman society. The worship of false gods and goddesses were connected to different aspects of life, similar to the veneration of Catholic saints today. Romans believed these gods influenced their daily lives so they worked to honor and exalt them through ceremonies and various blood sacrifices.

After Constantine declared Catholicism the state religion, the pagan temples in Rome were converted overnight into Catholic churches, with statues of pagan gods, reflecting the influence of Greek mythology on Roman culture, repurposed as statues of saints. Roman and Greek lowercase "g" gods are always demons. The Catholic faith was installed through a man-made governmental executive order, the word "government" directly translates to "mind control." Cold religion like this has pushed million if not billions away from Jesus.

Roman polytheistic paganism and Christianity completely merged under Constantine's decree, forming a distinct divergence from biblical teachings. Some Catholics perceive their faith as separate from other Christian denominations, viewing others as misguided, when in reality they are the most misguided. The diversion away from the early church model and the simple Gospels of Jesus and Paul, grieves God. Jesus died to end man-made fallen religion and not expand it.

The perception of Catholic exclusivity has led to an unfortunate division within the broader body of Christ since the 3rd century. This is why Martin Luther, a German monk and theologian, had to famously nail his Ninety-Five Theses to the door of the Castle Church in Wittenberg on October 31, 1517. In his theses, Luther challenged the practices of the Roman Catholic Church, particularly regarding the sale of indulgences. Indulgences were fake certificates sold to reduce the punishment for sins and shorten the time spent in nonexistent purgatory, leading to abuses and financial gain for the church.

This was all the evil operation of man to stop people from dealing with the Father directly for the remission of sins. This and many other unbiblical activities by the Catholics pushed Christians away from a real relationship with the Father and from the blood of Jesus.

Luther's act was the catalyst for the Protestant Reformation, and Luther's ideas spread around the world overnight and led to a significant shift in Christian theology and practice. Luther successfully redirected most of the body of Christ, back towards the simple Gospels of what Jesus did.

The Romans did this because infiltration over invasion has always been effective in the art of war, satan knows this.

The Bible shows us in the Old Testament two times hat the way to get future generations to serve false pagan gods is through merging and intermarrying.

Exodus 34:16 KJV

*And thou take of their daughters unto thy sons, and their daughters go a whoring after their gods, and make thy sons go a whoring after their gods.*

Deuteronomy 7:3-4 KJV

*Neither shalt thou make marriages with them; thy daughter thou shalt not give unto his son, nor his daughter shalt thou take unto thy son. For they will turn away thy son from following me, that they may serve other gods: so will the anger of the Lord be kindled against you, and destroy thee suddenly.*

Corruption is always the result of unbiblical mixture. Catholicism aside, the denominations as a whole in Christianity have caused a lot of division and separation in the body of Christ, rather than unification.

Unbiblical churches have allowed demons, lowercase "g" gods to enter congregations worldwide, a shadow and a type of the first seal of Revelation where false religion and false peace is rampant. There are also many churches with leaders that are secretly or subtly (or overtly) celebrating the new age, tarot, the gay and trans agenda, witchcraft, or freemasonry (also witchcraft). That's the level of infiltration that the enemy has had into local churches.

The Kingdom is not easily found by many (Matthew 7:14). The Bible says that God's children, His followers, are holy and set apart. Just as Jesus is not of this world, believers also become set apart from the world, losing interest in the fallen, sinful, and worldly culture as they surrender more to Jesus instead of the world.

1 John 2:15 ASV

*Do not love the world, neither the things that are in the world. If any man love the world, the love of the Father is not in him.*

As we near the conclusion of our journey, let's recap the significance of fellowship and the strength found in numbers. In a world where sinful behaviors like promiscuity, fascism, communism, domination and submission programs, self-promotion, vanity, violence, greed, substance abuse, and the pursuit of instant gratification prevail, being part of the body of Christ is a profound honor. Finding fellowship in the one faith serves as a protective shield against the world. Remember, the company you keep influences your future. Just don't substitute talking about your relationship with God with your actual relationship with God.

Just as Jesus is not of this world, believers are called to be in the world but not of it (John 17:14-16), losing interest in the fallen, sinful, and flesh-driven culture that surrounds them. The desires of the flesh war against those of the Spirit, highlighting the internal struggle between sinful impulses and living in alignment with God's will.

Romans 7:15 KJV

*For that which I do I allow not: for what I would, that do I not; but what I hate, that do I.*

Amidst a world and churched world culture that promotes sinful behaviors like fame-seeking, enmity, exploitation, materialism, and instant gratification, the influence of finding honest brothers and sisters who are set apart from the world cannot be understated. This sense of belonging values fosters joy, healthy relationships, deep connections, and the potential for finding a spouse.

If a spouse is not found before the end of the Church Age, just know Jesus is your ultimate spouse, that you should be consecrated, holy and set apart for today, and He's coming soon on the clouds to bring you home. He is the blessed hope.

He is more than enough and always will be.

# Ch. 17 STEP IN ALL THE WAY YOUR DESTINY AWAITS

I encourage you to acquire a Bible and read through the whole New Testament. After you have done that read the whole thing from Genesis to Revelation. All the text may not be immediately clear, particularly without embracing Jesus and the Holy Spirit. As mentioned in chapter 16, when the Holy Spirit resides within you, the Scriptures will unveil more meaning. The Holy Spirit is the interpreter of the deep codes in the Bible.

When do you avail yourself to the transformative influence and wisdom inherent in God's Word, you will see the entire unified and progressive narrative that spans thousands of years of history. This will enable you to see where you are currently placed in the story.

By immersing yourself in the Scriptures with an open heart and a desire to seek God's guidance, you will discover profound truths that can shape and enrich your faith journey. You will never get to Heaven and regret reading too much Bible. You may get to hell and regret reading too little.

While it may not fully make total sense initially, especially without formally accepting Jesus and the Holy Spirit, you can spend some time with worship music to familiarize yourself with the Holy Spirit, the least understood man in the threefold Holy Trinity that most denominations ignore.

When more of the Holy Spirit is flowing inside of you the words on the page will begin to make more sense. The Bible was written through the divine inspiration of the Holy Spirit, dwelling inside of righteous men.

Developing as a Christian means being able to go back to God's Word when you need clarity and guidance. The Holy Spirit will be able to tell you which Scriptures you need to read to understand your life with the clarity and the sound mind of God. Bible verses will come to you in prayer.

Another effective method to invite the Holy Spirit to work within you is by attending a church that emphasizes both the Word of God and the presence of the Holy Spirit. Some churches prioritize the study of Scripture primarily and others place emphasis on experiencing the presence of the Holy Spirit through worship primarily.

The ideal is going to be a balance of Spirit and Truth. Such a church places importance on both the presence of God's Spirit and rightly dividing His Word. It's essential to always remember that His Church, the bride encompassing all true believers, supersedes the structure of any local church. Many mix the two concepts when they are very different.

A building is a little "c" church. Jesus' bride that's on fire for Him is the capital "C" Church, there is no other church and no other ministry.

John 4:24 KJV

*God is a Spirit: and they that worship him must worship him in spirit and in truth.*

Through the blend of Spirit and Truth one will be turned into a disciple of Jesus. You can be healed by Jesus, set free, and full of supernatural joy. The true disciple of Jesus Christ walks in the authority of God and not any man-given authority. For the authority to come upon you by God Himself, you must remember who God is and what he did for you, and always keep it in memory. God's authority was granted through Jesus blood and the Holy Spirit.

Christians do that through communion, which is a spiritual act of remembrance of what He did for you and it's not a pagan ritual of eating flesh and drinking blood (Romans 14:17). The Catholics look at it this way because we are discussed transubstantiation in the previous chapter.

Luke 22:19 ASV

*And he took bread, and when he had given thanks, he brake it, and gave to them, saying, This is my body which is given for you: this do in remembrance of me.*

The Bible is a book of remembrance. The truth is God is good, He died for us, in our place, to pay the sin debt that we could never pay ourselves. No matter how hard we try by our own power we can never reverse the curse of the fall. You will understand the truth in the Word by receiving communion and His presence in the room. You will feel the unity, love, reverence, and holiness in the atmosphere. You will truly appreciate what He did for you.

When the Holy Spirit is in the room and everyone is loving it, the whole room feels like a glimpse of Heaven, it feels electric. If your church doesn't feel like this during the time of prayer, praise and worship, then you may want to keep looking. Keep looking until you find a church that has this type of Heavenly atmosphere. If you can't find this don't be discouraged you are always in the true Church and you can learn the Bible, pray, and praise with the help of YouTube Bible teachers like Robert Breaker and worship with YouTube channels like Upperroom and Worshipmob. If you want a Bible mentor or other authentic Christian friends, you can pray for that and God will provide that. If He did it for me, He will do it for you.

The presence of God is a big gift not to be taken for granted and all the credit goes to the Holy Spirit for creating that sweet aroma, that loving and healing atmosphere, that feels like the opposite of a filthy city street.

It's a healing you can't find anywhere else, whether spiritual, emotional, mental, or physical. I can say that with confidence because after exploring many new age traditions outside of God, I never found anything that comes close. I am very grateful that I gave my life to Jesus after years and years of seeking relief in the new age realm.

I am very thankful that I did not complete the kabbalah class I took because it was attempting to lock the tree of death, which they wrongly call the tree of life, into my DNA. Some new age traditions are more dangerous than others because they actively want to stunt you and lock fear and death codes into your DNA.

The only tree of life, book of life, and river of life are in Heaven.

It's probably obvious at this point but do whatever you can to stay away from Eastern meditation, yoga, tarot, witchcraft, divination, psychics, crystals, astrology, and kabbalah among other fallen practices.

Knowing your enemy and where your enemy is hidden is crucial. You do not want your energy being harvested by entities outside of the Holy Trinity. Only the Holy Trinity is the life-giving source of all. In Christian theology, the Greek word "zōē" (/zoh-ay/) holds profound significance as it encapsulates the essence of life itself. This term goes beyond mere existence to encompass the fullness of life, both in a physical and spiritual sense. "Zōē" points to the abundant and eternal life that believers receive through their relationship with Jesus, who is the ultimate source of life. It signifies not just mere survival or biological existence but instead stewarding a flourishing and vibrant life that is rooted in God's love and sustenance.

As we dwell in this life-giving source, God Himself, we experience true fulfillment and purpose, finding our identity and vitality in Him who is the giver and sustainer of all life. Through Him and only Him we found our way home.

Stay centered on the Holy Trinity, avoid distractions that may lead you astray, and focus as much as you can on only following the leading of the Lord while continuing to worship His goodness. The path to righteousness may be narrow, and only a few find it. By prioritizing your relationship with God and staying committed to His ways, you will find true fulfillment and walk in His divine purpose for your life. When you are walking in God's authority you can even command angels to war and protect on your behalf.

The religious spirit mentioned earlier is the root cause of division within the body, leading to various man-made approaches to Christianity. In reality, the original followers of Jesus simply identified themselves as followers of the Way, with the label "Christians" bestowed upon them by pagans.

The key distinction lies between human-influenced interpretations of Christianity and the authentic presence of Jesus and the Word of God. The true reality is found in the genuine presence of Jesus and the teachings of Scripture. Outside of the Holy Trinity, no other spiritual tradition carries positive eternal significance; rather, the fallen traditions of humanity always bear negative eternal implications. There are no exceptions.

Droves of churches throughout America contain lukewarm elements that water down the uncompromising truth found in the Word of God to prevent causing confusion among their members. Many churches are hesitant to challenge their congregations with uncomfortable Bible truth for fear of affecting their financial contributions. They prefer congregants that are great tithers who religiously occupy the seats, but never actually share the Gospel outside of the church. Most church goers in America seldom share the faith with others outside of the four walls. Not every church is this way, there are certainly churches that are on fire for the Lord and have active evangelism efforts, but most Churches are preaching to the quire week after week as opposed to sharing Jesus with the lost world.

Local church leaders often emphasize tithing (part of the Jewish law) and attendance over the importance of the depth of prayer, worship, Bible study, and confronting the lost world. They shy away from leading individuals to a place of holy repentance and are reluctant to break away from man-made indoctrination. In both the business and church worlds, one of the most perilous mindsets is the adherence to the phrase, "we have always done it this way."

Quality worship often looks like King David shamelessly dancing and quality Bible teaching often looks like the Apostle Peter on the day of Pentecost in Acts 2:38-41. Peter's powerful message led to the conviction and conversion of three thousand souls who heard him preach the truth.

2 Samuel 6:14-16 KJV

*And David danced before the Lord with all his might; and David was girded with a linen ephod. So David and all the house of Israel brought up the ark of the Lord with shouting, and with the sound of the trumpet.*

Peter's journey from denying Jesus' deity three times to eventually boldly proclaiming the Gospel at Pentecost highlights the profound truth that God can use anyone, regardless of past failures or shortcomings. This transformation underscores the incredible grace and redemptive power of God, demonstrating that He can work through imperfect individuals to accomplish His purposes and bring about significant impact in the world.

Peter's story serves as a powerful reminder that God's calling and empowerment can transcend human limitations, showing that He equips and empowers those who are willing to serve Him faithfully.

Acts 2:38-41 KJV

*Then Peter said unto them, Repent, and be baptized every one of you in the name of Jesus Christ for the remission of sins, and ye shall receive the gift of the Holy Ghost.*

*For the promise is unto you, and to your children, and to all that are afar off, even as many as the Lord our God shall call.*
*And with many other words did he testify and exhort, saying, Save yourselves from this untoward generation.*

*Then they that gladly received his Word were baptized: and the same day there were added unto them about three thousand souls.*

In the book of Acts, which narrates the early Church's history, it is noteworthy that systematic tithing is not emphasized as the primary method of giving. Many Christians today confuse stepping all the way in with giving their local church their last dollar. A lot of this has to do with the "seed faith" principle that says, "give to get." When on the contrary the early believers were guided by the Holy Spirit to give generously through love offerings to support fellow members of the body of Christ, addressing their practical needs such as shelter, food, and clothing without expecting to get anything back. Acts serves as God's blueprint for the Church Age operating under the dispensation of grace. It's God's New Testament church order, and it's barely followed by local churches. The focus was not on centralized authority on an exalted altar but on the well-being and care of the community, reflecting the essence of brotherly love and unity. It was a blend of various saints with different Holy Spirit led gifts like teaching, equipping, healing, casting out devils, and prophesying

Acts 2:44-45 KJV

*And all that believed were together, and had all things common; And sold their possessions and goods, and parted them to all men, as every man had need.*

The traditional format of church services adopted by the majority of churches today, resembling Catholic style systematic services, along with the Catholic style missions, have, unfortunately, hindered the effectiveness of the body of Christ and its outreach to the world. Only a limited number of churches have fully embraced the concept of Acts-style love offerings to support fellow believers in meeting their needs. Only a few churches empower various saints to use their Holy Spirit led gifts. They emphasize that God's authority only works through the leadership and that leadership requires everyone's total submission, bordering on man worship. The body needs to work together in a spirit of unity and not through master-slave programs.

Moreover, 95% of local churches have overlooked the importance of engaging in one-on-one "disciple making" in accordance with the direct model of Paul and Timothy. The modern church often labels training as "discipleship" a watered down term, when in reality it needs to be much more intentional. That's why "disciple making" is a more accurate term than discipleship. Disciples are followers, learners, and sharers. In modern churches the master-slave program has taken root, and disciples are never trained up to be new leaders. Jesus always wanted there be a multiplication of trained up individuals that are empowered with the Holy Spirit, filled with gifts, ready to spread the Spirit and Truth with the world.

The Greek word "mathētés" (/mah-thay-tace/) means "disciple" or "learner."

Mathēteía encompasses the idea of being made into a disciple who is actively engaged in learning from a mentor or elder. In the context of Christianity, mathēteía refers to the intentional process of learning, growing, and following Jesus Christ as His disciple.

Paul and Timothy shared a mentor-disciple relationship in the early Christian community; Paul assumed the role of a spiritual father to Timothy. Despite not being biologically related, Paul took Timothy under his wing, offered guidance, teaching, and financial support in Timothy's ministry and spiritual journey. He trained him up and sent him out into the world to be effective for the Gospel to then train others. That's Jesus' method of multiplication local churches missed.

This model is the example of disciple making: to nurture and equip saints for their roles in spreading the Gospel and building up the body of Christ. Modern churches expect believers to be trained from one thirty minute generalized sermon a week. It's not possible. Training happens in an intentional one-on-one relationship with an apostolic mentor, also known as an elder in the faith.

The most exemplary churches around the world are characterized by leaders and students who are passionately devoted to God, placing the truth of God above personal status or fame. Jesus never sought fame.

Consistently, after He would facilitate a remarkable miracle, He would say don't tell anyone. These churches that prioritize robust disciple-making initiatives have broken out of the confines of regular church gatherings – through this better model of making disciples individuals new to the faith can receive invaluable guidance and training from experienced mentors without any financial burden (Matthew 10:8), fostering spiritual growth and maturity within the community more efficiently.

If you feel called to explore churches then attend a service, be attentive to discern whether you experience the healing touch of the Holy Spirit in the midst of the group. If you do not perceive His presence, peace, joy, and righteousness then continue with your search until you discover a local church where you sense the genuine healing atmosphere of Jesus, and not only that, a clear method of building disciples, without being discipled the path is much more difficult. This book will help you to be equipped, and then the next step is finding a one-on-one elder in the faith that has a history of making new disciples.

If you need to relocate to another part of the country to find such a church, it may be a good idea if you feel the leading of God to do so, as being in an environment of God's glory can bring significant breakthroughs and new freedom. Do it now while you can because during the tribulation the churches will be either shut down or government monitored by the antichrist's AI system. They are already doing this with AI in state-allowed churches in China, this is why most of the church in China is underground and hidden from the government.

Finding healing in church isn't about discussing ideas at an intellectual level like in traditional psychotherapy. It's about allowing the truth found in the Word of God, and the Holy Spirit's fire to refine

354

and align you with His will. In other words, finding the supernatural operation of God to work in your life rather than the operation of man, which often manifests in trying to do it through your own strength.

The operation of God operates in the supernatural in ways that defy human understanding. Despite the seeming impossibility, His power is evident and effective when you find it. Whether inside a Spirit-filled church or not, you can encounter the Father's overwhelming presence and power. The supernatural power of Jesus can transform any issue or affliction you've been dealt in life. So don't be afraid to leave shame, guilt, embarrassment, and pride behind, and humbly bring any issue to the Son for reconciliation and healing.

There is only one ministry and it's the ministry of reconciliation.

2 Corinthians 5:18 KJV

*And all things are of God, who hath reconciled us to himself by Jesus Christ, and hath given to us the ministry of reconciliation.*

Isaiah 53:6 KJV

*All we like sheep have gone astray; we have turned, every one, to his own way; and the Lord hath laid on Him the iniquity of us all.*

Isaiah 54:4 KJV

*Fear not; for thou shalt not be ashamed: neither be thou confounded; for thou shalt not be put to shame: for thou shalt forget the shame of thy youth, and shalt not remember the reproach of thy widowhood.*

The time of youth, the time of immaturity - the season when we were walking without Jesus (in widowhood), when the enemy was happiest, when the enemy stole the most from us, when we wore the grave clothes, is now under the blood of Jesus.

If you have begun to accept the blood by reading this book I now proclaim and decree over your life that the mourning, the time of guilt and shame, is now over! Hallelujah!

Jesus drank in all of that sin for you, all of that iniquity, and all of that fallenness to set you free!

He willingly drank the cup of sin, bearing its poison on our behalf.

Matthew 26:39 KJV

*And he went a little further, and fell on his face, and prayed, saying, O my Father, if it be possible, let this cup pass from me: nevertheless not as I will, but as thou wilt.*

In the moment when Jesus prayed, "Father, if you are willing, take this cup from me; yet not my will, but yours be done," in the Garden of Gethsemane, He revealed that it was through His sacrificial act that redemption became possible. Despite His human desire to avoid the excruciating burden of bearing the sins of the world—past, present, and future—Jesus, fully human and fully divine, acknowledged the natural inclination to evade suffering. However, by submitting to God's will, He exemplified the necessity of confronting challenges directly as part of life's journey. This exchange granted us the opportunity for genuine spiritual growth and complete redemption. In this poignant moment, Jesus expressed profound anguish and entreated God to spare Him from the impending suffering symbolized by the "cup," representing the sacrifice, agony, and imminent crucifixion He knew awaited Him. Jesus, in His humanity, bore the weight of the forthcoming trial, encompassing physical pain, emotional turmoil, and spiritual separation from God that He would endure on the cross. His experience of hematidrosis, where blood is excreted through the skin due to extreme stress, underscores the intensity of His emotional and physical anguish. Ultimately, Jesus yielded to the Father's will, showcasing obedience and surrender to God's redemptive plan through His sacrificial death on the cross. Jesus willingly chose to drink the cup of humanity's sin, prioritizing the Father's will above His own, selflessly taking on the burden of sin for our sake.

The grave clothes, the sin, the fallen actions, the guilt, the shame, were taken on inside of Him when His precious blood was shed for us.

Now that you know the truth of the Gospels of Jesus you no longer need to wear the grave clothes. You no longer need to be bound by the past, weighed down by the chains of sin and shame.

It's your time to shed the grave clothes of your old self and embrace the new life that awaits you as a born again Christian.

Take up the garments of righteousness, grace, and forgiveness that have been generously given to you.

Walk in the light of God's love, knowing that you are a new creation in Christ, draped in His mercy, His grace, His peace, His joy and His righteousness that has brought you into total redemption and reconciliation.

Don't look back step in all the way into the fullness of God's purpose for your life, adorned in the beauty of His grace.

The Father is for you. He has always been there in every single moment.

The Christian path is the sweet spot between being loved and having a deep God-given purpose.

Jesus fills in that God-sized hole.

Nothing else in the world can fill that void.

When we get a taste of Jesus, when we experience His blood, redemption, healing, signs, and wonders, we wonder how we managed without Him before.

Furthermore, the journey with Jesus unfolds and deepens over time in a manner that surpasses any other spiritual experience.

It is a deep relationship with the Holy Father, and that relationship will continue to refine, mature, and deepen in complexity and richness as you walk with Him.

I've was shown so much grace by God in a short two and a half year time that I had to spend the last two and a half years writing this book.

I am only five years into being born again by Jesus and I can't wait to see what the next five years holds – hopefully the rapture and eternal life in Heaven. The birth pains are very large today with depravity rampant across society, global 1,000 year floods, earthquakes, tsunami alerts, wars, and the two-state solution almost finalized.

No other spiritual tradition has the worship, praise, and affection towards God like Christianity does. I can listen to worship music for twelve hours straight. I can read the Bible for twelve hours straight. Christianity is that meaningful, because it's the only one that's true.

Revival is stirring across America at this present time. Notably, college campuses and public high schools have witnessed spontaneous gatherings for multi-day worship events. These occurrences serve as tangible evidence of revival taking place, with numerous individuals turning to Jesus during this significant moment in history, it's a great honor to be living in the last days before Jesus comes back on the clouds for His Church. Throughout history, there have been notable periods of spiritual awakening marked by large-scale revivals where many souls have come to Christ.

This surge of spontaneous worship is a direct result of the Holy Spirit attentively responding to the pure adoration and heartfelt prayers of the people, fervent and desperate. A genuine outpouring of praise and adoration, stemming from a place of pure reverence and love for God, devoid of ulterior motives, is what facilitates a move of God.

The Holy Spirit's supernatural presence is always palpable, creating a profound sense of goodness and rightness. Finding an atmosphere saturated with the Holy Spirit's presence will prepare you for an eternity in Heaven where you get to worship God.

Engaging in worship infuses your life and every aspect of life with the supernatural elements of God, leading to spiritual growth and a deeper connection with Him.

Your day job, your special projects, your hobbies, your income, your relationships, your spouse, your sense of purpose and meaning, every area will be touched by Jesus by stepping all the way in.

When people say there is real transformation through the cross they aren't kidding.

I was a broken person before Jesus. Now my life has eternal meaning.

Praising the Lord, receiving prayers, and walking in a daily Christian lifestyle has healed my mind, body, soul, and every area of my life. It's not a perfect journey up Mt. Zion, the Bible doesn't promise a perfect nor easy life, only God is perfect, but I take this life over my old life every single time. What matters is you are on Mt. Zion.

"It is well within my soul" are lyrics from a worship song.

Is the clearest description of following Jesus that I can communicate to you.

If you genuinely seek Him, if you want to discover deep peace, if you want to receive total redemption and restoration, then take this opportunity to give your life, all of your life, every single area of your life over to Jesus and embrace the blood and the work on the cross.

He will never let you down.

If you haven't said this prayer yet, declare this out loud with boldness and authority:

*Jesus, I accept that you were wounded and died on the cross and rose from the dead three days later for all of my debts, sins and iniquities. I deeply ask for your blood to cover and blot out all of my sins. I accept you as my Lord and Savior. My defender. My King. I give you all of my heart so that I may begin to heal and be delivered from all the evils in my life. Please place me Lord on the right course aligned with you and your perfect will for me. Jesus I need the Kingdom of God:*

*your peace, your joy, and your righteousness to invade my mind and my heart. I lay down all pride. I surrender all. I no longer want chaos. I no longer want my plan. I want your plan. Holy Spirit come and live inside of me and baptize me with fire. Come and rest on me so I may turnover any and all burdens, whether known or unknown, to you for healing and transformation. I want to be a new creation in Christ that honors you. Father, I take rest in your everlasting goodness all the days of my life. I have faith that you have me in your embrace and that you are hearing my cries for a new lease on life. I want a sound mind and a beautiful life that honors you. Thank you for your work on the cross. Thank you for the blood. Thank you for keeping me alive to accept the salvation of my soul. Fortify my faith. Please permanently live inside me Holy Spirit and keep me away from any negativity or temptation the enemy may manufacture against me. I want only you as my Lord and Savior Jesus. I cast down every idol and false god I ever placed faith in. I never want to grieve you Holy Spirit. I place you Jesus on the throne of my heart. I trust you are the same always and forever. Captivate my heart. Do not allow me to backslide and go back into the sinful ways of the flesh. Give me the greatest measure of the Holy Spirit I can handle, so I am buffered away from sin. I trust you are the living Holy God of Israel and you provided me the Holy Bible so that I can turn my life around, yes even a wretch like me, I want my new identity in Christ as a son [or daughter] of the King to rewrite my mind. I am washed new into a saint of God through the blood of the Lamb. Direct me in all my ways, pointing me only towards the Son, so I never stumble, and faithfully run the race to the end of the age with persistency and perseverance. Thank you for receiving me back to you, Father. Fan the flames and form me into your image through the blood of Jesus Christ! In Jesus Holy name, Amen!*

Walking in the footsteps of Jesus is the ultimate journey of finding your way back home to faith, hope, and love, all the way into eternity.

He will never let go of you as a saint, just hold onto Him too. The Father is for you. Jesus is right here, closer than your own DNA.

The Holy Spirit is your friend, your helper, your healer, from this day forward and into all the days of your life.

Learning to know the voice of the Holy Spirit and being led by Him should be one of your primary concerns pertaining to your growth as a maturing child of God. It's all part of that lifelong pursuit to know Him and His resurrection power as you press into the high calling in Christ Jesus!

Colossians 1:13-14 KJV

*Who hath delivered us from the power of darkness, and hath translated us into the kingdom of his dear Son: In whom we have redemption through his blood, even the forgiveness of sins.*

2 Corinthians 5:21 KJV

*For he hath made him to be sin for us, who knew no sin; that we might be made the righteousness of God in him.*

God looked at the cross and saw you. God looks at you and sees Christ in you, the hope of glory!

Philippians 1:6 KJV

*Being confident of this very thing, that he which hath begun a good work in you will perform it until the day of Jesus Christ.*

I Stand by the Door
*By Sam Shoemaker*

I stand by the door.
I neither go to far in, nor stay to far out.
The door is the most important door in the world -
It is the door through which men walk when they find God.
There is no use my going way inside and staying there,
When so many are still outside and they, as much as I,
Crave to know where the door is.
And all that so many ever find
Is only the wall where the door ought to be.
They creep along the wall like blind men,
With outstretched, groping hands,
Feeling for a door, knowing there must be a door,
Yet they never find it.
So I stand by the door.

The most tremendous thing in the world
Is for men to find that door - the door to God.
The most important thing that any man can do
Is to take hold of one of those blind, groping hands
And put it on the latch - the latch that only clicks
And opens to the man's own touch.

Men die outside the door, as starving beggars die
On cold nights in cruel cities in the dead of winter.
Die for want of what is within their grasp.
They live on the other side of it - live because they have not found it.

Nothing else matters compared to helping them find it,
And open it, and walk in, and find Him.
So I stand by the door.

# The Names of God: Who God Is

SAVIOR: (Luke 2:11) For unto you is born this day in the city of David a Savior, which is Christ the Lord.

SEED OF WOMAN: (Genesis 3:15) And I will put enmity between thee and the woman, and between thy seed and her seed; it shall bruise thy head, and thou shalt bruise his heel.

SHEPHERD AND BISHOP OF SOULS: (1 Peter 2:25) For ye were as sheep going astray; but are now returned unto the Shepherd and Bishop of your souls.

SHILOH: (Genesis 49:10) The scepter shall not depart from Judah, nor a lawgiver from between his feet, until Shiloh come; and unto him shall the gathering of the people be.

SON OF THE BLESSED: (Mark 14:61) But he held his peace, and answered nothing. Again the high priest asked him, and said unto him, Art thou the Christ, the Son of the Blessed?

SON OF DAVID: (Matthew 1:1) The book of the generation of Jesus Christ, the son of David, the son of Abraham.

SON OF GOD: (Matthew 2:15) And was there until the death of Herod: that it might be fulfilled which was spoken of the Lord by the prophet, saying, Out of Egypt have I called my Son.

SON OF THE HIGHEST: (Luke 1:32) He shall be great, and shall be called the Son of the Highest: and the Lord God shall give unto him the throne of his father David.

SUN OF RIGHTEOUSNESS: (Malachi 4:2) But unto you that fear my name shall the Sun of righteousness arise with healing in his wings; and ye shall go forth, and grow up as calves of the stall.

TRUE LIGHT: (John 1:9) That was the true Light, which lighteth every man that cometh into the world.

TRUE VINE: (John 15:1) I am the true vine, and my Father is the husbandman.

TRUTH: (John 1:14) And the Word was made flesh, and dwelt among us, (and we beheld his glory, the glory as of the only begotten of the Father,) full of grace and truth.

WITNESS: (Isaiah 55:4) Behold, I have given him for a witness to the people, a leader and commander to the people.

WORD: (John 1:1) In the beginning was the Word, and the Word was with God, and the Word was God.

WORD OF GOD: (Revelation 19:13) And he was clothed with a vesture dipped in blood: and his name is called The Word of God.

JEHOVAH: (Isaiah 26:4) Trust ye in the LORD for ever: for in the LORD JEHOVAH is everlasting strength.

JESUS: (Matthew 1:21) And she shall bring forth a son, and thou shalt call his name JESUS: for he shall save his people from their sins.

JESUS OF NAZARETH: (Matthew 21:11) And the multitude said, This is Jesus the prophet of Nazareth of Galilee.

JUDGE OF ISRAEL: (Micah 5:1) Now gather thyself in troops, O daughter of troops: he hath laid siege against us: they shall smite the judge of Israel with a rod upon the cheek.

THE JUST ONE: (Acts 7:52) Which of the prophets have not your fathers persecuted? and they have slain them which showed before of the coming of the Just One; of whom ye have been now the betrayers and murderers.

KING: (Zechariah 9:9) Rejoice greatly, O daughter of Zion; shout, O daughter of Jerusalem: behold, thy King cometh unto thee: he is just, and having salvation; lowly, and riding upon an ass, and upon a colt the foal of an ass.

KING OF THE AGES: (1 Timothy 1:17) Now unto the King eternal, immortal, invisible, the only wise God, be honor and glory for ever and ever. Amen.

KING OF THE JEWS: (Matthew 2:2) Saying, Where is he that is born King of the Jews? for we have seen his star in the east, and are come to worship him.

KING OF KINGS: (1 Timothy 6:15) Which in his times he shall show, who is the blessed and only Potentate, the King of kings, and Lord of lords.

KING OF SAINTS: (Revelation 15:3) And they sing the song of Moses the servant of God, and the song of the Lamb, saying, Great and marvelous are thy works, Lord God Almighty; just and true are thy ways, thou King of saints.

LAWGIVER: (Isaiah 33:22) For the LORD is our judge, the LORD is our lawgiver, the LORD is our king; he will save us.

LAMB: (Revelation 13:8) And all that dwell upon the earth shall worship him, whose names are not written in the book of life of the Lamb slain from the foundation of the world.

LAMB OF GOD: (John 1:29) The next day John seeth Jesus coming unto him, and saith, Behold the Lamb of God, which taketh away the sin of the world.

LEADER AND COMMANDER: (Isaiah 55:4) Behold, I have given him for a witness to the people, a leader and commander to the people.

THE LIFE: (John 14:6) Jesus saith unto him, I am the way, the truth, and the life: no man cometh unto the Father, but by me.

LIGHT OF THE WORLD: (John 8:12) Then spake Jesus again unto them, saying, I am the light of the world: he that followeth me shall not walk in darkness, but shall have the light of life.

LION OF THE TRIBE OF JUDAH: (Revelation 5:5) And one of the elders saith unto me, Weep not: behold, the Lion of the tribe of Juda, the Root of David, hath prevailed to open the book, and to loose the seven seals thereof.

LORD OF ALL: (Acts 10:36) The Word which God sent unto the children of Israel, preaching peace by Jesus Christ: (he is Lord of all)

LORD OF GLORY: (1 Corinthians 2:8) Which none of the princes of this world knew: for had they known it, they would not have crucified the Lord of glory.

LORD OF LORDS: (1 Timothy 6:15) Which in his times he shall show, who is the blessed and only Potentate, the King of kings, and Lord of lords.

LORD OF OUR RIGHTEOUSNESS: (Jeremiah 23:6) In his days Judah shall be saved, and Israel shall dwell safely: and this is his name whereby he shall be called, THE LORD OUR RIGHTEOUSNESS.

ADAM: (1 Corinthians 15:45) And so it is written, The first man Adam was made a living soul; the last Adam was made a quickening spirit.

ADVOCATE: (1 John 2:1) My little children, these things write I unto you, that ye sin not. And if any man sin, we have an advocate with the Father, Jesus Christ the righteous.

ALMIGHTY: (Revelation 1:8) I am Alpha and Omega, the beginning and the ending, saith the Lord, which is, and which was, and which is to come, the Almighty.

ALPHA AND OMEGA: (Revelation 1:8) I am Alpha and Omega, the beginning and the ending, saith the Lord, which is, and which was, and which is to come, the Almighty.

AMEN: (Revelation 3:14) And unto the angel of the church of the Laodiceans write; These things saith the Amen, the faithful and true witness, the beginning of the creation of God.

APOSTLE OF OUR PROFESSION: (Hebrews 3:1) Wherefore, holy brethren, partakers of the Heavenly calling, consider the Apostle and High Priest of our profession, Christ Jesus.

ARM OF THE LORD: (Isaiah 51:9) Awake, awake, put on strength, O arm of the LORD; awake, as in the ancient days, in the generations of old. Art thou not it that hath cut Rahab, and wounded the dragon? (Isaiah 53:1) Who hath believed our report? and to whom is the arm of the LORD revealed?

AUTHOR AND FINISHER OF OUR FAITH: (Hebrews 12:2) Looking unto Jesus the author and finisher of our faith; who for the joy that was set before him endured the cross, despising the shame, and is set down at the right hand of the throne of God.

AUTHOR OF ETERNAL SALVATION: (Hebrews 5:9) And being made perfect, he became the author of eternal salvation unto all them that obey him.

BEGINNING OF CREATION OF GOD: (Revelation 3:14) And unto the angel of the church of the Laodiceans write; These things saith the Amen, the faithful and true witness, the beginning of the creation of God.

BELOVED SON: (Matthew 12:18) Behold my servant, whom I have chosen; my beloved, in whom my soul is well pleased: I will put my spirit upon him, and he shall show judgment to the Gentiles.

BLESSED AND ONLY POTENTATE: (1 Timothy 6:15) Which in his times he shall show, who is the blessed and only Potentate, the King of kings, and Lord of lords.

BRANCH: (Isaiah 4:2) In that day shall the branch of the LORD be beautiful and glorious, and the fruit of the earth shall be excellent and comely for them that are escaped of Israel.

BREAD OF LIFE: (John 6:32) Then Jesus said unto them, Verily, verily, I say unto you, Moses gave you not that bread from Heaven; but my Father giveth you the true bread from Heaven.

CAPTAIN OF SALVATION: (Hebrews 2:10) For it became him, for whom are all things, and by whom are all things, in bringing many sons unto glory, to make the captain of their salvation perfect through sufferings.

CHIEF SHEPHERD: (1 Peter 5:4) And when the chief Shepherd shall appear, ye shall receive a crown of glory that fadeth not away.

CHRIST OF GOD: (Luke 9:20) He said unto them, But whom say ye that I am? Peter answering said, The Christ of God.

CONSOLATION OF ISRAEL: (Luke 2:25) And, behold, there was a man in Jerusalem, whose name was Simeon; and the same man was just and devout, waiting for the consolation of Israel: and the Holy Ghost was upon him.

CORNERSTONE: (Psalm 118:22) The stone which the builders refused is become the head stone of the corner.

COUNSELLOR: (Isaiah 9:6) For unto us a child is born, unto us a son is given: and the government shall be upon his shoulder: and his name shall be called Wonderful, Counsellor, The mighty God, The everlasting Father, The Prince of Peace.

CREATOR: (John 1:3) All things were made by him; and without him was not any thing made that was made.

DAYSPRING: (Luke 1:78) Through the tender mercy of our God; whereby the dayspring from on high hath visited us,

DELIVERER: (Romans 11:26) And so all Israel shall be saved: as it is written, There shall come out of Zion the Deliverer, and shall turn away ungodliness from Jacob.

DESIRE OF THE NATIONS: (Haggai 2:7) And I will shake all nations, and the desire of all nations shall come: and I will fill this house with glory, saith the LORD of hosts.

DOOR: (John 10:7) Then said Jesus unto them again, Verily, verily, I say unto you, I am the door of the sheep.

ELECT OF GOD: (Isaiah 42:1) Behold my servant, whom I uphold; mine elect, in whom my soul delighteth; I have put my spirit upon him: he shall bring forth judgment to the Gentiles.

EVERLASTING FATHER: (Isaiah 9:6) For unto us a child is born, unto us a son is given: and the government shall be upon his shoulder: and his name shall be called Wonderful, Counsellor, The mighty God, The everlasting Father, The Prince of Peace.

FAITHFUL WITNESS: (Revelation 1:5) And from Jesus Christ, who is the faithful witness, and the first begotten of the dead, and the prince of the kings of the earth. Unto him that loved us, and washed us from our sins in his own blood,

FIRST AND LAST: (Revelation 1:17) And when I saw him, I fell at his feet as dead. And he laid his right hand upon me, saying unto me, Fear not; I am the first and the last.

FIRST BEGOTTEN: (Revelation 1:5) And from Jesus Christ, who is the faithful witness, and the first begotten of the dead, and the prince of the kings of the earth. Unto him that loved us, and washed us from our sins in his own blood,

FORERUNNER: (Hebrews 6:20) Whither the forerunner is for us entered, even Jesus, made an high priest for ever after the order of Melchisedec.

GLORY OF THE LORD: (Isaiah 40:5) And the glory of the LORD shall be revealed, and all flesh shall see it together: for the mouth of the LORD hath spoken it.

GOD: (Isaiah 40:3) The voice of him that crieth in the wilderness, Prepare ye the way of the LORD, make straight in the desert a highway for our God.

GOD BLESSED: (Romans 9:5) Whose are the fathers, and of whom as concerning the flesh Christ came, who is over all, God blessed for ever. Amen.

GOOD SHEPHERD: (John 10:11) I am the good shepherd: the good shepherd giveth his life for the sheep.

GOVERNOR: (Matthew 2:6) And thou Bethlehem, in the land of Juda, art not the least among the princes of Juda: for out of thee shall come a Governor, that shall rule my people Israel.

GREAT HIGH PRIEST: (Hebrews 4:14) Seeing then that we have a great high priest, that is passed into the Heavens, Jesus the Son of God, let us hold fast our profession.

HEAD OF THE CHURCH: (Ephesians 1:22) And hath put all things under his feet, and gave him to be the head over all things to the church.

HEIR OF ALL THINGS: (Hebrews 1:2) Hath in these last days spoken unto us by his Son, whom he hath appointed heir of all things, by whom also he made the worlds.

HOLY CHILD: (Acts 4:27) For of a truth against thy holy child Jesus, whom thou hast anointed, both Herod, and Pontius Pilate, with the Gentiles, and the people of Israel, were gathered together.

HOLY ONE: (Acts 3:14) But ye denied the Holy One and the Just, and desired a murderer to be granted unto you.

HOLY ONE OF GOD: (Mark 1:24) Saying, Let us alone; what have we to do with thee, thou Jesus of Nazareth? art thou come to destroy us? I know thee who thou art, the Holy One of God.

HOLY ONE OF ISRAEL: (Isaiah 41:14) Fear not, thou worm Jacob, and ye men of Israel; I will help thee, saith the LORD, and thy redeemer, the Holy One of Israel.

HORN OF SALVATION: (Luke 1:69) And hath raised up an horn of salvation for us in the house of his servant David.

I AM: (John 8:58) Jesus said unto them, Verily, verily, I say unto you, Before Abraham was, I am.

IMAGE OF GOD: (2 Corinthians 4:4) In whom the god of this world hath blinded the minds of them which believe not, lest the light of the glorious Gospel of Christ, who is the image of God, should shine unto them.

IMMANUEL: (Isaiah 7:14) Therefore the Lord himself shall give you a sign; Behold, a virgin shall conceive, and bear a son, and shall call his name Immanuel.

MAN OF SORROWS: (Isaiah 53:3) He is despised and rejected of men; a man of sorrows, and acquainted with grief: and we hid as it were our faces from him; he was despised, and we esteemed him not.

MEDIATOR: (1 Timothy 2:5) For there is one God, and one mediator between God and men, the man Christ Jesus.

MESSENGER OF THE COVENANT: (Malachi 3:1) Behold, I will send my messenger, and he shall prepare the way before me: and the Lord, whom ye seek, shall suddenly come to his temple, even the messenger of the Covenant, whom ye delight in: behold, he shall come, saith the LORD of hosts.

MESSIAH: (Daniel 9:25) Know therefore and understand, that from the going forth of the commandment to restore and to build Jerusalem unto the Messiah the Prince shall be seven weeks, and threescore and two weeks: the street shall be built again, and the wall, even in troublous times. (John 1:41)

He first findeth his own brother Simon, and saith unto him, We have found the Messiah, which is, being interpreted, the Christ.

MIGHTY GOD: (Isaiah 9:6) For unto us a child is born, unto us a son is given: and the government shall be upon his shoulder: and his name shall be called Wonderful, Counsellor, The mighty God, The everlasting Father, The Prince of Peace.

MIGHTY ONE: (Isaiah 60:16) Thou shalt also suck the milk of the Gentiles, and shalt suck the breast of kings: and thou shalt know that I the LORD am thy Savior and thy Redeemer, the mighty One of Jacob.

MORNING STAR: (Revelation 22:16) I Jesus have sent mine angel to testify unto you these things in the churches. I am the root and the offspring of David, and the bright and morning star.

NAZARENE: (Matthew 2:23) And he came and dwelt in a city called Nazareth: that it might be fulfilled which was spoken by the prophets, He shall be called a Nazarene.

ONLY BEGOTTEN SON: (John 1:18) No man hath seen God at any time; the only begotten Son, which is in the bosom of the Father, he hath declared him.

OUR PASSOVER: (1 Corinthians 5:7) Purge out therefore the old leaven, that ye may be a new lump, as ye are unleavened. For even Christ our passover is sacrificed for us.

PRINCE OF LIFE: (Acts 3:15) And killed the Prince of life, whom God hath raised from the dead; whereof we are witnesses.

PRINCE OF KINGS: (Revelation 1:5) And from Jesus Christ, who is the faithful witness, and the first begotten of the dead, and the prince of the kings of the earth. Unto him that loved us, and washed us from our sins in his own blood,

PRINCE OF PEACE: (Isaiah 9:6) For unto us a child is born, unto us a son is given: and the government shall be upon his shoulder: and his name shall be called Wonderful, Counsellor, The mighty God, The everlasting Father, The Prince of Peace.

PROPHET: (Luke 24:19) And he said unto them, What things? And they said unto him, Concerning Jesus of Nazareth, which was a prophet mighty in deed and Word before God and all the people.

(Acts 3:22) For Moses truly said unto the fathers, A prophet shall the Lord your God raise up unto you of your brethren, like unto me; him shall ye hear in all things whatsoever he shall say unto you.

REDEEMER: (Job 19:25) For I know that my redeemer liveth, and that he shall stand at the latter day upon the earth:

RESURRECTION AND LIFE: (John 11:25) Jesus said unto her, I am the resurrection, and the life: he that believeth in me, though he were dead, yet shall he live:

ROCK: (1 Corinthians 10:4) And did all drink the same spiritual drink: for they drank of that spiritual Rock that followed them: and that Rock was Christ.

ROOT OF DAVID: (Revelation 22:16) I Jesus have sent mine angel to testify unto you these things in the churches. I am the root and the offspring of David, and the bright and morning star.

ROSE OF SHARON: (Song of Songs 2:1) I am the rose of Sharon, and the lily of the valleys.


Dear friend,

You are blessed for reading this book and learning more Scripture: the living, breathing, Word of God.

2 Timothy 3:16-17 KJV

*All scripture is given by inspiration of God, and is profitable for doctrine, for reproof, for correction, for instruction in righteousness: That the man of God may be perfect, throughly furnished unto all good works.*

The Bible is the only book you can never finish because it's alive. Jesus was and is the Word, in person, in Spirit and in Truth.

This Christian book simply scratched the surface on what's in the Bible.

I encourage you to keep growing and learning the Word.

It's the ultimate source of Truth. There are many applications of the Bible, but there is only one Holy Spirit confirmed interpretation. No Scripture is of private interpretation (2 Peter 1:20).

Find a community of believers that also read, study, believe, and behave the Bible as soon as you can. There's no point in waiting. Your new life in Christ awaits you. Come as you are. You can join a community of other disciples at https://t.me/godsdisciples

Luke 11:28 KJV

*But he said, Yea rather, blessed are they that hear the Word of God, and keep it.*

Be blessed, be bold, be Holy, and know that you have overcome through the blood of the Lamb and your testimony.

Revelation 12:11 KJV

*And they overcame him by the blood of the Lamb, and by the Word of their testimony; and they loved not their lives unto the death.*

Shed your grave clothes and embrace your new raiment in Christ!

Go forth and walk in the eternal truth of His victory. Amen!

Hallelujah!
Andrew